UNIVERSITY OF CALIFORNIA
PUBLICATIONS IN HISTORY

VOLUME LXX

THE POLITICS
OF CONSERVATION

Crusades and Controversies

1897-1913

BY

ELMO R. RICHARDSON

UNIVERSITY OF CALIFORNIA PRESS
BERKELEY AND LOS ANGELES
1962

University of California Publications in History
Advisory Editors: R. N. Burr, Brainerd Dyer, W. T. Jackson, D. S. Landes,
J. R. Levenson, J. W. Olmsted

Volume 70

Submitted January 11, 1961
Issued October 16, 1962
Price, $4.00

University of California Press
Berkeley and Los Angeles
California

◇

Cambridge University Press
London, England

FOR
MY PARENTS
AND
MY BROTHER

PREFACE

THE MOVEMENT for the conservation of natural resources was one of the most popular reforms in the recent history of the United States. Beginning as an idealistic theory shared by a few men, in less than a decade at the turn of the century it was transformed into a pragmatic policy of government that changed the course of the country's economic development. Because it depended upon technical planning and administration for the most efficient and equitable use of resources, the conservation crusade might be called the epitome of the Progressive Era. Moreover, it embodied the principal aim of that generation of Americans who were determined to destroy the evils of economic and political monopolies by enlarging the responsibility and power of government. The movement thus had a dual nature: a technically complex program dependent upon a simple, emotional appeal.

Public acceptance of federal resource conservation was based upon a variety of motives, methods, and participants. In order to attract the widest possible support, it was then and thereafter described in oversimplified terms. The conservationists were looked upon as altruistic and invariably right; all who doubted them were irresponsible at best, and subversive at worst. In reality, the policy evolved in a process of trial and error, and was subjected to the personal ambitions and political interests of both the crusaders and their critics. The oversimplified explanation of the movement facilitated popular approval, but it also obscured the complex basis of resource administration. At the time, these distortions gave rise to numerous controversies. Since then, they have persisted in the histories of conservation. The writings on the subject have, until recently, relied upon the viewpoints of the leaders of the crusade or been based upon a few secondary sources. Only in the last few years have trained researchers drawn upon official archives and manuscript collections in order to describe more accurately the complex nature of conservation and to assess its significance in the context of recent history.

This book is intended as a contribution to the larger project of historical assessment. It examines the specific theme of conservation as a political issue and offers several new perspectives. Until now, the success of the movement has been ascribed to the actions of a few men, and the political repercussions of their policy have been viewed from the vantage point of the nation's capital. This study draws upon documents and letters not only in national depositories, but also in the archives and historical societies of the states west of the Rocky Mountains. Although the economic and political conditions of that region obviously influenced the formulation of resource policies, these sources have never been extensively used by the students of conservation history. Examination of evidence in the West as well as the East reveals facts which belie the oversimplifications of the past. The traditional view of the West as the opponent of resource regulation must be carefully revised. Actually, there were many interests in that region, economic and political, which accounted for support as well as criticism. In spite of the noise made by orators and editors, opposition to conservation was neither solid nor effectively organized. Indeed, the movement was given decisive assistance by westerners. A host of citizens— governors, publicists, businessmen, educators, and political opportunists of every description—were instrumental in securing essential local coöperation with federal administrators.

In the context of these new facts, conservation as an issue in the arena of national politics must also be reanalyzed. The most significant influence upon that issue, the famous Ballinger-Pinchot controversy, has been described so often that it has become a historical cliché. Yet these accounts invariably have been limited by selected evidence and reasoning after the fact. (See the bibliographical note at the end of chap. iv.) Another topic, the West's claim on the post of Secretary of the Interior, similarly may be viewed in a broader context. Lastly, by using sources from the West, including the newly opened Ballinger Papers, this study examines the relationship between the conservation controversy and the Progressive revolt against the Taft administration. Consideration of all these subjects will emphasize the basic role of politics in the transformation of the ideal of a few into a national institution.

I would like to acknowledge the generous assistance of many persons in the West and the East. The staffs of the manuscript depositories listed in the bibliography were patient, courteous, and efficient in making their holdings available in spite of physical obstacles and time limitations. I am particularly indebted to the following curators for information about local materials and for hours of cordial conversations: Richard Berner, of the University of Washington Library; Clara Beatty, of the Nevada State Historical Society; Eugene Gressley, of the University of Wyoming Library; Richard Nesbit, of the Washington State Archives; Edna Reinbach, of the Eastern Washington Historical Society; Jane Smith, of Interior Records, the National Archives; and George Warren, of the Colorado State Archives. C. Raymond Clar and David Stratton gave me useful details from their own research projects. Other information cited herein was furnished by H. B. Embach, F. Lee Kirby, L. F. Kneipp, William H. Mondell, Thorton T. Munger, Mrs. Reed Smoot, and Oswald West. My former colleagues in the history department of the University of Kansas used their hatchets skillfully and beneficially on a part of the manuscript. The editors of the *California Historical Society Quarterly*, the *New Mexico Historical Review*, and the *Pacific Northwest Quarterly* kindly gave permission to include excerpts from my articles in those journals. Finally, by his realistic comments and his own example, Professor George E. Mowry, of the University of California at Los Angeles, helped me shape the initial version of this study.

ELMO R. RICHARDSON

Los Angeles
April, 1961

CONTENTS

I. Trials and Errors 1

II. Roosevelt, Pinchot, and Their Disciples 17

III. Ballinger's Beginnings 47

IV. Pinchot's Gambit 65

V. The Critics' Campaign 86

VI. The Limits of Reaction 105

VII. On the Progessives' Band Wagon 121

VIII. The Democrats' Opportunity 145

Notes 163

Bibliography 189

Index 201

CHAPTER I

TRIALS AND ERRORS

THE WEST'S INTERESTS

IN FEBRUARY, 1897, Thomas H. Carter of Montana stood at his desk in the Senate Chamber and denounced the President of the United States. Grover Cleveland, he asserted, had shown "contemptuous disregard" for the people's interests and the wishes of their representatives by ordering the withdrawal of twenty million acres from the public domain for forest reservations. Although Congress had empowered the President to create such areas six years before, the law had been used sparingly. By issuing his proclamations two weeks before the end of his second disappointing term in the White House, Cleveland seemed to be making a gesture of righteous defiance. For several years the West had been the breeding ground for disloyalty to the administration. Many former Democrats of that region, already alienated by Cleveland's economic policies and no longer constrained by party fidelity, readily joined in the barrage of protest against the "useless protection of dead timber." The Republicans were particularly offended by what they described as a blatant coup made by the discredited leader of a party that had suffered defeat in the national elections a few months before. The westerners therefore had a double reason for criticizing the executive orders during the weeks of debate in the Senate.[1] Carter found great comfort in the assertion that the administration which had committed the outrage was, "by the providence of God and the act of an intelligent electorate," about to pass beyond the power to "harass and annoy the American people." His colleague, Senator John L. Wilson, of Washington, assured the suffering West that the new President, William McKinley, and Cornelius Bliss, his Secretary of the Interior, were wholly in sympathy with the needs of their region. In order to convince these executives that westerners were fully opposed to the forest reservations, the personal arguments of congressmen were supplemented by memorials passed in many state legislatures. Responding to these pressures, McKinley agreed to a modification of Cleveland's actions a few weeks after he took office. Senator William S. Stewart, of Nevada, who had left the Democratic party over the issue of free silver, joyfully confided to an agent of the giant Anaconda Copper Company, of Montana, that a complete revocation of the reserves would soon be passed by the Republican Congress. In May a bill written by the senators from Wyoming, Francis E. Warren and Clarence D. Clark, was adopted and signed by the President. By its terms, the actual creation of the new forests was held in abeyance for one year. Shortly thereafter Congress specifically prohibited the future establishment of forest reserves except for the protection of timber and watersheds.[2]

Viewed superficially, these events implied that the West was united in its opposition to a federal policy of withdrawing lands from the public domain for reservations. In reality, the subject had received only scattered and languid notice before Cleveland's proclamations were announced. Indeed, the comments made at that time in Western newspapers revealed substantial approval of the idea, if not the suddenness of executive initiative. The influential Portland *Oregonian* maintained that there was a real need for vigorous measures which would prevent further depredations and fires in the forests. The editor had no patience, however, with those who were interested only in preserving pastoral scenery; action should be taken, not by these "sentimentalists," but by local leaders who were familiar with practical interests. In Montana, the Great Falls *Leader* agreed that the reserves could serve as proper protection for vitally needed watersheds once their boundaries were redrawn to exclude nontimbered lands. In San Francisco, the conservative *Argonaut* went even further by claiming that the "scientific conservation of forests" constituted the "real and permanent interests of the people—not only of the West but as far East as the Mississippi Valley." The *Deseret Weekly*, of Salt Lake City, although staunchly Republican, decried the revocation of the reserves as an act of blind selfishness on the part of Western senators. In addition, some of the most prominent citizens of the region were appalled by this legislative frustration of the policy. In California, the author and naturalist John Muir privately fumed over the "bad lot" of senators who had voted "on the Holy Sabbath day for old fashioned diabolical destruction of forests." Partly because of his efforts, California's delegation asked that the suspension not be applied to reserves in their state. Muir confidently assumed that continued pressure by himself and his friends would eventually secure the preservation of all such areas; but, he lamented, "how long O Lord . . . must the destruction go on."[3]

The diversity of opinion concerning federal responsibility for forest protection and other land use problems reflected the complex conditions existing in the West. Although that vast region was divided into eleven political parts, economically speaking it consisted of widely scattered and overlapping interests. On many arid plateaus, agriculture was limited by intermittent water supply, while forested mountain ranges not only supported lumbering and mining, but also served as watersheds and cover for stock grazing. Throughout a generally sparsely settled area, there were islands of population, many of which were then experiencing accelerated increases in the number of residents and in the accompanying problems of urban life. Within the boundaries of a state, therefore, most of the land might be devoted to one pursuit at the same time that the majority of the residents were dependent upon another. A variety of economic interests existed in every state, but one of them usually exercised a dominant influence. The mining industry accounted for much of the wealth of Montana, Colorado, and Nevada, although these states contained vast agricultural acreage and supported a large proportion of the sheep and cattle raised in the West. Timber of greatest commercial value was located in Washington, Oregon, and California, but many other economic conditions there gave rise to the largest cities: Seattle, Portland, San Francisco, and Los Angeles. The only other metropolitan centers were Denver, the gateway for commerce to the West, and Salt Lake City, the crossroads of the central Great Basin. In Wyoming and New Mexico the absence of natural advantages and the presence of unclaimed stretches of rangeland accounted for the paramount position of the stock-raising industry. In every instance these economies were in an exploitative phase and, although it was customary to criticize the intrusion of nonresident owners, in fact the West relied upon investment from the East in all of its commercial activities. As a consequence of these many interests, the use of lands and resources was subject to conflicting claims in every part of the region. Thus, a forested area was at once the source of lumber, an impediment to mineral development, a shelter for forage, and a cover which could impound a water supply and prevent erosion of the soil.

The West was also in a formative stage politically. Most of the states had been organized less than thirty years before. Two of them, Wyoming and Utah, had just entered the Union, and New Mexico and Arizona were still territories under federal control. In many instances, representative government was subjected to the control of an oligarchy whose influence was enhanced by poor communications across the great distances and by the sparsity of population. At the turn of the century, moreover, the time-honored traditions of patronage and jobbery were practiced by both political parties. Only in the urban centers were those customs being challenged and replaced by the demand for government based upon direct popular participation. It might be said that westerners were generally content with traditional practices because their viewpoint was either provincial or selfish. They were willing to let the successful citizens speak for them, except when success was owing to inordinate greed or oppression. The acquiescence of the majority was basically a matter of self-preservation. In most communities all property and order depended upon the maintenance and growth of a particular economic interest; the representatives of that interest therefore veritably expressed the attitudes and hopes of their fellow citizens. In this way the Northern Pacific Railroad dominated the economy of the Pacific Northwest, and much of the commerce of California relied upon the Southern Pacific Railroad. The copper-mining empires of Montana and Arizona were as influential as the iron- and coal-mining enterprises of Colorado in securing the support of their local and state governments. Even though the prestige of these corporations had recently been tarnished by the attacks of the muckrakers and reformers, their economic importance remained unchanged. More commonly, farmers' and stock raisers' associations guided the actions of state legislatures; in Wyoming and New Mexico, especially, the cattlemen and sheepmen dominated politics and government. Moreover, new economic interests were then appearing in the West—those based upon the use of watercourses for the irrigation of arid lands and the generation of electric power. As a result, numerous land-development and power corporations were organized, often with no other assets than the potential advantage of access to natural resources on the public domain.

In every case these economic organizations and their political spokesmen claimed that they spoke for the people of the West. Their solicitude for the settler was in part hypocritical, insofar as they sought to use individual entry and claim to the public lands for the enlargement of their own special interests. Lumbermen, for example, often paid homesteaders to take up acreage in forested areas and then transfer their plots to the lumber company. For the most part, however, westerners generally shared the traditional belief in the freedom of the small landowner and ambivalence toward governmental restrictions. Like state legislatures, newspapers in the region were often controlled by one or more economic groups, but their editors usually defended the traditional attitudes. Especially in urban centers, newspapers which circulated among residents with a variety of interests used arguments which were purposely vague in order to appeal to the opinions, not the practical interests, of their readers. On the other hand, the editorials in small-town journals were more outspoken and more pungent, even if they represented the viewpoint of a minority.

Considering the comparatively primitive economic and political conditions which prevailed in the West, it is possible to understand why the subject of responsible resource regulation became a vital, although confused, issue in that region. The first indication of the new federal policy occurred in 1896 when the National Academy of Sciences sent a special forestry commission through the West to survey the timbered areas of the public domain. Many westerners sincerely hoped that the information thereby assembled would facilitate a modification of antiquated land laws. When Cleveland used the commission's recommendations to create, suddenly, vast reserves, their hopes gave way to exasperation. "Why should we be everlastingly and eternally harassed and annoyed and bedeviled by those scientific gentlemen," Senator Wilson demanded. "They admit that they had no knowledge, and that they hurried through the country in Pullman Palace cars," he added, as if to remind his colleagues that the East was too impractical and effete to be trusted with the responsibility.[4] Such criticism was based not only upon the feeling that vital decisions were being made by men not familiar with local conditions, but also upon a political fear: the federal program was conceived by technologists and administrators who resented or were indifferent to the coteries which controlled governments. Protests against resource policy consequently were made as a defense of the political *status quo* which the new policy ignored or threatened to replace.

One substantial bulwark stood against the inroads of the so-called sentimentalists and theorists who sought to reform the government's land use policies. For decades, federal administration of the public domain had depended upon the machinery of Western politics. The Department of the Interior, which executed the acts of Congress affecting lands and resources, had long been subject to the personal attitudes and friendships of the Secretaries of the Interior and their subordinates.[5] The advent of the new administration naturally did not alter that tradition. McKinley's appointment of Bliss seemed to make an unfortunate truth out of the observation of that perceptive Irish-American, "Mr. Dooley." "The Sicrety iv th' Interior is an important man," he assured his countrymen. "If possible, he ought to come fr'm Maine or Florida. At anny rate, he must be a resident iv an Atlantic seacoast town ... If he gets th' idee there are anny white people in Ann Arbor or Columbus, he loses his job."[6] Bliss was a wealthy New York merchant who had served on the Republican National Committee which secured McKinley's nomination; he had contributed generously to the campaign chest from his personal fortune. He was at first reluctant to take a Cabinet post, but finally accepted the one for which he was perhaps least qualified. In deciding upon the problems before the

Department of the Interior, Bliss's paramount interests were party harmony and patronage. Apart from these considerations, his understanding of such matters as forest conservation was summed up by Muir's bitter observation: "There seems to be precious little arboreal bliss in Bliss—Dry goods and dry rot mostly.'" The hopes of the West were thus dampened once again. From the time that the region was first settled, its residents had wished to see a westerner become Secretary of the Interior, but, with the exception of the three-year tenure of Henry M. Teller, of Colorado, during the administration of Chester A. Arthur, that portfolio had been given to men from states east of the Missouri River—men, in every instance, whose knowledge of conditions in the transmontane West was superficial and secondhand,[8] and whose interest in its problems was usually political.

President Benjamin Harrison was the first to acknowledge the West's claim when, in 1893, he appointed Thomas Carter, of Montana, to be Commissioner of Public Lands. The Land Office was a clearinghouse for every detail of land disposal and use, and it was the first to handle the administration of the new forest reserves and the federal projects for the reclamation of arid lands. For many westerners the Commissioner's policies were more important than those of his superior, the Secretary of the Interior, or any other federal official. Because of a succession of inept or sympathetic Secretaries, the Commissioners before and after Carter were able to gain a position of dominant influence over administrative matters and patronage. McKinley's appointee to the head of the Land Office, former Congressman Binger Hermann, of Oregon, readily welded his bureau and the new Division of Forestry into a political machine which Bliss was reluctant to disturb.[9] Although personally hostile to the idea of forest reservations, Hermann was more familiar with the problems of land use than either Bliss or his successor, Secretary Ethan A. Hitchcock. During the years of his legal and political career in Oregon, he had direct experience with the ways in which federal land laws enabled large corporations to exchange claims in federal reserves for better lands elsewhere in the public domain. The inequities of these lieu land laws constituted one of the principal sources of complaint coming from the West.

On lower administrative levels, the agents of the federal bureaus were usually appointed on the basis of political preference and local economic power. Like their superiors, they believed that the disposal of the public domain was essential to the growth of their region. Most of them were trained in the legal profession because of the direct relationship between private property and land laws, and consequently they viewed existing statutes with mixed feelings. On the one hand, they willingly manipulated the ambiguous phraseology of the laws for their own advantage and that of their clients. On the other, they insisted upon a strict and clear interpretation of the letter of the law to protect existing properties. Many of the lawyers in the West who specialized in land and resource litigation therefore wished to continue the general policies of the past, but desired to adjust them to the needs of the region's changing economy. They insisted, however, that such adjustment could be formulated and applied only by westerners. Their administration of federal laws was essentially conservative in purpose and technique, and they regarded the technical plans and new personnel required by the dynamic resource policy as wholly undesirable. During the initial period, then, conservation was actually represented in the West by the men who were least sympathetic with its purpose. Although westerners complained that government agents were incompetent, corrupt, or tyrannical, they were themselves partly responsible for the mistakes and malpractices. Because they insisted upon political considerations and economic interests as the criteria for appointment, local positions went to men without skills or ethics.[10]

As a result of administrative shortcomings, a body of criticism was conceived by the spokesmen of the West. The bureaus in charge of land use policy—the Land Office, the Division of Forestry, the Reclamation Service, and the Geological Survey—had limited funds and incomplete information for carrying out their assignments. They were consequently unable to maintain adequate supervision over the use of natural resources, or to educate the residents of the area in the realities of ecology. Westerners were quick to point to cases of depredations on the public domain and eager to ridicule such a concept as reforestation. They resented what seemed to be a program conceived in the East— which had wasted its own resources—and administered by a handful of ambitious theorists who sought to control a vast empire from a distance of two thousand miles. During the next decade the complaints heard in the West and in Congress reiterated these misconceptions until they were stripped of every rational meaning.

THE POLITICS OF PROTEST

After the creation of the Cleveland forest reserves, scores of debates erupted in the West over the question of the desirability and effects of federal regulation. To offset the arguments for forestry associations, Governor William P. Lord of Oregon asked John Minto to put his literary talents at the service of the state's sheep industry. Minto, a pioneer settler and naturalist, echoed the feelings of many Oregonians whose stock was excluded from the new reservations. He did not object to the idea of resource conservation in general, but he preferred the Australian system of individual-proprietor caretaking instead of government administration. He did, however, disagree emphatically with the Academy of Science's commissioners on the subject of the relation between rainfall and forest growth. Although mostly concerned with the problem of grazing in the reserves, Minto's writings referred to other considerations. In one of his articles, for example, he warned against "The Dangers of the Use of Power Without Knowledge"—the title being an allusion to Cleveland's actions—and demanded the reduction of the Cascade Reserve in Oregon. For many months, his statements were given sympathetic coverage in the pages of the *Oregonian,* edited by Lord's friend Harvey Scott, a prominent Republican. As a member of the state Board of Horticulture, Minto also submitted a report which condemned the American Forestry Association's surveys in the state. Praising all who opposed federal interference, he hailed the new McKinley administration as "the most potent agency in staying a course . . . not only injurious but alarming to the citizens of the range states." These arguments did not, however, represent the attitude of all Oregonians. During the same period the Portland Chamber of Commerce joined the newly organized state forestry association in support of federal policy. Even the potent woolgrowers' association admitted that only the government could bear the expense of forest protection and act as fair judge of the rights of the many persons who used the reserves. John Muir came up from California to denounce the sheepmen, but Minto's point of view prevailed. The division of opinion revealed by the controversy would persist in Oregon for several years.[11]

Similar debates occurred in states whose economic and political power was dominated by grazers. Governor William A. Richards of Wyoming, himself a stock raiser, publicly denounced absentee administration of forest reserves which, he disdainfully observed, had been selected by "college professors and landscape gardeners." The only proper alternative to the "farce" of federal regulation, he asserted, would be the cession of all public lands to the states. That suggestion would grow into a major controversy within the decade. Richards' successor continued to support this attitude by approving a legislative memorial opposing the exclusion of grazing in the forests and the proposed leasing of rangeland.[12] In New Mexico Territory the demands of the stock interests enjoyed the personal solicitude of Governor Miguel A. Otero. When the Gila Reserve was created in March, 1899, he formally requested that the establishment of this and all other reserves be suspended until the uncertain economic conditions in the area could be remedied. Then, after visiting the Manzano Mountains in the center of the territory, he convinced Commissioner Hermann that no reserve should be established there. Successful in that instance, he then recommended the creation of a reserve elsewhere.[13]

The political leaders of states with extensive mining interests also contested federal policy. Governor Frank Steunenberg of Idaho told his legislature that the reserves were made at the worst possible time. "With immigration practically ceased and outside capital withdrawn," he complained, "we are to a considerable extent thrown upon our own resources. . . . The pretext that our lands and forests are the just inheritance of posterity is not only hackneyed, but illogical and overdrawn." During the tenure of his successor, Frank W. Hunt, the state executive coöperated with Idaho's members of Congress in blocking the establishment of a Shoshone Falls National Park. Fully aware of the potential value of the area, Hunt proudly observed that three million acres had been saved for the wealth and population of the state.[14] In Colorado, criticism of the reserves was initiated by the Fort Collins *Courier*. Arguing that the policy was contrary to previous land laws and that it locked up areas already entered by settlers, the *Courier's* editorials denounced the theorists and sportsmen allegedly reponsible for the withdrawals and maintained that lumbering actually improved watersheds. Every local problem, from fires to unemployment, was blamed on the government; when a boom time did occur, the government was charged with hindering it. When the Trans Mississippi Commercial Congress met at Cripple Creek, in 1901, Colorado cattleman Elias M. Ammons demanded a full investigation of the effects of the reserves upon near-by communities.[15] The prevalence of complaint and doubt about the policy enabled local political and economic interests to exercise an influence which they might not have enjoyed in normal times. In New Mexico, for example, Thomas B. Catron, of Socorro, promoted the cause of citizens whose holdings were threatened by the reserves and sent an associate to Washington, D.C. to plead, successfully, their cases. Business and civic organizations in the towns of western Washington State were also able to convince the McKinley administration that the Olympic Reserve was unnecessarily large. As a result, it was greatly reduced in size in 1900 and again in 1901.[16]

In seeking to modify federal policy, local interests sometimes worked at cross purposes, thereby harming their own prosperity as well as impeding adequate administration. Nothing exemplified this better than the controversy which began in Arizona in 1898. In that year the Atlantic and Pacific Railroad joined with two lumber companies in securing the establishment of the Black Mesa, San Francisco, and Grand Canyon Forest Reserves. According to the stockmen in those areas, the railroad and the lumber companies were more interested in obtaining lieu land selections than in protecting timber. Fearful of being barred from the reserves, the grazers gave the forestry agents a hostile reception. According to A. B. Hermann, supervisor of the Grand Canyon Reserve and brother of the Land Commissioner, the editor of the Williams *News* suggested that the best form of retaliation against the government would be to hang "these U.S. tree agents" to the trees they had come to protect. The sheepmen were also opposed, however, by the irrigationists of the Salt River Valley, to the south, for these land-holders were anxious to have their watersheds preserved.[17]

The sheep raisers concluded that they must protect their livelihood by strengthening the Arizona Sheep Breeders and Wool Growers Association. Under the leadership of E. S. Gosney, the organization was reconstituted as the Arizona Woolgrowers Association, with a large membership and a new sense of mission. Gosney, a lawyer, banker, and sheep owner, presided over the group for more than a decade and gave it an aggressive, responsible leadership. Like the members of the territorial government, he had no faith in Secretary Hitchcock's knowledge of Western range conditions, and therefore decided to deal with the controversy on the local level. Traveling to Phoenix, he and his associates tried to talk to the irrigationists themselves and also addressed numerous meetings to explain the sheepmen's attitude. In open letters to the "fair minded people" of the valley, he criticized the distortions being made by the local press and admitted that a gradual application of the reserve system was a desirable policy. But practical forestry would actually be retarded, he added, if "our well meaning friends continue to force upon us iron clad theories and regulations however scientific they may look in the studio or have proven in some eastern or foreign forest." If that system should be applied forcibly, he warned, "a generation may pass before public confidence and patriotic earnest co-operation of the citizen with the government can be restored."[18]

Anxious to repair the rupture of public relations to which Gosney referred, Gifford Pinchot, the head of the Division of Forestry, came to Arizona in 1900 and was cordially welcomed by the sheepmen. Unlike his superior, Secretary Hitchcock, Pinchot was a trained forester, familiar with Western conditions and cognizant of the way in which forests could be used for grazing under proper regulations. For these reasons Gosney and Albert F. Potter, the secretary of the Arizona Woolgrowers Association, gave him their full confidence. Pinchot not only carried their formal demands back to Washington but also induced Potter to join the forestry bureau as an adviser on grazing problems. Hitchcock remained adamant about excluding sheep from the reserves, however, and it seemed to the Arizonans that Pinchot had not pressed their claims strongly enough.

During the seasons which followed, fires further reduced the rangelands and drought intensified the conflict over water use. In 1901 the woolgrowers of Coconino County, an area around Flagstaff which supported the largest number of sheep in the territory, decided to send special representatives to the White House to seek a solution to the crisis. As the *Coconino Sun* anticipated, effective political avenues were thereby utilized, and Hitchcock was ordered to hold a full hearing on the controversy. At that session the sheepmen agreed that forest preservation was necessary, but they objected to the lumber companies' seemingly profiting from the reserves while their own interests were ruined and their communities made bankrupt. Representatives of the irrigation projects of Phoenix insisted that the reserves were essential for future urban and agricultural expansion. At the conclusion of the hearing the Secretary was so obviously unconvinced that Pinchot and Potter went to the new President, Theodore Roosevelt, and directly requested him to permit grazing in the San Francisco Reserve, outside Flagstaff. According to their recollection of the meeting, Roosevelt heard their arguments, pressed a buzzer summoning his secretary, and dictated a brief but unquestionable directive to Hitchcock: "From information which has just reached me, it is my opinion that sheep should not be excluded from grazing on the San Francisco Mountains Forest Reserve."[19] Although prohibitions against grazing were not rescinded elsewhere for several years, the Arizona controversy proved to be a significant episode. Out of the chaos of conflicting claims within the state and between users and the government, a precedent was clearly established. From that time on, the efficacy of personal coöperation between economic organizations and men with decisive influence in government was to be demonstrated repeatedly.

THE LIMITS OF LOCAL INITIATIVE

Although the initial reaction to federal resource regulation in the West was not always negative, it was invariably controversial. Several of the states had begun programs of administering resource use on their own domains years before the Cleveland reserves were created. As early as 1886 California and Colorado established forestry commissions, but these were primarily fact-finding bodies which sometimes coöperated with such national organizations as the American Forestry Association.[20] In January, 1897, Governor Robert Smith of Montana urged the passage of legislation for the maintenance and rental of grazing lands in the state, and suggested that provisions be made for timber sales, mineral claims, and homestead claims. Unlawful denudation of timber on state lands in Washington continued at such an alarming rate that Governor John H. McGraw asked his legislature to create a Land and Forest Commission which would be staffed with technicians and not political appointees.[21] In Utah the vital problem of watershed protection accounted for the formulation of a broad conservation program. Through the personal efforts of Governor Heber M. Wells, Salt Lake City's need for protective reserves was submitted to the Division of Forestry and ultimately fulfilled in Cleveland's proclamations. To supplement federal policy, Wells also obtained state laws for reforestation.[22]

Civic, professional, and business organizations in the larger cities of the region also supported resource regulation. In Colorado, petitions from these groups helped secure the establishment of the first federal reserves in 1891 and 1892. In Seattle and Tacoma, Washington, and in Portland, Oregon, commercial and mountaineering clubs sponsored campaigns for the reservation of the watershed areas which served those communities. The wasteful lumbering operations of the United Verde Mining Company near Prescott, Arizona, aroused local fears for watershed cover and elicited a unanimous petition for the creation of the Prescott Reserve and its subsequent enlargement. When the Fourth National Irrigation Congress met in Albuquerque, New Mexico, in 1895, the delegates—representatives of towns, farm areas, and land development companies—adopted a resolution which demanded the extension of the few existing federal forest reserves. Throughout the West the desirability of more reservations was publicized by the lectures of scientists and scholars at the University of California, the University of Southern California, and the state universities of Washington and Utah.[23] The listing of similar activities could be continued at great length. Nevertheless it is obvious that the sum of all of these efforts over the course of a decade was a mere fragment of the solution to the problem of resource conservation.

The most striking example of the limitations upon local action was the crusade led by John Muir in California. By an act of Congress, the state had been given jurisdiction over the vast Yosemite Park and the adjoining Sequoia and General Grant forests, and a Yosemite Commission had been established to administer the areas. In 1890 formal charges of maladministration were brought against that agency by Charles D. Robinson, a member of the lower house of the legislature. The controversy that followed eventually spread beyond the boundaries of the state. Muir, whose career was closely involved with the exaltation of the magnificent mountain valleys of the Yosemite, naturally assumed a leading role among those who criticized the commissioners. During the public discussions of the charges, the accusers denounced the Southern Pacific Railroad, which allegedly controlled the Yosemite Commission along with every other part of the state government, and blamed sheepmen who grazed their flocks in the park for destroying its natural beauty. Muir concentrated his personal attack on one of the commissioners, John P. Irish. A former state senator, Irish was sincerely interested in preserving the Yosemite forests, but he entertained opinions about resource use which were unscientific and often superficial. He believed, for example, that underbrush should be cleared away, because the pioneers had cleared the land by fire and ax for farming. Such naïveté confirmed the conclusion of the Muir men that the commission looked upon the park as little more than a "prolific lumber patch and cattle ranch." Assailed by articles at home and in the prestigious columns of *Century*—edited by Muir's friend Robert Underwood Johnson—Irish was glad to have the support of Gifford Pinchot, then a young professional forester. Pinchot inspected conditions in the park and decided that the arguments against the commissioners were erroneous. He promised to vindicate Irish in an article he would send to Johnson's magazine, but after talking with Muir before leaving California, he never wrote the promised defense. In time, Irish realized that the attacks were not directed against him personally, but were designed to force the appointment of a trained forester to administer the park. The barrage of correspondence and newspaper editorials was the means to that end; that aim was far more important for the crusaders than the probability of ruining the reputations of men who were not directly culpable. The use of similar tactics by conservationists during the subsequent years would have significant consequences.[24]

The emotionalism practiced by the Muir men aroused strong resentment in the state. The conservative San Francisco *Chronicle* labeled their campaign a "prevalent tin can and pig pen delusion." For the most part, however, Californians feared that the crusade was aimed at wresting control of Yosemite Park from the state. Reaction reached a high point when the state Board of Forestry was dissolved because of the controversy and burning of underbrush was publicly defended. In agricultural Tulare County, an Anti-Park Association was formed by several communities. Shortly thereafter, delegates from three counties attended a so-called forestry convention, and resolved that stock raising was more important than the preservation of scenery. As a newspaper in Kern County expressed it, commerce and lumbering could not be sacrificed so that "some fine-spun theory be experimented [with] and proved of little if any value."[25] Muir dismissed these opponents as "unregenerate sons of Adam"—the man who had broken into nature's first reserve. In the opinion of Assemblyman Robinson, such resistance was "the last breathings & spasmodic struggles of that senile, dying old dragon—States Rights."[26]

In 1893 the conservationists were greatly strengthened by the adherence of the Sierra Club of San Francisco. Founded by Muir in 1889, this society of outdoorsmen included many of the most influential economic and political leaders of the state. Depending upon their support, Muir began a campaign to have Yosemite Park re-ceded to the federal government.

In the beginning, the recessionists believed that nine-tenths of the people of California would approve of their aim, but they admitted that the remaining tenth were the hardest fighters because their economic interests were "touched to the quick" by the proposition. The park seemed to be threatened from all sides during 1894 and 1895. The government considered the desirability of reducing its size and permitting mining and farming within its boundaries. At the same time, Governor James H. Budd tried to get the legislature to cut substantially appropriations for maintaining the area. For once, the commissioners joined their critics to protest that action, and they later agreed to employ a skilled landscape architect as the conservationists demanded. The publicity given to these issues helped dissolve public apathy by bringing an increasing number of visitors to the Yosemite Valley. Muir was pleased with that development, but he continued to enlist additional support for the campaign. In order to supplement his ranks in the north, he secured the assistance of Theodore P. Lukens in southern California. A resident of San Bernardino, Lukens had for many years explored the forests adjacent to Los Angeles, making notes, replanting, and lecturing in near-by communities on the need for an adequate forestry policy. His services were especially welcome when a bill for the recession of Yosemite Park was introduced into the state legislature in January, 1897. The campaigners found, however, that mere publicity could not reach inside the Assembly Chamber. The measure failed of passage because few members favored it, and because the majority admittedly did not understand the importance of the transfer. Undaunted by this defeat, Muir believed that his crusade would eventually win: "things refuse to be mismanaged long."[27]

The action taken by President Cleveland a month later should have impressed the recessionists with the efficacy of federal initiative, but Muir personally distrusted the man in the White House and doubted the wisdom of appealing to government officials. The events of the next two years should have induced him to revise his attitude. A large number of sheep were taken into Yosemite Valley during 1898; state agents ultimately had to expel 80,000 of them. In order to solve that problem, Senator Stephen M. White began discussions with Commissioner Hermann concerning the granting of grazing permits for the area, while Congressman Curtis Castle asked Secretary Bliss to open the Sequoia forest to grazing because of the existing drought. "Sheep & fire destruction are going merrily on," Muir lamented in a letter to editor Johnson, of the *Century*. When he learned that Pinchot opposed military supervision of the park and that sheepmen had sent lobbyists to Washington, he commented bitterly that it was "a fine year for the forests, a fine J. P. Irish . . . sheep year."[28] Muir failed to notice the limitations of a movement based upon the verbal zeal of a handful of citizens. The California conservationists would not be successful in their crusade until both public sentiment and political influence were sufficiently aroused in the West and in the nation's capital.

The years of discussion and publicity in California did create a climate of opinion conducive to local organization. In the winter of 1898 Muir became despondent over the way in which the Sierra Club had defected from the campaign to prohibit grazing in Yosemite Park. Because that group seemed to be "half dead," he suggested to Lukens that the conservationists in the southern part of the state establish another "Alpine Club." "The more clubs, the better," he explained, "for we are going to have a good deal of work in the reservations." Two seasons of inadequate rainfall and forest fires in the south underscored the need for greater public support. In April, 1899, Lukens' adherents sent out a formal call to all citizens who were "interested in protecting our mountain forests and the water sheds below them," and a meeting was held to formulate a "general plan of forest protection and water storage for Southern California." Besides Lukens, the sponsors of this meeting included William Knight, a publicist and the earliest associate of Hubert H. Bancroft; Abbot Kinney, whose pioneering work in popularizing conservation equaled his accomplishments as a real estate promoter; and William Kerckhoff, the operator of a lumber mill and owner of an electric power company in the Los Angeles area. Three months later, the group held a larger convention and organized the Forest and Water Society, electing Kerckhoff president and Lukens secretary. In 1900, the society was reorganized under the leadership of Kinney and Knight, and was renamed the Forest and Water Association of Los Angeles County. Membership was subsequently extended to many prominent businessmen and political leaders and to others such as George Maxwell, one of the first advocates of reclamation projects in the Southwest. In order to promote greater coöperation between Californians and federal officials, the association held many meetings which attracted statewide attention and provided excellent opportunities for speakers like Pinchot to educate the public on the subject of conservation. As might be expected, the organization was occasionally accused of entertaining political prejudices, but its officers insisted that forest despoilers, "rich or poor, Democrat or Republican, should be put in jail." In significant contrast to Muir, they did not hesitate to utilize political channels. Senators Thomas R. Bard and George C. Perkins were asked to convey several resolutions to Congress protesting any diminution of federal forest reserves in California. Other petitions on the subject of land use regulations were sent to the Secretary of the Interior and the Land Commissioner.[29] The success and popularity of the Los Angeles association evidently encouraged conservationists elsewhere in the state. In 1899, delegates representing commercial, stock, lumbering, and farming interests held a convention in San Francisco and soon afterward founded the California Forest and Water Association. Its subsequent activities included the distribution of pamphlets on many aspects of resource conservation, as well as the publication of a periodical, *Water and Forest*. In view of all of these activities, it is easy to understand why Pinchot found the state a "friend of forestry" when he came there in 1899.[30]

Considering the numerous problems encountered by the conservationists, and recognizing the fact that there was a limited number of such zealous leaders as Muir and Lukens, it seems clear that local initiative could be no more than a supplement to the conservation policy. As the Yosemite controversy revealed, the task of educating the public, even under the optimum conditions which existed in the growing communities of California, was a long-term one. Finally, the ultimate power of politics and government was an advantage enjoyed by the opponents of the movement, not by its supporters. Each of these influences—public approval, leadership, and political effectiveness—would have to improve before a conservation program could be applied in the West.

CHAPTER II

ROOSEVELT, PINCHOT, AND THEIR DISCIPLES

THE NETWORK OF ADMINISTRATION

RESOURCE CONSERVATION did not win popular support until almost a decade after President Cleveland issued his forest reserve proclamations. Yet, within a few years of that action, a policy of regulation and use had been established and was being applied not only by the federal government, but by many of the states of the West. During those years a group of men who were extraordinarily adept at the art of politics assumed positions of executive power and, by working together, laid a pragmatic foundation for federal resource administration. A few of them fully understood the potential value of the program to the future of the country; most were aware of its essential role in economic development; all recognized that conservation depended upon administrative techniques that would have to be applied within the limits of traditional politics. These executives shared a palpable personal relationship as well—one which was inspired by ambition as well as idealism. Their contribution was substantial precisely because their motives were an inextricable mixture of these two qualities.

The cornerstone of this structure of politics and personalities was Theodore Roosevelt. Looking back on his significant career while composing an autobiography in 1913, Roosevelt decided that the adoption of federal conservation was the greatest contribution he had made to the domestic policies of the United States. Long before he entered politics, his interests and experiences had prepared him for that role. In the 1880's, the young New Yorker left personal disappointments in the East and sought emotional and physical regeneration in the range country along the border between the Montana and Dakota territories. He became familiar with the stark conditions of living in the West during several subsequent seasons as a stock raiser and many hunting trips along the Kootenai and Yellowstone rivers. Further travels in the Mountain states familiarized him with the conflicting claims of farmers, stockmen, and other users of lands and resources. These realities at once strongly appealed to his interest in the natural sciences and stimulated his passion for the testing ground of individual worth that lies in the shadowy borderland between law and adventure. The West and the people who lived there became an important part of his thoughts. Even after he returned to New York, he not only continued to consider himself a westerner, but was so regarded by the many friends he made in both regions. In later years, they rallied around him as members of the Rough Riders and as political supporters. He also enjoyed the intellectual company of such influential scientists as Clarence King the geologist and Bernard Fernow the forester, as well as the enthusiastic writers on the Western scene—John Muir, John Burroughs, Stewart Edward White, and Owen Wister.[1]

During the first phase of his political career, Roosevelt was able to transform these personal interests into governmental action. While he was governor of New York his understanding of the theory of conservation was broadened through association with two young specialists in resource problems, Gifford Pinchot and Frederick Newell, a promising civil engineer. In consequence, his messages to the state legislature often included requests for the enlargement of forest reserves and the establishment of administrative sites for the protection of other resources. It was as governor, also, that he learned his first lesson in the politics involved in conservation policy. In 1900, a controversy broke out in the Forest and Game Commission, whose members were all too amenable to party pressures. When the affair seemed to threaten the security of his whole administration, Roosevelt intervened and reorganized the agency in such a way that its activities were removed from the realm of patronage. While doing so he perceived that public understanding of the commission's technical duties could not be quickly or directly improved. Confident that he was acting for the best interests of all citizens, he could more effectively deal with such a critical problem by exercising the authority of his office.[2] Similar issues beyond New York further demonstrated to him the essential role of executive initiative. Watching the controversy over the Yosemite Commission in California, he urged Cleveland's Secretary of the Interior to have the park placed under federal control. Roosevelt was pleased with the President's subsequent creation of new forest reserves, but he felt that the action should have been based upon the consent of the West's representatives in Congress.[3] Both of these controversies must have impressed him with the fact that a great chasm of failure yawned between the conservationists and their goals—a gap that could be bridged only by personal politics.

When Roosevelt was suddenly elevated to the Presidency in September, 1901, he assured the country that the policies of his predecessor would continue. His first message to Congress a few months later revealed, however, that he was contemplating changes in programs and administrative techniques. Calling attention to existing federal jurisdiction over the public domain, he asserted that this responsibility could best be fulfilled if the Division of Forestry were reorganized and staffed with scientists who could formulate a permanent policy. In the following year, he reminded the legislators of widespread violations of land laws by private economic interests, promised a more watchful administration of the statutes, and asked for corrective measures.[4] He also endorsed passage of Senator Francis G. Newlands' bill which subsequently established reclamation projects throughout the arid West. Privately, however, the President had slight confidence in legislative action after observing the customary inertia of congressmen and the hostility of members from the West. He continued to recommend specific legislation, but his most significant accomplishment came from his skill in the politics of administration.

Roosevelt was anxious to build up popular support for his administration during his first term in office. Consequently, he did not overlook the possibility of public reaction to decisions in resource matters. In some instances, he was able to handle potentially dangerous issues with characteristic forcefulness. In 1902, for example, he was warned by Governor George Chamberlain of Oregon and editor Scott of the *Oregonian* that lumber and mining companies in the state were manipulating land laws to get choice tracts from the public domain. Appointing Francis J. Heney, a Californian, as special investigator, the President directed him to search out evidence which would lead to the conviction of every malefactor. The prosecutions stretched out over three years and involved most of the members of Congress from Oregon as well as Land Commissioner Binger Hermann. When Senator Charles Fulton anxiously advised Roosevelt that the affair was damaging the Republican party in the state, he was told that the trials would continue, no matter where they led. Ultimately, Fulton's colleague, Senator William Mitchell, was convicted as an accomplice in the timberland frauds, and Commissioner Hermann, who was accused of burning official correspondence, resigned from his office.[5] By acting quickly and boldly the President gained in public esteem for his handling of the scandal. Despite the reply to Fulton, he was not unmindful of the security of his party. When Democrat Newlands claimed credit for the Reclamation Act of 1902, for example, the President promptly wrote to several friends and asserted that he had initially consulted with the senators from Montana and Wyoming and with Congressman Franklin Mondell of Wyoming. These men, he insisted, had prepared the bill and secured its passage. Once the subject was out of the realm of Republican politics, however, Newlands' contribution to reclamation and continued support of the administration's resource policies received just acknowledgment. In his autobiography Roosevelt praised the senator's work and denounced Mondell's subsequent opposition to conservation.[6]

In the spring of 1903, the President traveled through the West, mending political fences for the coming election, greeting old friends and making new ones. In many localities, he noticed evidence of waste or monopoly of lands, water, minerals, and forests, and he was advised of conflicts among the various users of these resources. When he reached California, for example, he was confronted with the still smoldering controversy over Yosemite Park. In significant contrast to his decision about the Oregon cases, he found it necessary to handle this issue with caution. While he camped with Muir on the floor of the magnificent valley, Roosevelt heard the arguments for immediate federal control over the park and left with his earlier belief in that solution soundly confirmed. Unlike Muir, however, he was more than a naturalist, and he realized that he could not safely bring about recession until there was a strong sentiment for it. As he pointed out to his camping companion, it was rarely wise to force such opinion. He did not add the obvious fact that it was especially unwise to attempt the task before an election. Instead, he was content to rely upon administrative procedures which were beyond the reach of public controversy. By executive proclamations, he brought much of the area adjacent to the park under federal jurisdiction. Forest reserves were created, and care was taken that their boundaries should not immediately damage the prestige of conservation among local residents. He had no sympathy with complaints against existing regulations, however, and personally ordered government officials to tolerate none of them. By the time of his reëlection, in 1904, the President's policy had the support of Governors Henry Gage and George Pardee. Moreover, he learned from consultations with the senators from California that the people of the state were generally convinced that local control of the park was expensive as well as controversial. A series of meetings between state and federal officials was sponsored by Governor Pardee and Congressman James Needham; shortly afterwards, Representative James Gillett introduced a recession bill into the House. By 1906 Muir and his adherents could rejoice over the passage of the measure for which they had fought for more than a decade.[7] Because of his skillful use of administrative details and political influence, Roosevelt deserved at least as much credit as Muir for the outcome of the controversy.

As an experienced executive, the President understood the importance of having competent assistants. In the course of the four years between 1904 and 1908 he gathered around him a group of young lieutenants who may properly be referred to as "the Roosevelt men" because of their personal devotion to him, or because they shared his enthusiastic interpretation of executive power and political diplomacy.

The circumstances surrounding the selection of one of these advisers well illustrates the relationship between Roosevelt and his subordinates. By 1902, the smoldering discontent of stockmen in the West had been rekindled by the enlargement of forest reserves and the enforcement of use regulations. In Wyoming, fires were set off in the forests, meetings called in several counties, and petitions sent to the White House. Sheep owners near Yellowstone National Park even sent a personal representative, A. A. Anderson, to carry their objections to the President. After Roosevelt heard his statement, he ordered the boundaries of the local forest redrawn on the basis of Anderson's information and then appointed him to be superintendent of the new reserve. When Anderson returned home, however, the scorn of his neighbors was turned against him; within a few months his only defenders seemed to be "Buffalo Bill" Cody, who was editor of the Cody, Wyoming, *Enterprise,* and Roosevelt. When the sheepmen warned that federal policy threatened the stability of the Republican party in the state, the President asked William A. Richards to come to Washington. He had met the former governor during his western trip and, while discussing the controversy, found him to be outspoken, yet cordial and unpretentious. Assured by Richards' knowledge of economic conditions in the West and his earnest desire to end the controversy over federal policy, Roosevelt asked him to take the office of Commissioner of Public Lands, recently vacated by the discredited Hermann. Richards accepted and, before long, established a close working relationship with his colleagues Pinchot, of the Bureau of Forestry, and Newell, the director of the new Reclamation Service. Drawing upon his knowledge of local interests, he was able to smooth the way for forestry and irrigation projects. Although criticism continued in Wyoming, hostility there and in other range states was greatly assuaged by the extension of grazing privileges in the reserves.[8]

Realizing that the controversies in various parts of the West were all symptoms of the inadequate functioning of existing land use laws, Roosevelt designated Richards, Pinchot, and Newell to form the Public Land Commission. Officially, they were directed to survey the effects of present laws and to recommend changes to Congress. Privately, they intended to use the information to enlarge the scope of administration exercised by their own bureaus. In September, 1903, Wyoming became the site of their first examination, after Governor Fenimore Chatterton attacked Pinchot and the reserves in a speech delivered before a state industrial convention in Sheridan. Copies of his remarks were sent to the forester in near-by Billings, Montana, and Pinchot came to the meeting immediately. There he faced a barrage of questions from the delegates and, as Chatterton later recalled it, conducted a poor defense of his policy under fire. Although two additional ranges were opened in the forests shortly afterwards, the governor did not alter his opinion of Pinchot as the sheepman's enemy. In October, the two other members of the Public Lands Commission joined their colleague in a special convention at Cheyenne, the state capital. They had prepared themselves for the encounter by talking with Senator Francis Warren, but they were overwhelmed by the reception Chatterton prepared for them. At the Capitol they found a crowd of state officials, lawyers, editors, and businessmen from almost every county in Wyoming. In the course of a session which lasted all day, these representatives denounced the reserve system, blamed it for the recent loss of a million sheep which had been moved out of the state, and described it as a general menace to the livestock industry everywhere in the West. Then, by a unanimous vote, they registered their opposition to the proposed repeal of existing land laws and demanded cession of the public domain to the states. The commissioners left Wyoming with disturbing apprehensions about the real strength of hostility to federal land and resource policy. As they traveled through the rest of the West, however, they encountered few who were so firmly opposed to regulation as Chatterton, whom Pinchot privately scorned as a "yellow dog." For the most part, they observed that spokesmen of economic and political interests were generally vague or divided on the subject of desirable legislation. Their findings undoubtedly confirmed Roosevelt's belief that the most effective program of conservation and use would come through executive action.[9]

After his immediate future was assured by the election of 1904, the President turned to reorganizing the Department of the Interior and the Bureau of Forestry, the agencies which directed resource regulation. His immediate problem was the Secretary of the Interior. McKinley had chosen Ethan A. Hitchcock, a former St. Louis industrialist, to replace Cornelius Bliss in 1899. Although Hitchcock displayed slight imagination in initiating new programs, he executed existing laws with a keenly developed sense of responsibility and with a moralistic concern for the integrity of his Department. Perhaps the shock of the Oregon timberland frauds accentuated these personal characteristics; after that scandal, his directives were customarily rigid and his judgments revealed a suspicion of anyone connected with land and resource development. Most of his immediate staff and some of the agents in the field reflected their chief's distrust of applicants and petitioners. As a result many westerners formed a prejudice against everyone connected with the Department. The Secretary did not usually join with Richards, Pinchot, and Newell in intimate consultation with the President. Indeed, Roosevelt seemed to prefer to deal with his Land Commissioner and then have the matter brought to Hitchcock's attention. Older, more unbending, and far less enthusiastic than his colleagues, Hitchcock evidently resented their growing influence over matters which had theretofore been his own province.

On their part, the Roosevelt men came to regard the Secretary as an anachronism whose brittle attitudes constituted an obstacle to a dynamic resource program. On more than one occasion Pinchot complained to the President about Hitchcock's intransigence over forestry matters under the jurisdiction of the General Land Office. Moreover, the Secretary's particular form of zeal proved to be politically clumsy. His annual report publicized his belief that "the higher the offender, the greater the crime against society and law, because of the force and influence of the higher example." For that reason he had no patience with the vanities of Western political leaders. When Roosevelt asked him to investigate illegal fencing of the public domain in Wyoming, Hitchcock pursued the case with characteristic righteousness. Aware of the President's statement that he did not "give a rap whether the man hit be Democrat or Republican, Senator or private citizen," the Secretary eventually drew up indictments against several influential Republicans in Congress, including Senator Warren. Roosevelt, then occupied with the plan for reorganization, was greatly upset by the course of the investigation. The Interior Department had "gone to pieces," he confided to Richards with obvious disgust; "nothing but fraud gets attention." When further indictments mentioned the Commissioner himself, Roosevelt decided that it was Hitchcock who was dispensable. Early in 1907, he received the resignation of the man who was obviously unsuited to the new ways of the Roosevelt men.[10]

James R. Garfield, then Commissioner of Corporations, was chosen to preside over the renovation of the Department. When he accepted the post of Secretary he was already a member of the inner circle of advisers to the President—a fact which seemed to be the principal reason for his selection. A son of the late President James A. Garfield, the new executive had been raised in the world of Ohio politics, where he learned how to gauge men's temperaments and dissolve their antagonisms with cordial but firm assurances. While negotiating the intricate and often touchy agreements for the Bureau of Corporations, he de-

veloped an agility in dealing with administrative politics that earned
the admiration of Roosevelt. These characteristics were revealed by the
tone of the Secretary's first annual report in 1907. After describing the
more efficient structure erected as a result of the reorganization, Garfield presented a hopeful declaration of purpose for federal land policy,
including the statement that "The highest use of lands is the making
of homes." In significant contrast to his predecessor, he recognized the
real sources of Western opposition and assured the people of the West
that Interior agents were not detectives and were not used as such. The
beginning of a new official attitude toward the region was particularly
marked by the Secretary's assertion that administrative successes during the year were made possible by federal reliance upon men with
Western experience.[11] Apart from his undoubted abilities, the principal
reason for Garfield's accomplishments was his intimate friendship with
the man who was the guiding spirit of the conservation crusade.

In physical appearance, tall, lean Gifford Pinchot was a striking contrast to Roosevelt; in limitless energy and executive skills, he was the
President's twin. As a young man he had found in the new profession
of forestry the means of expressing an intense ambition to do some great
moral task. After studying European forestry methods, he returned to a
series of unique opportunities in the United States. Serving first with
private owners, he later surveyed the timberlands of states east and
west, thus acquiring a store of scientific data unmatched by any naturalist in the country. Because of his experience, he was asked to join the
federal Bureau of Forestry in 1896, but he decided to wait for a more
advantageous position. At that time, he became the most prominent advocate of a full program of planned resource use based upon the authority of the federal government. Although he did not originate the
concept that was later called conservation, Pinchot's influence gave that
policy a pragmatic meaning. As secretary to the forestry commission
of the National Academy of Sciences which surveyed western timberlands for the Cleveland administration, he came into conflict with older
men who adhered to the tradition of preservation of natural resources
from further use. Although he was unable to overcome their influence
at that time, his selection as chief of the Bureau of Forestry in 1898
provided him with the opportunity to transform a minor governmental
concern into a major domestic policy.

When Pinchot took over the Bureau, he found it a small agency
operating on a paltry budget and impeded in its vital work by the
shortcomings of an untrained staff and the suspicions of westerners.
Until he could obtain necessary changes from Congress and the admin-

istration, Pinchot proceeded cautiously, compromising on petty issues and explaining his program as a solution to the prevailing discontent in the West. Within a few years, political deftness and administrative competency enabled him to intensify his publicity. Never before had a subordinate official enjoyed such an opportunity to preach to men of every occupation everywhere in the country. An endless procession of statesmen and politicians, critics and crusaders, came to his office and home in Washington, D.C., and to his many temporary headquarters in hotel rooms or forests in the West. They complained, argued, listened, and departed with a healthy respect for the forester's sensibility and persuasiveness, if not for his theories. His detractors described him as the epitome of egotistical, theoretical, Eastern bureaucracy, yet few men in the country understood the problems of multipurpose use of resources as fully and accurately as he did. At least once every year he traveled through the West, calling at isolated ranger stations, small towns, and farms, making voluminous notes on the use and abuse of forests, grass, and water. He was as much interested in the possibilities of future action which local residents might take as he was in finding subjects for federal regulation. There were dozens of westerners whose knowledge of specific areas or problems was more detailed, but none who knew the total complex of conditions in the West so well as the chief of the Bureau of Forestry.[12]

The relationship between Roosevelt and Pinchot might be described as ideological and political symbiosis. The President readily identified his own interests as a naturalist and his faith in dynamic executive power with the forester's personal crusade for planned conservation and use of resources. Pinchot, as a secondary official, had slight means to implement his programs, but because he was Roosevelt's most trusted adviser, his proposals were encased in the authority and prestige of the Presidency. By securing an act transferring jurisdiction over forests from the Interior Department to the Department of Agriculture, in 1905, Roosevelt removed the last obstacle to the fulfillment of Pinchot's ambitions. He retained McKinley's Secretary of Agriculture, James Wilson, of Iowa, as a valuable friend of the farmers and a reliable administrator. Pinchot was appointed Chief Forester of the newly organized Forest Service in the Department and although he was subordinate to Wilson, his influence was second only to that of the President. The jurisdiction of his bureau extended over 160 million acres of federal reservations, now wisely renamed national forests, and encompassed the use of water, minerals, grasses, and right of ways within them. With the dedicated adherence of Garfield and Newell, and with the force of Roosevelt behind him, he assumed a dominant, and some-times domineering, position in the government.[13]

Like the President, the Chief Forester was publicly solicitous for the welfare of the settler—that universally defended man—but, like his chief also, he relied upon the decisive advantage gained by enlisting the support of men with great economic and political influence. Some of these, such as Judge Thomas Burke, of Seattle, eagerly assisted him during the early period of the movement, but subsequently became discouraged by the growth of his personal power. Others, like Senator Reed Smoot, of Utah, were permanently converted to the cause of fed-eral conservation. The experience of C. Watt Brandon was typical of the working relationship cultivated by Pinchot. As editor of a small-town newspaper in Wyoming, Brandon first wrote to Pinchot to reg-ister local complaints against use regulations. Pinchot's reply and their subsequent correspondence encouraged Brandon to arrange for con-sultations between federal agents and resident stockmen. In doing so he initiated a procedure that soon became a regular practice for set-tling grazing problems in the area. Pinchot was, however, wary of the motives of some supporters. For example, it seemed to him that Senator Jonathan Bourne, of Oregon, was assuming a friendly attitude in order to advance his own political influence in the administration. It was impossible to gain the trust of a small coterie of westerners, but Pinchot was able to work with these irreconcilables when he could not bypass their power. Representative Franklin Mondell, of Wyoming, for ex-ample, consistently opposed the growth of federal authority over the public domain and, although he had supported the transfer bill, was particularly hostile to the Forest Service. As chairman of the House committees on resources and departmental expenditures, however, Mondell had to be in continual communication with Pinchot. Mondell's son later recalled that whenever the two reached an impasse over some issue they would take a box lunch to Rock Creek Park and work out their difficulties in the peaceable and pastoral surroundings there.[14]

Under Pinchot's vigorous direction the Forest Service enlarged its field staff and selected officers of every rank from residents of the west-ern states. Generally, these agents were trained in the fundamentals of forestry. If local political pressures were involved in their appointment, however, Pinchot kept them under surveillance until he was certain that their paramount loyalty was given to the Forest Service. By 1907, when the reorganization plans were completed, most of the federal officials serving in the West were conscientious, faithful admirers of their chief. Regularly reporting to or corresponding with the headquarters in

Washington, they exchanged not only information of a scientific nature, but also instructions concerning local demands and politics as well. The educational tracts which the Service distributed to them in return were inserted into newspapers as fillers or delivered as speeches to meetings of ranchers, businessmen, and civic leaders. By these procedures the Forest Service was able to gauge Western sentiment and concentrate its efforts on specific areas. After several years, it had gained the enthusiastic support of many prominent men in every economic pursuit. These disciples of Pinchot included J. B. Killian, of Colorado, and Dwight B. Heard, of Arizona, both large cattle raisers; private foresters E. T. Allen, of California, and Joseph N. Teal, of Oregon; and editors Will Cowles, of the Spokane, Washington, *Spokesman-Review*, and Clarence P. Dodge, of the Colorado Springs, Colorado, *Gazette*. Some of these friends served in official capacities: for example, Arizona stockman Albert Potter became head of the Grazing Division in the Forest Service. Others, like Malcolm Moody, of Oregon, acted as personal emissaries for Pinchot in the Northwest.[15] Standing at the center of this vast network of information and support, the Chief Forester was able to learn of changes in public opinion as soon as they were manifest, and could take every means available to him to stimulate or discourage them.

THE CRITICS AT BAY

The administrative reorganization of the federal bureaus occurred at a critical time. Although discontent had simmered in the West for many years, inadequate regulations and lax enforcement convinced many residents that the irritating federal policy would ultimately be abandoned. After 1905, however, resource users were confronted with a dismaying phalanx of new rules, additional reserves, and—most outrageous of all—an assessment of fees for grazing and irrigation. Moreover, the traditional indifference of agents who were political appointees was now replaced by the responsible, often righteous, attitude of Forest Service officials and Interior Department field employees. Before, the average stock raiser or landowner had found it necessary to obey federal directives once or twice a season; now, every person who entered the reserves for any reason found himself watched, disciplined, and taxed at frequent intervals.

For the next two years the region echoed with indignant cries and grim warnings. Governor Bryant B. Brooks of Wyoming told a sympathetic legislature that a great disturbance would occur unless the new regulations were applied more gradually. A delegation of cattlemen from the state went to Washington to argue against the grazing fee, but their trip was futile. When the tax was applied in spite of remonstrances, Wyoming woolgrowers joined the cattlemen in passing resolutions of protest.[16] Local public opinion was hardly in a light-hearted mood, but a bit of strained doggerel appeared in a Cheyenne newspaper:

> Bury me not on the range,
> Where the taxed cattle are roaming,
> And the angry coyotes yelp and bark,
> And the wind in the pines is moaning.
> On the Reserve please bury me not,
> For I never would then be free:
> A forest ranger would dig me up,
> That he might collect his fee.[17]

Arizona coyotes were barking for the same reasons. Although many men of the Forest Service were well known to the residents of the territory, they were criticized as representatives of a policy that had abolished traditional range customs. Even Roosevelt, the idol of many, was denounced along with Pinchot. Arizonans were ready to believe that the two officials had "gone nutty about this forest conservation business" when they established the Tucomcori Reserve in an area of brush vegetation. At a meeting of citizens in Nogales, one rancher offered his impression of the seemingly insane policy: "Looks like every time one of the government scouts finds a tree in the West he wires Pinchot and Pinchot gallops into Teddy's office and says: 'Oh, Teddy, we've found a tree in the What-the-Hell mountains; let's create a new forest!'" Local rangers were nicknamed "Teddy's Pets" during those tense months, and were viewed as a distinctly low form of life.[18]

In those parts of the West where grazing, lumbering, and mining were coincidentally practiced, opposition was even more pronounced. In southwestern Montana residents defiantly informed the rangers that as "free American citizens" they would cut timber and run stock as they had done in the past. Roosevelt's popularity was eclipsed by the issue there, as elsewhere, and many Montanans believed that as soon as the Democrats took the reins of government this "crack pot scheme of politicians in Washington" would be abolished.[19] Early in 1907 Governor Joseph Toole discussed the controversy with members of the state legislature. Quoting an unidentified informant, he asserted that the use regulations were being enforced "with such severity and disregard of business methods long settled and with such arrogant assumption of authority as to amount to petty but intolerable tyranny." No one doubted the wisdom of having forest reserves, he assured the lawmakers, but the needs of a "flood of settlers" and the vital mining industry should not be hampered by federal policy. As a Republican, the governor could not repeat political threats, but he suggested that the state's delegation in Congress protest against the size of "these indiscriminate reserves." If the allegedly tyrannical enforcement of regulations was brought to the President's attention, Toole believed that Roosevelt would speedily correct the condition.[20] In Oregon, Governor George Chamberlain took a similar stand in his address to the legislature. Much of the area included in reserves which occupied one-fifth of the total domain within the state could, he stated, properly be opened to settlement, cultivation, and grazing. In a region where rainfall was always heavy, additional withdrawals for watershed protection were unwarranted. Many citizens of the state agreed with John Minto's preference for local forestry protection instead of federal control. "The only advantage I can see in the formation of these forest reserves," one of his adherents wrote, "is in keeping the land out of the hands of timber monopolies."[21] The substance of all these arguments seemed to indicate that a large part of public opinion in the West was still preoccupied with the limited policy of reservation of the preceding years and that westerners were wholly unprepared to accept the new programs of the Roosevelt men.

The political leaders of the states, particularly those in the Northwest, were primarily responsible for the absence of local understanding about conservation. In the state of Washington the legislature belatedly acted upon the recommendation of former Governor McGraw by establishing a Board of Forest Commissioners in 1905. Within a year the agency showed itself adept at the old art of forest depletion through political chicanery. Even when the members made responsible recommendations, they were blocked by the state land commissioner, E. W. Ross. A jealous defender of the landed assets of Washington, especially school sections, Ross was an implacable foe of the encroaching Forest Service. His opinions were widely reprinted in newspapers over the state, and he was in turn praised by vested interests as the defender of the people's rights. Ross seems to have persuaded other officials to share his hostility toward federal interference; E. T. Allen told Pinchot that the state fire warden refused to answer any communications from the Forest Service. When Allen himself tried to explain the policy to the legislature, he was interrupted by a verbal attack from Ross and was hustled out of the chamber. If the state had an opportunity to vote on the subject of national forests, Allen concluded sadly, ninety per cent of the people would want them abolished.[22]

In February, 1907, Governor Albert Mead gave the President a solemn warning about federal conservation in Washington State. Admitting that reckless lumbering methods were wrong, he maintained that the practices of the past did not justify wholesale withdrawals of forest reserves, especially since natural reforestation was so rapid in the rain-drenched state. Pointedly reminding Roosevelt that the voters there had given him a majority of 75,000 votes in the election of 1904, Mead testified that the citizens felt that federal officials were using their authority to "work injury to the best interests" of the state. The President asked for Pinchot's opinion on the nature of opposition in Washington, and was told that it rarely came from actual homesteaders. He sent a copy of this response to the governor and, for additional emphasis, pointed to the fact that speculators had seized valuable lands when the Olympic Reserve was opened to entry a few years before. By implication, it was they, not the ordinary citizens, who now opposed federal restrictions. Mead was so angered by this reply that he sent copies of the whole correspondence to the state Senate and asked for the creation of a special commission to receive complaints from settlers in the national forests. He intended to forward these statements to Roosevelt and Pinchot, and particularly to the new Commissioner of Public Lands, Washington's own Richard Ballinger. Because his official summary of the arguments against federal control revealed the hand of Ross by referring to the alleged nullification of school land titles, it represented nothing more than the views of a coterie of state officials.[23]

No state had better cause to take up arms against the federal policy than Idaho. Containing a sparse population which was directly dependent upon lumbering, mining, and grazing, it was blanketed with national forests which covered almost forty per cent of its total area. With few exceptions, persons of every occupation in all parts of the state scorned the new use regulations. Sheepmen refused to restrain their herds from damaging the rangeland; miners who were accustomed to prospecting anywhere took advantage of the rangers' unfamiliarity with isolated areas; even some employees of the Forest Service left their posts or sided with their neighbors in local disputes. Idaho Democrats blamed every economic problem on Roosevelt, the "Forest Reserve Autocrat," and jeered at their opponents for being afraid to say the same.[24]

Republicans in Idaho were indeed in an uncomfortable position during these years. Whether from solicitude for their party or for their own reëlection, many of them learned to dissemble their personal views on the issue. William E. Borah, for example, developed that political art to a degree that was, in some instances, appalling. During federal prosecutions for timberland frauds in the state, the young attorney had found himself the accused as well as the prosecutor. His personal experience with the zealots of the Interior Department during the trials accounted for his subsequent antipathy toward federal resource administration. Although accused of complicity in the frauds, Borah aroused enough local support to be elected to the United States Senate in 1906. After taking his seat there, he was further disgusted to learn that the Forest Service was appointing Democrats who in turn were choosing their supporters for local jobs.[25] The senator often denounced the Service for the edification of his colleagues, but his remarks about forest policy, when he was talking to constituents, were necessarily equivocal. Many towns in the southern part of the state, such as Pocatello, supported federal protection of watersheds which supplied farms with irrigation water. These farming communities did not share the views of the small mining towns in the north.

Speaking at a rally in Idaho City, Borah warmed up to a damnation of federal policy in general and the Forest Service in particular. When the meeting was over, one of his listeners stepped up and congratulated him, adding that the speech had been meticulously copied down by a newspaper reporter. The senator fell for the ruse. "My God, I must get hold of him right away," he exclaimed, "before he publishes anything that will create a false impression as to my views and position." After scurrying around the hall with a distracted air, he decided to telephone friends in Boise to have a roadblock set up. The trickster finally admitted that the whole thing was a hoax designed to find out whether Borah really meant all the things he said about conservation.[26] The oratorical assaults of many other Western politicians may properly be viewed with this incident in mind. Moreover, if politics encouraged such behavior in a state which was strongly critical of federal regulations, practical hypocrisy must have been even more common in those areas where more diverse economic and political interests existed.

Idaho's other senator had no such qualms about attacking the conservation policy of the Roosevelt administration. Weldon B. Heyburn began his career as an attorney for mining investors in the "Panhandle," the northern part of the state. He carried his belief in the traditional disposal of resources to the Land Office, where he served in the Division of Mines, and to the Senate Chamber. The solicitude he showed for capital investors in his own state and in adjacent Washington earned him the respect of many conservatives. One of them, at least, thought that the senator would make an excellent Secretary of the

Interior. In 1903, aroused by a proposal to enlarge forest reserves in Idaho, Heyburn dispatched letters to his friends to find out how they felt on the subject. The correspondence indicated that his constituents considered the withdrawals desirable only if they excluded noncommercial timber and grazing lands, did not otherwise damage future economic development, and were circumscribed by boundaries drawn by westerners. His informants were not only fearful that the reserves were "likely to remain forever," but were also opposed to the influx of "minions with little brief authority" who would administer them. After his personal views were confirmed by this survey, Heyburn soon matched Senator Carter, of Montana, in intemperate criticism and earned for himself the title of "the Objector." In 1904, he introduced a bill to prohibit the future creation of forest reserves and, when the measure was not acted upon, blocked approval of proposed withdrawals in the area near his home town of Wallace, Idaho.[27]

During the next two years, he turned his fire upon the federal executive and bombarded the offices of Roosevelt and Pinchot with lengthy protests against the reserves. At the same time, he decided to avoid any allegation that he was personally connected with resource users, and wisely declined any financial and legal association with investors seeking confirmation of claims and use permits. His self-assurance in approaching the President was bolstered by the facts that he had campaigned for Roosevelt's reëlection and had helped sponsor the Pure Food and Drug Act, a showpiece of the administration. When he warned the federal executives that their resource policy would damage Republican strength in Idaho, they refused to be intimidated. Just as Roosevelt had admonished Senator Fulton, of Oregon, he now submitted evidence that belied Heyburn's allegations about public sentiment in the state and asserted that the reserves were guaranteeing future growth of the West instead of stifling it. Political interests, the President added, would be heeded whenever proper, but he would not "for one moment consent to sacrifice the interests of the people as a whole for the real or fancied interests of any individual or political faction." The particular interest of the people in the West was conservation: "I believe they cordially approve it; I do not intend to abandon it."[28]

In order to offset the influence of Heyburn and his adherents, Roosevelt cultivated the coöperation of other party leaders in Idaho. Senator Fred Dubois, from the agricultural community of Pocatello, remained a soft-spoken, but useful supporter until his retirement in 1906. He not only served as a reliable source of information about conditions in the state, but also issued a public denial of his colleague's distorted version of the effect of conservation there.[29] Great effort had to be made, however, to secure the support of Governor Frank Gooding. A member of the Idaho Woolgrower's Association, he found it difficult to discuss the Forest Service's actions with moderation; with fist clenched and face flushed, he spoke to a receptive audience whenever the organization held a meeting. After his election to the governorship, however, Gooding showed restraint in his public remarks, a fact which encouraged Pinchot to call on him in the fall of 1905. After a series of lengthy private conversations, the Chief Forester agreed to let Gooding exercise the initiative in proposing future changes in the administration of resources in the state. In return, the governor abandoned his hostile attitude and encouraged the Idaho legislature to adopt measures for the prevention of wastage in lumbering operations and the protection of watersheds. His own land commissioner, C. J. Munson, was responsible for the fulfillment of related administrative tasks. His office gathered evidence, for example, which the governor used to prosecute fraud and restrict private claims on the state's public domain. In acknowledgment of Gooding's valuable coöperation, Roosevelt sent his friend William H. Taft, the Secretary of War, to speak on behalf of the governor's reëlection in 1906. These events seemed to confirm Gooding's later statement: federal conservation would be successful whenever the states were made "interested parties in the development of their own natural resources."[30]

By the end of 1906 the President had assumed that opposition to conservation was disappearing in the West. This judgment soon proved to be premature. Early in 1907, the Senate took up the annual appropriations bill for the Department of Agriculture. A coterie of Western irreconcilables immediately used the provisions relating to Forest Service expenditures as grounds for a full attack upon federal resource policy. Heyburn, Carter, Fulton, Clark, Piles, and Thomas Patterson dredged up every economic, political, and personal argument polished by a decade of usage and hurled them against the entire structure of conservation. Borrowing the idea Heyburn had used three years before, Fulton then attached to the bill a rider which threatened to prevent future expansion of the central part of the program. By its terms, no forest reserve could thereafter be created or enlarged beyond the timber line in Oregon, Idaho, Montana, Wyoming, Washington, or Colorado except by act of Congress. Significantly, those states where support for conservation was already strong—California, Nevada, and Utah—were not included in the measure. By voice vote, the Senate approved the bill with the rider and sent it to the President. Faced with the necessity of having to sign the essential appropriations bill, Roosevelt called Pinchot

to the White House and, armed with statistics on all remaining unreserved forested lands in the six states, created or enlarged thirty-
two national forests. Then he signed the bill which removed the power
of his successors to establish reserves in those areas.[31] No single action
could more dramatically illustrate the ultimate advantage of administrative power over legislative intentions.

The critics of conservation were so enraged by Roosevelt's sweeping
withdrawals that they took the first step toward organized opposition.
Drawing upon the currently popular device of the annual commercial
convention, they planned a regional meeting which would record the
West's demand for a just land and resource policy. Because such a
gathering would, at least by implication, be critical of the Roosevelt
administration, only one state in the predominantly Republican region
could act as host without political embarrassment: Colorado. After
1905, the application of the fee for grazing privileges had forced the
stock raisers in that state to join the mining interests in loud denuncia-
tions of federal land policies. When the Colorado Cattle and Horse
Growers Association passed a vigorous resolution against the fee,
Pinchot sent his assistant, Albert Potter, to the state. Conferences with
Elias Ammons, spokesman for the stockmen, and with a special committee of the association failed to satisfy anyone. When Senator Patterson carried Ammons' arguments to the President soon afterward, he
was informed that the Attorney General had sustained the legality of
the fee. "If the stockman wants the forest reserve for grazing purposes,"
Pinchot added, "let him pay the people of the country a little rental.
The people of the country at large are paying for the Forest Service,
and very few of them receive any direct benefit." By going to Denver
himself, the Chief Forester succeeded in getting an endorsement of the
policy from a joint meeting of the American Stockgrowers and National
Woolgrowers associations. Such a quick victory caused the Denver
Republican to wonder editorially whether he was "a hypnotist," or
whether governmental control was "so just that it pleads its own case."
The administration's efforts failed, however, to mollify the majority of
Colorado Democrats, who felt sure that no real concessions would be
made until their party was in power. When the state cattle and horse
raisers met again in January, 1907, they resolved that if federal regulation and withdrawals continued the rights of the state would be dangerously encroached upon. About the time that Roosevelt's fiat exacerbated
the situation, W. G. M. Stone, of the Colorado Forestry Association,
had hoped to introduce a forest conservation bill into the legislature,
but he sadly concluded that there would be "squally weather" ahead.

That was an apt description of the storm that broke in Denver soon afterward.[32]

In April, 1907, the Democratic majority in the Colorado legislature appointed a special committee to make recommendations to the governor on the question of proper reaction to the President's withdrawal of fifteen million acres—or half of the area still open to settlement in the state. Acting on their instructions, Governor Henry A. Buchtel sent out a call for a convention to be held in Denver in June to discuss federal land policies. He was further directed to write to the governors of every state west of the Mississippi River, to consult with them on proposals which the meeting might consider, and to ask that they appoint delegates from any economic or civic organization in their states. Buchtel also extended invitations to Pinchot, Garfield, and Newell.[33] From his own state, he appointed representatives whose views exemplified the variety of opinion about conservation that existed in the West. One of them was F. C. Goudy, an organizer of the state Forestry Association and a loyal supporter of Pinchot and his policy. Another was D. C. Beaman, an officer of the Rockefeller-owned Colorado Fuel and Iron Company, which dominated many of the mining enterprises in the state. J. Arthur Eddy, a speculator in irrigation, water power, and coal lands, accepted an appointment with a letter filled with lamentations over alleged federal abuses. Assuring the governor that he had no financial interest in land policy, he also insisted that the issue transcended politics. Although he claimed to be a "strong Roosevelt man," he conceded that the President "does get off on some things & one of them is this fool Forest Reserve system."[34] Considering the motley character of these delegates alone, the convention promised to be a lively one.

Roosevelt examined letters from Forest Service agents and conservationists in Colorado, read the comments appearing in Western newspapers, and decided to accept the challenge of his opponents for a second time. His method in this case differed significantly, however, from the coup of the preceding year. He first discussed the threat with Garfield, Wilson, and Pinchot, and later talked with Senator Carter, who anxiously assured him that the convention would not be so hostile as was expected. The President handed a letter to the Secretary of Agriculture for possible use at Denver, but, because Pinchot had already scheduled a western trip for June, Wilson asked the Chief Forester to carry the message. In it Roosevelt stated the truths about federal land policy with characteristic forcefulness. Every acre of agricultural land in the national forest, he wrote, was open to settlement under the laws of Congress, laws made with the approval of the West's representatives. Even if the government did not sponsor reclamation projects, users would have to pay for the cost of water supplies. Finally, no such restrictions had yet been placed on coal-land entries. The men who maintained that federal regulation deprived the West of future development were, he asserted, the spokesmen for selfish special interests and the real source of harm to bona fide settlers. The people of the West could best bring about permanent growth in their region by supporting the administration's policies.[35] Even if Buchtel had not invited the Roosevelt men, it is likely that the President would have sent them, knowing full well how effective they were in the art of persuasion.

Watching the delegates assemble in Denver, the *Record-Stockman* of that city suggested that they hold their proceedings and make their decisions in secret sessions. As it happened, the Public Lands Convention was wide open. Western newspapers recorded the actions and remarks of everyone with loving detail. Any rumors, anecdotes, or complaints made by the most famous senator or the most obscure sheep owner constituted prime news copy. Editorial writers and cartoonists pooled their talents to crucify Gifford Pinchot. Senator Patterson's tabloid *Rocky Mountain News* set every headline in the largest block letters. "OPPOSE UNCLE SAM AS LANDLORD," one issue exclaimed, "STAMP OF DISAPPROVAL FOR ROOSEVELT LAND POLICY." Former Senator Teller's anguished cry warranted the same treatment: "ARE NOT MEN BETTER THAN TREES?" A large part of press coverage was devoted to the charges and accusations which filled the convention hall every day. The critics who had hoped to dominate the sessions charged that government agents were packing the meeting. Western conservationists in turn denounced the gathering as a group of selfish men whose opinions did not represent the true sentiment of the West. Actually, the critics' charge was less accurate than that of their opponents. Although some Forest Service officials attended and sat at committee meetings, the majority of the delegates came from Colorado—500 out of a total of 861—and Wyoming sent 104 of the rest. Moreover, these delegates did not represent an equitable cross section of opinion in many states; some towns, for instance, sent several sets of representatives. When the convention opened, organizations which supported federal policy, such as the National Livestock Association, were excluded from voting and were not permitted to use the rostrum. Only after making repeated protests against such treatment did the conservationists succeed in making a few short speeches toward the close of the meeting. A second charge that was bruited about alleged that the convention was being used for partisan purposes. One rumor, for example, had it that the meeting would somehow support the reëlection of Democrat Teller to his former seat in the Senate. A more reasonable rumor asserted that the gathering was designed to discredit the Roosevelt administration. Both Patterson and Teller denied this charge and pointed to the fact that a number of delegates were prominent Republicans. Apart from Colorado's predominantly Democratic representatives, however, no uniform political complexion could be ascribed to the delegations of any state.[36]

Judging from the speeches delivered at the convention, the issue of federal land policy had aroused the emotions of the critics, but had not freshened their store of distortions and clichés. From the floor and the rostrum, states rights doctrines were proclaimed, tales of oppression were told, and the worst possible motives were attributed to the Roosevelt men. Every uncomplimentary reference to Pinchot and the Forest Service was greeted with yells of delight. Patterson rose to accuse the government of driving American homesteaders to Canada, and Colorado's Democratic congressman, John A. Shafroth, unfurled a large map showing two thirds of the western slope of the Rocky Mountains covered with national forests. In every case, the critics' arguments condemned the whole federal policy because of particularly irritating regulations. Many of their listeners, however, could not accept that line of reasoning. They had no liking for such rules, but neither did they desire to return to the controversy and chaos of the past. The delegates from New Mexico, for example, were unimpressed with the histrionics of the speakers. Although unanimous in their opposition to the leasing of grazing lands, they combined a variety of interests in support of federal jurisdiction over resource use. One of the delegates was Solomon Luna, the largest stock owner in the territory; another was H. A. Jastro, a cattleman with landholdings in California as well as New Mexico and a close friend of the Chief Forester. Both these men welcomed the preservation of rangeland in the national forests. The delegation also included former Governors Miguel Otero and L. Bradford Prince, the latter a leading irrigationist in the Southwest. The New Mexicans took no part in the convention debates, preferring to wait to see what constructive alternatives to federal control might be proposed. They heard none that seemed feasible. The representatives of economic interests in California, Oregon, and Utah similarly disagreed with the critics' arguments and joined in an endorsement of conservation.[37]

The Roosevelt men played a decisive part in thwarting the hopes of the convention's organizers. Facing hostile audiences was, by this time, a familiar experience for Pinchot. As he came to the platform, he quipped, "If you fellows can stand me I can stand you," and the anger of many listeners seeped away in laughter. When a heckler shouted to him that a Forest Service official had been guilty of unwarranted abuse, the Chief Forester shot out an index finger and snapped, "Give me that officer's name, he will be discharged at once." His speech was a plainly worded explanation of the government's aims in public land policy, spiced with homely allusions and studded with facts that revealed his intimate knowledge of Western problems. One of his critics asked why the President had deliberately undermined the wishes of Congress by making the sweeping forest reservations of the previous May. Pinchot, sidestepping deftly, replied with force: "Theodore Roosevelt is not that kind of a man." Although the point was raised again later in the day, Pinchot's assurance made a lasting impression. When he finished, his boldness, reasonableness, and good humor had effectively destroyed the black image which many westerners had of him. His address and all the subsequent references to him were greeted with vigorous applause. The convention gave equal attention to the remarks of Land Commissioner Ballinger, especially because he was a westerner serving with the government. After discussing the complex problems involved in administering the land laws, Ballinger left no doubt as to where his own loyalties lay. "I, as a western man," he announced, "stand ready to challenge at all times, in season and out of season, any assertion that the President of the United States is not in hearty accord with the best interests of the citizens of the great West." By the close of the meeting, the federal officials were so cordially received that it almost seemed as if they had organized the convention themselves.[38]

Many of the leaders who had responded to Buchtel's invitation expressed the hope that the states would be able to agree upon a distinctly Western land policy at Denver. But, by the time the resolutions committee assembled for its deliberations under the chairmanship of E. W. Ross, no extraordinary suggestions had been offered from the platform, on the floor, or in private. After waiting until most of the conservationists had left the convention, the committee submitted resolutions which were surprisingly mild. Without specifically condemning the national forests, they merely admonished the government not to let the reserves infringe upon settlements, impede the free use of water courses, or include nontimbered land. They opposed the application of fees for grazing on lands outside the public domain, and asserted the right of the states to control their own irrigation and mining development. A parting shot was fired at all bureaucrats and secret agents, but no reference was made to Roosevelt. At the final session, a segment of the full delegations adopted these resolutions with something less than unanimity. Then the Public Lands Convention adjourned, "roaring as mildly as a sucking dove."[39]

Western newspapers disagreed about the real meaning of the Denver meeting. In Colorado, the Democratic press described it as a victory for the West and an obvious condemnation of the administration's policies. The Seattle *Post-Intelligencer* disagreed with favorite son Ballinger and upheld Ross as the true spokesman of Western sentiments. Another critic of conservation, the *Salt Lake Tribune,* denounced the convention as futile, not only because it had been thwarted by government agents, but also because the delegates had destroyed their own potential influence by endorsing federal resource administration. The Portland *Oregonian,* showing unusually favorable judgment, agreed that the convention had been a "frizzle" and observed that the faults of the conservation system did not justify its abandonment. At the other end of the spectrum, the Colorado Springs *Gazette,* owned by Pinchot's friend C. P. Dodge, emphasized the fact that the meeting had been controlled by men who sought the privilege of "tucking a fine parcel of rich Government land under their arms and walking off unobserved." The arguments of such "meanly selfish and exceedingly unpatriotic" citizens, the Phoenix *Arizona Gazette* pointed out, were wholly barren of constructive proposals for changes. Both of these gazettes insisted that the convention had not represented the real attitude of the West.[40]

Gifford Pinchot believed that the meeting represented a victory for the administration's land policies. Athough there were protests against the regulated use of water and unreserved range, the leasing system for other resources aroused slight attention at Denver. "We had a great time," he wrote to a friend a few days after leaving the city, ". . . and were by no means eaten up . . . . So far as the Forest Service was concerned, the resolutions were absolutely harmless or better." During the following weeks he traveled through the West with Garfield and received favorable receptions from press and citizenry everywhere. Similar favors prompted Ballinger to assert that, beyond Colorado and Wyoming, there was no substantial dissatisfaction with federal administration of public lands. Moreover, all three officials assured the President that the convention had no political significance.[41]

Many years later, the meeting was described as a safety valve which relieved the pressures of ill will in the West and helped define that region's attitude on the issue of federal land policy.[42] The events of the following years would show, however, that Western opposition to conservation was not relieved by such organizations, but rather through the explosion of political controversy. Moreover, the emotional distortions heard at Denver hardly defined any clear or realistic attitude for westerners, and the critics' hopes that the convention would "result in some good" were not fulfilled. They would have to try again.

The Fred Light case, one of many suits challenging the legality of Forest Service regulations, was the only immediate result of the Public Lands Convention. For several months before that event, federal court decisions in Montana, California, Idaho, and Arizona had upheld the government's right to make rules affecting the occupancy of national forests. Some of the edge was thereby taken off local hostility, but the matter was not yet settled for the West in general. While Pinchot was at Denver, he agreed to an idea suggested by Colorado stockmen that a "friendly suit" be brought against one of their number. Fred Light was a pioneer settler of Aspen and a member of the local and state stockmen's associations responsible for the scheme. After discussing the procedure for the suit with Garfield and Potter, he formally refused to pay for the use of unfenced grazing land in a near-by national forest. Early in 1908 federal agents duly brought the matter into the courts.[43] Although the case at first raised the hopes of the critics, the litigation was protracted over several years' time and consequently faded as a potential cause for the opponents of federal policy. Before a final decision was handed down, other controversies emerged to stimulate collective action in the West.

The Sources of Coöperation

The struggles leading up to the Public Lands Convention provided the Roosevelt men with excellent opportunities to gauge the character of their adversaries. Those experiences also confirmed the value of an administration based upon the participation of influential westerners. In securing the coöperation of these men, the conservationists were confronted by a variety of circumstances. The governors of Utah, for example, had personally supported conservation since 1903. In that year Heber M. Wells ordered the withdrawal of state lands enclosed by proposed forest reserves; he also informed timberland seekers that these areas would no longer be open to purchase and settlement. Thereafter Wells's supplementary work was enhanced by the assistance of Senator Reed Smoot. Although the senator shared the conservative economic views of the high-tariff Republicans, his acquaintance with Pinchot made him particularly sensitive to the protection of the resources which were so vital to the economy of Utah. John C. Cutler, the successor to Wells, continued the close connection between state and federal administrations, and sponsored legislation to preserve additional areas. The criticisms of forest reserves which appeared in the editorials of the *Salt Lake Tribune* prompted him to write to the President in order to explain that the editor was merely using the subject to discredit the administration. Evidently Cutler's opinions of federal control had greater influence in the state than those of the newspaper; none of its criticisms were copied by the small-town journals of Utah during these years.[44]

One of the most striking examples of personal conversion to conservation occurred in New Mexico Territory. In 1906 federal administration of land and resources in the territory was impeded by a tangle of local politics arising out of the actions of Governor Herbert J. Hagerman. A friend of his immediate superior, Secretary Hitchcock, Hagerman was similarly prone to treat resource users with arrogant distrust. Although he thought of himself as a reformer of the Roosevelt type, the governor had none of the President's political acumen and succeeded only in arousing the resentment of prominent New Mexicans. Many citizens were disgusted by the presence of a large number of special agents sent by the Interior and Justice departments to investigate alleged land frauds. Hagerman not only favored these inquiries; he revealed his intention of personally altering traditional administrative and political procedures. He began by dismissing several state land agents and legal officers. After receiving many protests from Republican leaders in the territory, Roosevelt concluded that Hagerman's actions were creating a situation that threatened federal prestige as well as party security. When the governor allegedly ratified a "grossly improper" acquisition of land in order to get the support of a Democratic faction, the President demanded his resignation. Pinchot, whom Hagerman asked to intercede on his behalf, privately regretted the outcome of the affair, but, he confided to stockman H. A. Jastro, the governor had offered no satisfactory explanation of his actions. He seems to have remained silent about both his own political intrigues and the misdemeanors of his opponents. Although the Roosevelt men did not like to lose such a zealot, they evidently considered political peace in New Mexico of paramount importance.[45]

In order to reunite party factions the President personally selected George Curry, a former Democrat, to be the new territorial governor. One of many New Mexicans who had joined the Rough Riders in 1898, Curry became a friend and appointee of Roosevelt, who privately described him as "one of the best men I know anywhere." A long-time resident of the territory, Curry had been out of the country recently and therefore had no connection with local factions, yet he knew the attitudes of the people well enough to act as harmonizer of discontent. When he was inaugurated at Santa Fe early in 1907, one of his friends, territorial Attorney General Albert B. Fall, announced that the future administration would bring an end to the disruption caused by federal investigators and would confirm continued development of natural resources. Curry certainly did not share Roosevelt's belief in federal conservation. As a stock raiser whose ranch in southern New Mexico adjoined the Lincoln National Forest, he considered use regulations detrimental and discriminatory. Shortly after assuming office, he revealed that the realities of local interests would determine his land policy. When Fall denied a federal contention that the Almagordo Lumber Company had fraudulently acquired 20,000 acres of timberland, Curry sustained him, and offered his own resignation as a gesture of protest against the charges of federal agents. Roosevelt recognized that such an action would further demoralize his party in New Mexico and, therefore, refused to accept the offer. Later, the case against the lumber company was quietly dropped, but Roosevelt insisted that Curry ask Fall to resign. This agreement proved to be mutually satisfactory.[46]

Doubtlessly flattered by the outcome of this affair, the governor turned his attention to the primary source of local discontent: federal forest policy. After reading letters of complaint from citizens in his home county, he asked regional Forest Service officers to go there so that they would be impressed with the real needs of the small settler. When dissatisfaction deepened, he sent a personal protest to the Chief Forester, whose work he respected, but whose understanding of Western problems he doubted. Curry maintained that his people were suffering from abusive procedures used in the reserves and had no wish to see the forests enlarged. Asserting that he felt it to be his primary duty to protect the people of the territory, he threatened to appeal beyond Pinchot to Roosevelt and Congress, even if the action should cost him the governorship. Shortly after this letter was received, the President called him to the White House and agreed to another compromise to settle the unrest. Several pending investigations for land frauds were suspended, while Curry conversed with each of the Roosevelt men on the subject of conservation. When he visited Pinchot he was accompanied by a group of stockmen and political leaders from New Mexico. For all of them, the subject of forest administration was as important as the burning issue of statehood. The immediate result of this conference was the government's decision to open thousands of acres of proposed national forests south of Albuquerque to entry and use. Curry was so pleased with Pinchot's "corrected mistakes" that he thereafter readily consented to the withdrawal of other areas for forest reserves.[47]

The repetition of these experiences established a mutual trust and cordial friendship between the governor and the Chief Forester; upon that relationship federal conservation was firmly applied in New Mexico. Thereafter Curry personally attended to the complaints of forest users, obtained local referendums for the adjustment of boundaries, and promoted consultations between settlers and government agents. In March, 1909, he invited Pinchot to address stockmen and legislators at Santa Fe, and was confident that his friend would deal fairly with the people. Within a year the *New Mexican* admitted that the territory had "slowly and unwillingly learned that the forest reserves are good for it and its people." Curry was fully justified in being proud of his role as the popularizer of federal conservation. Roosevelt and Pinchot were equally well satisfied with the way in which compromise and adjustment served both the party and the policy in New Mexico.[48]

Of all of the disciples of Pinchot in the West, none was more valuable than George C. Pardee, of California. A physician by profession, his energetic, outspoken personality first brought him local political success and eventually helped him win the governorship in 1902. Because of his own observations of wasteful resource methods in the past, and because of the publicity created by the Yosemite controversy, Pardee became profoundly interested in the establishment of a comprehensive state conservation program. His inaugural message of January, 1903, included several suggestions for statutes to protect California's forests and water resources. The legislature quickly responded by re-creating the Board of Forestry and providing for a survey of conditions in state forests. Within a short time, the governor was exchanging information and advice with other conservationists, such as Abbot Kinney, of Los Angeles, and was consulting Newell and Pinchot about resource problems. By the time he left the executive mansion, in 1907, he had gained the admiration and personal trust of the Roosevelt men. Pinchot continued to correspond with him on resource and political subjects; writing his memoirs many years later, he described Pardee as "one of the pillars of the conservation movement."[49]

In 1905, a second Yosemite controversy erupted in California and threatened to shatter the new confidence in state-federal coöperation.

That year, the burgeoning city of San Francisco applied to the government for permission to use the Hetch Hetchy Valley in the park as a reservoir for future water supply. The plan at once aroused the militant opposition of John Muir and his former allies in the recession fight, and alarmed irrigationists in the surrounding area who depended upon the water sources of Yosemite for agricultural development. When the matter was referred to Pinchot, he was loath to do anything that might damage the prestige of federal policy among influential Californians. After consulting with the state's delegates in Congress, he announced that he did not think the project would seriously injure the resources of the park. Having secured his approval, city officials next sought a favorable judgment from the President. At that point, Muir wrote to his friend in the White House—his Yosemite camping companion of 1903 and helpmate in the recent victory for recession. Roosevelt's response was not encouraging. He confessed that it would be impossible for him to protect any areas unless there should be "a certain degree of friendliness toward them on the part of the people of the State" in which they were situated, and added that if an area were "used so as to interfere with the permanent material development" the result would be bad. California was for him a matter far different from Heyburn's Idaho:

I would not have any difficulty at all if, as you say, 9/10 of the citizens took ground against the Hetch Hetchy project, but so far everyone ... has been for it and I have been in the disagreeable position of seeming to interfere with the development of the State for the sake of keeping a valley which apparently hardly anyone wanted to have kept, under national control.

This letter convinced Muir of only one thing: the necessity of building popular sentiment against the plan. To do so he once again turned to R. U. Johnson, T. P. Lukens, and the Sierra Club. As before, their efforts were confined to articles and personal correspondence; they consequently failed to convince "politicians and office holders" like Pinchot and Garfield who had never seen the beauty of the Valley. Predictably, the Secretary of the Interior granted San Francisco permission to use water from Hetch Hetchy and the adjoining areas. Many conservationists must have shared Lukens' bewilderment over the stand taken by Roosevelt and Pinchot, but no real inconsistencies were involved. The federal officials were determined to base their policies on the pragmatic concept of multiple use of resources, and they did not wish to abandon the advantageous support of populous areas. For similar reasons, they approved of a plan whereby Los Angeles could use the Owens Valley, at the foot of the Sierra Nevada Mountains, for a municipal water supply. In a few years these decisions would bring significant political benefits.[50]

In view of these and other examples of state support for federal conservation, it is obvious that Roosevelt was not initiating the concept of coöperation when, in May, 1908, he called a White House Conference of Governors on Natural Resources. Instead, he hoped that the meeting would publicize the broad administrative structure of the policy. While he waited for Congress to appropriate funds for a national conservation association, the President encouraged the Western governors to create commissions in their own states.[51] Curry of New Mexico had anticipated that suggestion by appointing a territorial Conservation Commission that same month. A few weeks later his legislature made it a permanent agency of government; Curry then staffed it with representatives of New Mexico's principal economic interests and members of both political parties.[52] A similar commission was created by Governor Cutler of Utah at about the same time. His successor, William Spry, signified his determination to continue the policies of his predecessors by appointing leading state conservationists as well as mining, farming, and stock-raising authorities.[53] Wishing to "act in harmony" with federal resource administration, Governor Denver S. Dickerson of Nevada also secured legislation for a state Conservation Commission in March, 1909. State conservation, he announced, was an "object worthy of the highest endeavor."[54]

The official adherence of state governments in the West included a few distinct victories for the conservationists and at least two disappointments. Among the triumphs was the action of Governor Buchtel of Colorado. Seemingly hopeful of putting the experience of the Public Lands Convention behind him, Buchtel appointed a Colorado Conservation Commission as one of the last measures of his tenure in office. Moreover, he asked two of Pinchot's disciples, W. G. M. Stone and F. C. Goudy, of the state Forestry Association, to organize the work of the bureau.[55] In Oregon, the yeoman service of J. N. Teal brought about the conversion of many state officials, including Governor Chamberlain who created a state Conservation Commission in February, 1909. Perhaps because the organization was principally a fact-finding body, it received unanimous approval from the Oregon legislature. The lawmakers soon abandoned their earlier truculence for at least moderate praise of national forests, and made appropriations for state resource administration.[56] The commission idea was, however, bound to be debased by those who remained impervious to education and adjustment. In Montana, for example, local conservationists held vain hopes that the new governor, Edwin L. Norris, would prove himself a friend of federal policy. Apart from allowing the state Conservation Commission to advise the legislature on the subject of timberland protection, Norris soon revealed that he had no intention of relying upon the advice of federal administrators. Expressing the opinions of Montanans who were interested in private power development, he denounced Pinchot's influence in the Interior Department and opposed further withdrawals of water-power sites from the public domain.[57] In Washington State, Governor Mead also undermined the purpose of his commission by staffing it with men who had consistently opposed the idea of conservation. Although the state Forestry Association submitted a list of names with the hope that he would avoid political selections, he nevertheless appointed Land Commissioner Ross, former Senator Wilson, and lumber baron J. J. Donavan—all inveterate critics of Pinchot's policy.[58]

The beginnings of coöperation were only a step in the right direction, as the Roosevelt men well recognized. The future maintenance and expansion of federal resource policy depended upon the ascendency of conservationists in the West and in the nation's capital. Just as the circumstances of controversy and politics had accelerated the application of conservation measures, those same influences would secure the continuation of the policy after Roosevelt left the White House.

Chapter III

BALLINGER'S BEGINNINGS

Roosevelt's Land Commissioner

The network of personal relationships erected during these formative years accounted for the swift application of federal resource policy in the West. A system of government dependent upon the coöperation of a group of dedicated men, it also contained a potentially dangerous weakness. If one highly placed member held differing views of purpose or procedure, his hesitancy and dissent could create confusion enough to disrupt that system. A difference of opinion was therefore not merely a source of inefficiency; in the rarefied atmosphere of the conservation crusade it was viewed as a potential threat to the public interest.

Shortly after Roosevelt left office, early in 1909, one of the former members of his administration became the source of such disruption. Richard A. Ballinger had entered the federal service in 1907 when the President asked him to head the Public Land Office. The incumbent, William A. Richards, retained the friendly regard of his associates, but he was not the administrator needed to renovate that bureau as part of Garfield's reorganization of the Interior Department. Late in 1906 Richards had signified his readiness to resign as soon as a replacement could be found. Pinchot at once submitted the name of Malcolm Moody, his disciple in Oregon, thereby revealing that he was intensely interested in having the right man in the office. Pending a selection, he even considered taking the post himself, with the distinct understanding that he would reassume his place in the Forestry Service after the Land Office was overhauled. The President responded to this suggestion with characteristic tact: he would like to go farther, he confided, and make Pinchot Secretary of the Interior. He hesitated, because Pinchot was a New Yorker, and added that the West had a claim to both offices. Evidently he had deemed Ohio sufficiently western when he appointed Garfield a few months before. For several weeks, an alternative idea of Pinchot as First Assistant Secretary was discussed, but nothing came of it. Perhaps to please him, Roosevelt offered the commissionership to another Pinchot supporter, Philip Stewart, of Colorado, but the offer was declined. As Secretary of the Interior, Garfield properly deserved the courtesy of being consulted in the matter; it was he who suggested that the post be tendered to Ballinger. Uncertain whether that man would accept, the President asked Pinchot to look for possible alternative candidates in the meantime.[1]

Ballinger's experience and character undoubtedly accounted for his selection. The son of an Abolitionist editor in Illinois, he had moved with his family to Larned, Kansas, in 1873. There he helped his father in the newspaper business and worked as a cowhand in the western part of the state. Between 1877 and 1880 he attended the University of Kansas at Lawrence and Washburn College in near-by Topeka. With the encouragement of Senator John J. Ingalls, he later enrolled to study law at Williams College in Massachusetts. Among the friendships he made there were those with Harry Garfield and his younger brother James. After receiving his degree Ballinger moved to New Decatur, Alabama, and within a short time became city attorney, with a reputation as an enemy of dishonesty in public office. By 1889, however, he was attracted by the possibilities of a future career in the newly admitted state of Washington, and he soon settled in the growing community of Port Townsend, on Puget Sound. Through the patronage of Federal Judge Cornelius Hanford, he secured an appointment to the United States District Court, and was later elected to serve on the bench of the Superior Court of Jefferson County. By the end of the 1890's, Judge Ballinger was one of many Washingtonians who were convinced that Port Townsend was being outstripped by Seattle in the race for control of the state's commerce. In 1897, therefore, he moved his law practice and residence to Seattle, where he joined several established attorneys to form the partnership of Ballinger, Ronald, Battle, and Tennant. The business of the firm brought him into contact with civic leaders, specifically those who were anxious to end Seattle's reputation as a wide-open town. In 1904, the leaders of the Republican organization asked him to accept their party's nomination for the office of mayor. Ballinger was subsequently elected on a reform platform and, by the end of his two-year term, he had satisfied every hope of his sponsors. As an executive he was known to be honest and judicious; as a reformer he performed his duties without the fanfare usually associated with advocates of good government. His accomplishments as mayor brought him to the attention of party leaders in the state and beyond, among them Roosevelt and Garfield. But Ballinger was not contemplating a future career in politics. Finding slight personal satisfaction in public office, he declined to run for a second term in 1906, and instead accepted the presidency of the Seattle Bar Association.[2]

During these years, Seattle attained the position of hub city of the Pacific Northwest and gateway to the vast, undeveloped riches of Alaska Territory. The principal sources of income for its residents were the expanding harbor facilities, the railroad systems, coal mining, and lumbering. They naturally viewed the future development of these activities with an optimism engendered by seemingly boundless opportunities. All promoters of enterprise required extensive legal assistance in matters concerning transportation, landownership, and the use of natural resources. Because Ballinger's law firm specialized in such subjects, it flourished with the growth of Seattle's far-flung domain. The records of the partnership indicate, however, that its prosperity came from service to a variety of clients rather than a few large corporations paying large fees. Ballinger acted as a temporary adviser more often than as long-term counsel; he wrote charters and ordinances, drew up deeds and corporate agreements, and interpreted points of law. He was also the proud author of a commentary on community property law and the codifier of the statutes of the state. During the course of this practice, he acquired small amounts of railroad and bank securities, often in lieu of fee, and was able to purchase real estate in and around the city. Perhaps the most valuable advantage he received from handling commercial litigation was a detailed knowledge of federal and state land and resource laws. Like the businessmen he associated with and the government agents he consulted, he was deeply interested in modifying these regulations, securing their adjustment to new conditions, and defending those which were vital to the material interests of the region.[3]

Similarly, Ballinger shared the views of his associates who were prominent in the economic oligarchy which dominated the politics and government of the state. For these men, both progress and public welfare were based upon the unhampered expansion of their enterprises. Ballinger's personal experiences as a city attorney in Alabama and as a reform mayor somewhat tempered this ideology in his own mind with a sense of righteousness and integrity. "We have too many captains of industry," he once wrote, "who undertake to square extortion and oppression by philanthropy."[4] Because he was not a keenly ambitious man by nature, he was not enamored of positions of power and influence; indeed, he seems to have been distrustful of unrestrained political power. Apart from professional prejudices, therefore, he had more faith in the letter of the law than in the men who used it for their own purposes. Yet his sense of loyalty was strong toward those whom he believed were honest men engaged in legitimate enterprise, whether in business or government.

In January, 1907, the President's invitation was transmitted to Ballinger through Senator Samuel Piles, of Washington. Reluctant to leave his private affairs for the discomforts of public office, Ballinger replied that he could not take the commissionership. Garfield immediately dispatched a personal telegram to his old school friend, asking him to reconsider. Then, while the attorney was consulting his associates, Roosevelt sent what amounted to a command, a message couched in terms that a man of Ballinger's sensitivities could not resist. It was clearly a matter of duty, the President wrote, for him to help the work of the administration by accepting "this peculiarly responsible and important post." "It seems to me," he added, "that I should receive all the support possible from the men who believe in my way of handling things and the only way you can support me is to take this position." After that appeal, Ballinger agreed, but he wanted the public to know that he had not solicited the office for himself. Both Garfield and Roosevelt were greatly pleased with their success. "I am glad you are here," was the President's greeting when the new Commissioner arrived in the capital, "and do not offer any apologies for making you come here. Any man who could clean up Seattle as you did can clean up that Land Office."[5]

In personal characteristics, Ballinger was a significant contrast to his associates Garfield and Pinchot. His physical make-up revealed years of quiet, comfortable living relieved by slight recreation—riding, perhaps, for he once bought a hurdle horse from Roosevelt. With cold eyes and full mustache, his countenance suggested a man who was aware of his abilities, but the absence of flamboyant expression or attire implied an equal pride in the caution and sobriety of his profession. These external impressions were confirmed by his correspondence. Strongly worded statements and levity rarely appeared there, even in letters directed to close friends. He best expressed himself in the prepared brief, and his speeches were similarly constructed with care, sprinkled with only such anecdotes as were appropriate to the time and the audience. He was especially restrained in public expression, preferring to wait until a matter was safely in hand before committing himself. Unlike Pinchot, he did not perform very well in a sudden or heated exchange of views, or in the midst of public controversy.

Upon his arrival in Washington, D.C., Ballinger plunged into his work and, Garfield noted with satisfaction, took hold at once. He had briefed himself on needed changes in land policy by consulting with his associates in Seattle. Aware of their direct connection with the business of his office, he sought to protect himself from any future charge of impropriety. He therefore instructed his partner, A. J. Tennant, to see to it that any case involving public lands which the firm might subsequently handle not be credited to him as a member, nor any part of the fees be assigned to his name. Shortly thereafter, the firm itself was dissolved by mutual agreement, although two of the partners continued to practice law in Seattle.[6]

The new Commissioner soon found that, in terms of methods and organization, the Land Office had not yet entered the twentieth century. He discovered work bogged-down on the desks of elderly and pathetically hysterical women clerks whose output was decidedly limited. Even though some were the friends of previous Commissioners, Secretaries, and other federal officials, Ballinger had seventeen of them dismissed. When complaints about these and other sweeping actions reached the President, Roosevelt reportedly threw up his hands and exclaimed, "I can't help it, I can't help it. Ballinger has discharged a classmate of mine and also another classmate of Taft's. He's got the bit between his teeth and I'm not going to try to stop him." The Commissioner soon instituted modern accounting methods, reallocated work space, and secured merit raises and promotions. He was particularly anxious to discourage the customary red-tape treatment accorded to pending business, and he set an example by making his own working arrangements informal. From the first, he relied upon Assistant Commissioner Fred L. Dennett for coöperation, but within a short time many other members of the immediate staff showed their respect for their chief by their personal loyalty.[7]

Because of allegations made during the subsequent controversy, the details of policy suggested and applied by Ballinger warrant close examination. Pinchot later recalled that he, Newell, and Richards immediately found the new Commissioner opposed to the Roosevelt land policies.[8] It seems remarkable that Garfield made no references to such an attitude—an omission which is surprising in view of the fact that he carried on an extensive correspondence with Pinchot and others and also kept a diary for his private thoughts. In time, Garfield became aware that Ballinger differed with him on several matters, but his relations with his subordinate were always friendly. It was Pinchot who first expressed apprehension over Ballinger. As in the case of his criticism of Hitchcock, these complaints were few and somewhat petty, and for the most part were not sent to Roosevelt until the last months that the two were in office. On the other hand, Ballinger, as an executive, resented the inordinate influence Pinchot wielded in the Interior Department, and did not welcome the claims of the Forest Service in problems concerning public domain administration.

Ballinger first revealed a significant difference of reasoning when Garfield asked his opinion of Pinchot's suggestion that the Chugach

National Forest be created in southern Alaska. On the basis of reports from his own agents, the Commissioner replied that the region had sufficiently heavy rainfall to make forest reserves for water supply or reforestation wholly unnecessary. Pinchot's purpose, he argued, would not be approved by the "persons best informed in Alaska and in this country." Garfield quietly suggested that he might prefer to withdraw this written objection, but Ballinger declined to do so. While the Commissioner was traveling in the West several weeks later, he was informed that a Presidential proclamation had gone out, creating Chugach National Forest. Ballinger was irritated by the circumstances of the affair, but Pinchot took it more seriously. As he later testified, he was already convinced that Ballinger was too conservative, but it was the protest against the Chugach Forest which made him decide that the Commissioner was not trustworthy.[9]

Ballinger's views on the more important subject of federal leasing policy similarly differed from those of the Roosevelt men. The existing governmental emphasis upon lease rather than sale was unwise, he believed, because it attracted short-term investors and discouraged businessmen who sought permanent ownership; moreover, the policy was improper because the federal government was actually the guardian of lands and resources, not the proprietor. Specifically, he utilized these opinions when considering recommendations for coal-land legislation. After officially endorsing regulated sale of the deposits, instead of leases, he expected Garfield and Pinchot to "go through the roof," but Roosevelt urged him to repeat the suggestion in his annual report. During the subsequent controversy, the Pinchot partisans accused him of having shown undue favoritism to coal-land claimants from the Pacific Northwest. It was true that he knew several such men and, during his last months in office, corresponded with them concerning the status of their claims. Yet he showed no personal favoritism toward them beyond urging a rapid examination of their applications. The customary investigation of the claims in these cases may have caused him some slight embarrassment because he knew the applicants personally, but that same reason accounted for his official caution.[10]

The Commissioner's past experience made him particularly sensitive on the subject of dishonesty in public office. Yet he knew also that honesty was not necessarily determined by the loudness of protest or the volume of publicity. He felt that he could not be responsible for the actions of entrymen on the public domain once their claims had been approved and confirmed; generally, he thought of them as men of business acting in good faith. As a specialist in land laws, he was also aware of the common abuse of petty power by ambitious and corrupt federal agents. After he took over the Land Office, he was confronted with further instances of the fact that wrongdoing was not confined to either group. Hitchcock's agents had uncovered land frauds in Colorado which were by now in the charge of officers of the Justice Department. When the cases were brought to trial, however, the courts in Denver censured the methods used by the agents of both Departments, and the newspapers of that city readily publicized these charges. About the same time, a residue of ill will toward the government was left in the wake of accusations made by agents of Louis Glavis, of the Land Office, against Senator Borah, of Idaho. Moreover, such controversies tended to upset the stability of the Republican party in the states of the West.[11]

These subjects of disagreement within and beyond his office convinced Ballinger that he ought to return to private life. When he first accepted the appointment, he informed Roosevelt and Garfield that he would like to leave as soon as the reorganization of the Land Office was completed. In November, 1907, when that task was accomplished, he confided to the Secretary that he would resign the following March. Perhaps Ballinger had decided to heed the appeals of friends in Seattle who were anxious for him to resume his lucrative law practice. According to Pinchot, writing many years after the event, the Commissioner left office because he disagreed with the Roosevelt land policies. Yet, at the time, Garfield did not mention any such reason when he referred to the resignation in his diary.[12]

In the period between November and March, Ballinger seems to have relaxed his initial caution concerning relations with persons having business before the Land Office. In one of these applications, his old patron, Judge Hanford, was anxious to obtain lands near a reclamation project which would be used by the irrigation company of which he was president. His communications to the Commissioner demanded speedy action and implied that he would be personally and financially injured if he did not get official approval. Ballinger made no protest against such behavior, but the claims were not confirmed. Whether this decision was the result of an adverse report from the Reclamation Bureau's regional engineer or was determined by the fact that Ballinger was a former stockholder in Hanford's company cannot be determined. He seems to have compensated Hanford for this disappointment, however, by clear-listing certain other claims.[13]

The Commissioner's last weeks in office were congenial ones: he and Mrs. Ballinger were entertained at the White House and at the home of Secretary Garfield. Submitting his resignation in March, 1908, he thanked his superiors for their support, and from them he received words of praise for a year of work which had been of great benefit to the public service. At the time, the President confided to some of the Commissioner's friends that the government was fortunate in having hired a $20,000 man for a $5,000 salary. Just before leaving office Ballinger received the good wishes of many members of his staff—among them Louis Glavis. Secretary Garfield noted in his diary that the Commissioner left the capital with a reputation for "ability, industry & fairness."[14]

Just before he retired, the subject of needed coal-land legislation occupied Ballinger's attention. In March, testifying before Congressman Mondell's Public Lands Committee, he opposed the idea of substituting lease for outright entry and urged the passage of a bill which would facilitate the completion of legitimate claims. He was also consulted by Mondell, Senator Carter, and Frank Hitchcock of the Republican National Committee during the drafting of the Cale Bill, introduced by the delegate from Alaska to replace the Coal Act of 1904.[15] Later, when he returned to Seattle, several of the claimants for Alaskan coal lands asked him to interpret the way the pending legislation would affect their interests. Ballinger was aware of an Interior Department prohibition against any former employee's representing applicants within one year after resigning; he therefore wrote to tell Garfield that his advice was being solicited. In that same letter he expressed dismay over learning that the Secretary now opposed the Cale Bill, after initially favoring it. Indeed, Garfield had originally written the provision in it which recognized only bona fide entrymen, and had asked Senator Piles to support it. Three months later, however, he decided that a wholly new bill was necessary and approved a substitute measure which was then passed by Congress. Seemingly unaware of Ballinger's part in the writing of the Cale Bill, he assured his friend that he understood his opposition to leasing and stated that he was not disturbed by that fact. He had no comment, however, about the advice to the Alaskan coal claimants, a fact which may have caused Ballinger to assume that he was not disturbed by that information, either.[16]

In the months that followed several other claimants came to Ballinger's office—among them John McGraw and Miles C. Moore, former governors of Washington. It was at this time that he first met Clarence Cunningham, a mine owner of Idaho who had organized thirty-three claims in Alaska. Once again, Ballinger assisted these men in submitting their proofs and drawing up articles of incorporation for their projects. Later, on a trip back to Washington, D.C., he stopped at Garfield's home in Mentor, Ohio, and the two friends discussed the possibility that Land Office investigators might find the Cunningham claims to be faulty. It seemed to the Secretary that, although he filed affidavits for them, Ballinger was only casually interested in the claims.[17]

Ballinger also continued to assist such men as Hanford, who had claims before the Land Office, partly because of his friendship with the new Commissioner, Fred Dennett, his former assistant. Letters from Dennett also served to inform him that Pinchot's Forest Service was still interfering with the Land Office and that irresponsible field agents were still at work in the West. Ballinger was particularly upset over the publication of a sensational exposé of land fraud practices in Oregon in a book entitled *Looters of the Public Domain*. One of the authors, an agent of the Land Office, charged that Ballinger and Dennett had approved or had meant to approve many fraudulent entries in the state. Although Ballinger was puzzled by the motives for such an attack, he was angry enough to demand an investigation by Assistant Secretary of the Interior Frank Pierce (in Garfield's absence), and he suggested the dismissal of the author who was a land agent. Ultimately, it was found that only a fraction of the questionable claims had been filed. Of these, only a few had been approved; one had been rejected; the rest were still under investigation. Pierce did not make a formal investigation, perhaps because of the approaching Presidential election in November, 1908. A few weeks after that event, Dennett confided to Ballinger that several charges against the Land Office "could easily have gone wrong" during the campaign. In the course of the subsequent search for damaging evidence against Ballinger, this matter was not noticed.[18]

TAFT'S SECRETARY OF THE INTERIOR

As Roosevelt approached the end of his term, a cloud of despondency settled over the conservationists. They did not fear that their crusade would end when he left the White House. As Pinchot wrote, the movement was so well begun that it would be "extremely difficult to stop it if any one should try." It was obvious, however, that there could be no replacement for the intimate, efficient, personal administration which Roosevelt inspired. Like many other admirers of the outgoing President, they generally were pleased that his successor was to be William Howard Taft. As Secretary of War, Taft had proved to be an able administrator; he had great respect and affection for Roosevelt; and he was well aware of the President's paramount interest in conservation; and during the campaign of 1908 Taft promised to place his predecessor's executive policies on the firm foundation of legislation. Pinchot offered him information and advice on the subject of conservation, and privately assured his supporters that the policy would be continued during the next four years: "Taft is going to be with us in this work."[19]

After his victory at the polls Taft surprised the Roosevelt men by remaining silent about his choice of advisers for the new administration. Conservationists naturally expected that Garfield would be retained as Secretary of the Interior, if only because he was a fellow Ohioan and Cabinet colleague and a man highly esteemed by Roosevelt. This assumption was so strong that it was later alleged that Taft had promised Roosevelt that he would keep Garfield. If that commitment was made, it explains the anxiety of Roosevelt and Pinchot during these interim months. Although there is no proof of the promise, it was repeated as fact during the subsequent investigation in order to underscore Taft's disloyalty to his predecessor. At the time, Garfield hoped to remain in his post, but he decided not to embarrass Taft if his presence there was not wanted. After hearing several rumors to the effect that he would not be reappointed, Garfield talked to the President-elect late in January, 1909. Taft simply apologized for not retaining him in the Cabinet, and did so in a manner which Garfield thought was weak and insincere.[20]

Roosevelt and Pinchot were equally upset by this decision. Pinchot may have wondered whether his own place was secure—perhaps because he was even less intimate with Taft than Garfield had been. All three conservationists naturally wondered whether similar changes would be made in the ranks of their adherents in the federal services. They could do nothing to anticipate such changes, but they could shore up their policies. The three executives did not wait until January to take such steps. For many months surveys had been made to locate potential resources remaining on the public domain, plans laid for additional reclamation projects, and proclamations issued which withdrew thousands of acres for water power development and administrative sites in the national forests. These actions in no way differed from the procedures of preceding years, but the Taft men were noticeably unhappy with these fiats of an outgoing administration. Some of the advisers to the new President considered them to be dangerously improper.[21] Thus seeds of mutual suspicion were planted by these events and would soon grow in the fertile soil of controversy.

William Howard Taft wanted to construct a Cabinet of the best legal minds in the country, so that their experience with law would make them effective agents for the adoption of needed legislation. Secondarily, the President-elect was mindful of the tradition that the West, like the South, should be represented in his council. The Interior Department appeared to be the logical place for that particular appointment.[22] Of all the Western states, California had given him the largest support in the election, and some one of its favorite sons seemed to have the best chance of being chosen. Former Senator Thomas Bard and federal prosecutor Francis J. Heney, both Roosevelt men, were mentioned by the press, as were two of Taft's friends, Congressman James Needham and George Knight. The latter had been chairman of the Republican National Convention which nominated Taft and was the most strongly recommended of the four men. During the interim months, however, the already powerful group of reformers in California deluged the President-elect with protests against the selection of Knight, whom they considered a tool of the Southern Pacific Railroad.[23] Other names were mentioned in Western newspapers, including those of Scott, of the *Oregonian*, and Ballinger, but very few private suggestions were submitted to Taft from the West.

Ballinger was not moved by the resolutions and letters written by Seattle friends who hoped he would be appointed to the Cabinet. Immediately after the election he wrote to Frank Hitchcock, the Postmaster-General-designate and a principal adviser on patronage. Having recently declined to run for the governorship, Ballinger pointed out that his resignation from the Land Office signified that he had no desire to return to the strife of public affairs. Moreover, he had no wish to displace his good friend Garfield in the Interior Department, and he repeated that sentiment to Garfield in another letter written at the same time. In reply, Garfield merely declared that his feelings toward his former Commissioner had not changed and he told Ballinger not to worry about the matter. His tranquillity in this case might have been the result of the assumption that he was going to be reappointed himself. Ballinger's friends admired his concern for Garfield, but continued to urge him to accept the post if the Secretary was not a candidate. They agreed that he would have to sacrifice his personal affairs, but reminded him that it would be the opportunity of a lifetime and a proud heritage for his sons. In December Ballinger still insisted that he could not make the sacrifice, yet was willing to serve the new administration in any way.[24] It was at this time that Taft decided to appoint him Secretary of the Interior.

The President-elect announced his decision to Hitchcock and Philander C. Knox, the Secretary-of-State-designate, while they were with him at a winter retreat near Charleston, South Carolina.[25] Taft had already discussed Cabinet appointments with both men, but Ballinger was his personal choice. He had met the Commissioner whom Roosevelt and Garfield praised so highly. He knew him as an efficient administrator and was especially aware of his record as a lawyer and judge. Ballinger had also served as a member of the advisory staff of the Republican National Committee, as a state delegate to the 1908 convention, and as Taft's informant on affairs in the Pacific Northwest during the campaign. Moreover, Hitchcock had known him since the days of the Cale Bill and subsequently had received his personal support for the chairmanship of the Republican National Committee.[26] Before Taft made his decision, he inquired among his supporters to learn how the choice would be received. One of them, Congressman Needham, of California, admitted that he was not extraordinarily impressed with Ballinger, but felt that Garfield and Pinchot wanted him to get the appointment in order to guarantee their policies in the future. He therefore assured Taft that the selection would be "very agreeable to the Coast." Actually, the California Republicans knew nothing about Ballinger; they were interested only in preventing Knight from receiving the appointment. Considering Needham's response, Taft must have concluded that the Roosevelt men would be satisfied with the choice, yet he pointedly avoided asking their advice. Pinchot, he felt, would probably recommend "some transcendentalist" without any knowledge of the law, someone who had commended himself "because of some particular view that he has on a matter of sociology or political economy." Ballinger's record as an administrator and man of the law was especially appealing to Taft, who had also served in those capacities, and precisely fulfilled his desire to have legal experts in the executive council. Before the end of the year he sent John Hays Hammond, a wealthy mining investor and personal friend, to tell Ballinger that he was under consideration. When the President-elect left for a trip to Panama early in January, 1909, he asked Hitchcock to inform the candidate of the decision.[27]

When Ballinger came to Washington, D.C., later in the month, he called on Garfield and revealed, with evident embarrassment, that he had been asked to take the Interior portfolio. The Secretary did not show his personal disappointment; he declared that he had not been a candidate for the place, and advised his friend to accept it. For Ballinger, this assurance removed one of the two objections he had to coming into the Cabinet. A few days later he went to New York City to meet Hitchcock and Taft's brother, Henry. Their explanation of the President-elect's personal desire must have appealed to him in the same way as Roosevelt's insistence two years before. After this conversation, he agreed to give up his private affairs in order to serve the administration.[28]

The actual circumstances of the appointment take on a larger significance because of the allegations levied against Ballinger during the subsequent controversy. At the time the decision was being made, rumors were current—especially in the Northwest—to the effect that men interested in Alaskan investments were driving Garfield out of the Interior Department. Assisted by Hitchcock and by George W. Perkins, of J. P. Morgan and Company, the rumors continued, these men were also instrumental in having Ballinger appointed. Pinchot later testified that he was not certain about the reasons for the selection, but stated that the "common" explanation was that Hitchcock had promised "certain western interests a Secretary of the Interior with his sting drawn, and so Ballinger was produced out of a hat." He repeated this version in his memoirs and, because of the course of the controversy, it was subsequently accepted as fact.[29] Yet there is nothing in his own vast correspondence between January and March, 1909, that alludes to such influences. Even if Hitchcock had acted as the rumor claimed, that did not account for Taft's personal decision. The fact remains that Ballinger was not willing to take the post until after he talked with Garfield. In view of his sincere reluctance to accept the appointment and the actual circumstances of the case, it is easy to understand why he felt so bitter when his critics later insisted upon the existence of a conspiracy.

In the West, the choice was hailed as a just recognition of the political importance of the region and an acknowledgment of the need for a westerner as administrator of policies so vital to its welfare.[30] There were several expressions of dissatisfaction, however, even in Ballinger's home city. One Seattle businessman told a Forest Service officer: "If Ballinger is good enough for the Cabinet, we can recruit a dozen cabinets from the Seattle Bar." The implication was that a man of Ballinger's reticent character would not take full advantage of opportunities.[31] Those Washingtonians who looked upon the Forest Service as a "drag on Seattle's progress" hoped that the new Secretary would attend to the economic interests of his own region. Some of these well-wishers were obviously anxious to have the federal reserves opened for development, while others, including the Alaska investors, expected him to hasten confirmation of their patents. Mindful of such hopes, one of Ballinger's friends urged him to take the Department of Commerce and Labor instead, because in the Interior post he would have to use the "big stick" against men of his own state.[32]

Western friends of Roosevelt, Garfield, and Pinchot were naturally displeased by the change in the Cabinet. The President himself felt that it might be interpreted as a reflection upon Garfield and therefore hastened to praise his Secretary as the best man in the history of the Interior Department.[33] He said nothing about Ballinger, but a story which circulated later had it that he was critical of Taft's choice. Allegedly, Roosevelt stated in private that he would not have made Ballinger or any other westerner Secretary because such a man would have had to disregard his own opinions in order to carry out policy properly.[34] Garfield and Pinchot did not record their reaction to the appointment, although they both kept diaries and maintained extensive correspondence. There is evidence, however, that the Chief Forester was more than simply disappointed. Shortly after the selection was announced in January, Pinchot talked with Elbert L. Baldwin, assistant editor of *Outlook* magazine, and confessed that he would not be able to work with Ballinger as he had worked with Garfield. "Jim and I think alike concerning matters in which the Forest Service and the Department of the Interior are closely related," he said, and added, "Ballinger and I might clash." Baldwin, who was a friend of several men in the new administration, reported this comment to Taft.[35] Whatever the President-elect may have thought about it then is not known; he would have good reason to remember it a few months later.

Interpretations or Intentions

Richard A. Ballinger took the oath of office as Secretary of the Interior in a ceremony held at the White House on the morning of March 6, 1909. During the next few days he conferred with the chiefs of the bureaus, most of whom he had known as Commissioner, and spent several hours discussing pending business with Garfield and Newell. Although he admired and respected his predecessor, the new Secretary was a man with positive purposes and opinions of his own. He shared the President's determination to place the executive precedents of the Roosevelt administration upon the sound basis of legislation. Specifically, he was anxious to transform the broad outlines of Garfield's programs by practical adjustment of administration to laws. When newspapermen asked what his policy would be, he replied with a single statement: "I know of only one policy that pertains to an administrative officer and that is to administer the law as he finds it and enforce the highest efficiency on the part of his subordinates." Initially, he meant to concentrate his personal attention upon the strict application of facilities which were already operating and projects already begun. Ultimately, he would formulate suggestions for additional land and resource administration.[36]

When Ballinger took office, the Interior Department was preoccupied with the complex problems of protecting and enhancing water resources in the West. In order to implement the reclamation laws, several large projects had been finished, others recently commenced, and many more planned during the last years of the Roosevelt administration. In 1908 Garfield ordered an examination of potential power sites in Montana and adjacent areas and, on the basis of reports from field agents, secured the withdrawal of almost four million acres in seven states. Ostensibly, these sites were to be used for the administration of the future projects; actually, they covered large portions of the public domain. In many cases, the selections bordered on the holdings of private power and irrigation companies and interfered with the companies' plans for completing their enterprises. The Roosevelt-Pinchot-Garfield interpretation of the purposes of federal policy viewed these private interests as secondary in importance to the paramount object of federal reclamation for the common good. Apart from the promoters of local projects, water users generally welcomed governmental assistance in protecting watersheds, erecting dams, and insuring equitable distribution. All of them, however, objected to the details of regulation and payment involved in the administration of these reserves. In addition, federal agents, official and private civil engineers, businessmen, and agriculturalists disagreed upon the various merits of use fees, payment in scrip, leasing, priority of distribution, and the location and scope of the projects. Finally, the issues were subject to changing local political influences at every stage.

Newell, as a Roosevelt man, was generally unimpressed with Western objections in these matters and was consequently more anxious to complete the projects as planned than to adjust details which residents considered essential. He and Garfield emphasized their belief in the wisdom of this policy, but they failed to convert Ballinger. The new Secretary did not share their absolute faith in federal jurisdiction. The government, he wrote to Baldwin, of the *Outlook,* "cannot dictate to a State how non-navigable waters shall be used or whether they shall be used at all." This opinion was in part a reflection of his basic preference for and trust in the honest private enterprise. It was also the result of observations, made as attorney and Commissioner, of the machinations of irresponsible federal agents whose abuse of petty power soiled the name of the government in the West. Federal regulation of resources, as he interpreted the policy, was a means and not an end: "conservation without development has no substantial reason for existence."[37] Moreover, Ballinger doubted that even the existing statutes could be properly used to attack monopoly. He was sure that they did not authorize

the withdrawals of administrative sites. As Fulton's rider to the appropriations bill of 1907 had seemed to indicate, the sense of Congress was
prohibitive rather than permissive. Moreover, the Reclamation Act did
not give the Secretary power to innovate policy concerning the scope
or use of projects. After being reminded of Garfield's official brief upholding the broad interpretation of executive authority, Ballinger later
stated: "That doctrine is one that does not appeal to me as sound law
under the Constitution of the United States."[38] Unable immediately to
recommend legislation to define the extent of his power, he decided to
restore the sites to the public domain, have them reëxamined, and then
rewithdraw those that were of proper value. Until additional appropriations could be obtained, he meant to complete partially finished
reclamation projects rather than use existing funds to begin those
which were planned but not yet begun.[39] The possibility that these
changes would reflect upon the preceding administration of the Reclamation Service did not disturb him. Evidently his friendship with
Garfield did not alter his determination in the least.

In all of his opinions Secretary Ballinger had the loyal support of
his immediate staff. Assistant Secretary Frank Pierce, a westerner and
a Williams College graduate, and Land Commissioner Fred Dennett
agreed that his interpretation of policy was a matter of degree rather
than of kind. Oscar Lawler, Assistant Attorney General for Interior
affairs, fully shared Ballinger's strict interpretation of the Secretary's
powers. As a former federal district attorney from Los Angeles, Lawler
was well acquainted with the statutes relating to water and mineral
resources and, like his superior, was anxious to see the passage of more
adequate legislation. Believing that the executive branch could not
properly create law, he invariably posited his advisory opinions on the
prohibitions and limitations of existing laws. Like the Secretary also,
he felt that private enterprise must not be inhibited except in cases of
known fraud.[40] George O. Smith, Garfield's Director of the Geological
Survey, initially distrusted the new Secretary, but quickly overcame his
doubts. Unemotionally scientific by nature, he readily agreed with Ballinger's emphasis upon efficient procedures and responsible administration. Within a few months he was convinced that the policies of the new
administration were those of proper conservation.[41]

Conspicuously absent from this group were Newell and George Woodruff, the latter a confidant of Pinchot who had been replaced by Lawler
as legal adviser. When Ballinger began his work, he talked to Newell
and his assistant, Arthur P. Davis, and heard their objections to his
decision to review the sites. They argued that the proper worth of the

areas had already been taken into account during the investigations of 1908, and expressed their fear that if the sites were restored to the public domain, even temporarily, private companies would enter on them with full knowledge of their potential value. Desperately, Newell urged Ballinger to confine the restorations to tracts that were already privately claimed or obviously undesirable. If he did so, he could preserve continuity of purpose and avoid any reflections on the policies of his predecessor. In reply, the Secretary insisted that the proposed restorations were essential because the withdrawals had not been soundly based in law. He would not assume any supervisory authority not clearly granted by the statutes, and he refused to discuss the matter further.[42]

Privately, Ballinger viewed the Reclamation Service as the epitome of official irresponsibility and callousness. With its vaguely limited powers and seemingly irrational decisions, it was, with the exception of the Forest Service, the most controversial federal agency operating in the West. In addition, Ballinger's personal opinion about Newell was "deeply prejudiced," according to Davis. Recalling his experiences in the Land Office, the Secretary believed that both Newell and Woodruff were agents for Pinchot's interference in Interior affairs. Even before Ballinger was sworn into office, the press copied a rumor that Newell would be replaced by Robert Thomson, city engineer of Seattle. Like any new administrator, the Secretary hoped to build a staff which would be personally loyal to him. For all of these reasons, he therefore dispensed with Newell's advice on most matters.[43]

When Ballinger decided to restore the water power sites, late in March, 1909, Newell and Davis confided their fears to Garfield and Pinchot.[44] Garfield at first did not doubt the motives of his friend and successor, and concluded that he was listening to "malcontents" who were working through Hitchcock. The Secretary's evident desire to limit his own authority and that of the Department must have seemed strange, and Garfield doubtless was saddened by the way in which his policies were being questioned before Ballinger had full knowledge of the subjects involved. Pinchot had none of Garfield's charity, however. Several other reports had already reached him to confirm his initial distrust of Ballinger. He learned, for example, that the new Secretary had consulted Wilson of Agriculture about administrative sites under the jurisdiction of the Forest Service. After making further inquiries among his friends in the West, Pinchot saw other ominous signs: a proposed reclamation project at Grand Junction, Colorado, was being held up; the application of the Truckee Power Company, of Nevada, for use of the water from Lake Tahoe, California, was under serious consideration; and the Interior Department was palpably hostile to national forests in Alaska.[45] Pinchot and Garfield quickly concluded from these things that Ballinger would—willfully or not—undermine their past accomplishments and give aid and comfort to the opponents of federal conservation. Assuming that President Taft was squarely behind that policy, they appealed directly to him to modify the Secretary's narrow interpretation of executive authority. Taft spoke to Ballinger, but, with characteristic moderation, he softened the protests and merely suggested that the rewithdrawals could not safely be delayed until the examinations were completed. Ballinger later admitted that this was a wiser procedure than his original plan. By April, Pinchot and Garfield were convinced that he had seriously impaired his usefulness and would probably resign.[46]

Actually, there had been no substantial reason for their interference, and there were no grounds for their wishful thinking. Ballinger had done nothing more than reveal his intention of altering details of procedure and personnel—matters contemplated, but not executed. Yet his administration was being seriously compromised months before the subject of the Alaska coal claims became an issue. It is interesting to speculate whether the subsequent controversy and its political consequences might have been avoided if Taft had been more stern with him. In view of the strong convictions held by the antagonists, no other adjustment or compromise was likely. Before any reconciliation could even be considered, events plunged ahead.

CHAPTER IV

PINCHOT'S GAMBIT

SUSPICIONS AND CONVICTIONS

THE PUBLIC learned of the rift between Ballinger and Pinchot by the middle of May, 1909. In the West it received particular attention in the Republican press. Several editors of the region, already pleased by the contemplated overhauling of the Reclamation Service, quickly passed judgment on the new Secretary of the Interior after his first month in office. His policy was described as "safe, sane, and conservative ... without impeding the development of the great West and without hysteria in one direction or the other." Seattle's *Post-Intelligencer* exulted over the way the state's favorite son was turning policies "upside down," even though he had run afoul of Pinchot and "that interesting body of citizens identified in the popular mind with ... the 'uplift.' " Other editors gleefully assumed that the Chief Forester was being disciplined and his power curtailed. The rift seemed to be a "trial of the Roosevelt policy of conservation." For the most part, however, the public was not yet informed about the nature of the differences between the two officials. By July, Ballinger had merely acknowledged the existence of a divergence of opinion with Pinchot on the subject of national forests. In the following month, however, an expectant press was furnished with incendiary copy: the issue of the Cunningham claims.[1]

Shortly after Ballinger took office he was again approached by men from the Pacific Northwest who were investors in Alaskan development. They included Miles C. Moore, a former governor of Washington, who was one of a group backed by J. P. Morgan and mining magnate Daniel Guggenheim, the brother of Senator Simon Guggenheim, of Colorado. In 1902, Clarence Cunningham, an Idaho mine owner, filed thirty-three claims for this syndicate, covering 5,280 acres at the source of the Bering River in Alaska. The applications were entered and eventually recorded under the terms of the Coal Act of 1904, which required a declaration of good faith and prohibited subsequent consolidation. When Roosevelt withdrew 100,000 acres—almost all the known coal lands in the territory—in 1906 the value of the land in the Cunningham claims was greatly enhanced and their potential worth was estimated in millions of dollars. In order to hasten confirmations of the entries, the claimants sought endorsements from government officials—among them Senator Heyburn, of Idaho, who apologetically declined to become involved in what might develop into an embarrassing situation. When Ballinger took over the Land Office in 1907, he oversaw the customary examination of the claims by Louis Glavis, soon to be chief of the field division headquartered in Portland. After assuring the investors that their applications were proceeding rapidly, Ballinger at Glavis' request agreed to suspend clear listing—that is, approval. In order to explain the delay, he sent to the investors copies of Land Office correspondence about the investigation of the claims. In doing so, he may have exceeded the bounds of proper official practice, but similar courtesies had been often extended by Commissioners and Secretaries in the past. The notice that another delay would occur in January, 1908, caused the claimants to place their hopes in the passage of the Cale Bill—a fact of which Ballinger was certainly aware.[2] When he returned to his private practice in Seattle two months later, he became personally acquainted with the investors and, as indicated earlier, brought their claims to Garfield's attention.

The Cunningham applications were only a small fraction of the 963 Alaska coal-land entries pending before the Department of the Interior when Ballinger assumed office. From Moore, and from a report by Dennett, he learned that the investigations were still not completed and now involved additional agents and evidence. Moore was also dissatisfied with the terms of the Coal Act of 1908, the substitute measure introduced by Heyburn to replace the Cale Bill. Reminding Ballinger that the claimants had waited patiently during six years of delays, he pointed out that no irregularities had been uncovered and yet the patents were still not confirmed. He and his associates now hoped that the inequity and inefficiency of the Garfield period would be replaced by "a fairer interpretation and a higher respect for the law."[3] Ballinger was not pleased by these importunities and was anxious to avoid any possible doubt about his personal connection with the investors. He therefore ordered Pierce and Dennett to handle all matters relating to the Cunningham claims. He advised Dennett, however, that it would be better if a part of the many cases under investigation could be released so that the agents could concentrate on blatant violations. By employing quick action, he argued, the government's interests would be more effectively protected than if operations were spread over a wider field with less chance of certain success.[4]

When Moore next called on Ballinger he was shunted into Pierce's office. To his disgust, he found that the Assistant Secretary could tell him nothing new. Annoyed by this treatment, he complained to Ballinger in several letters and remarked pointedly that the claimants had expected better usage when their friend was appointed to the Interior Department. Unable to persuade Ballinger to change his attitude, Moore decided to circumvent him by asking Senator Jones, of Washington, to take the matter to the President. In June, Cunningham himself came to the Department when he learned that the Secretary would not make a planned visit to Alaska; he too was referred to Pierce and Dennett. Evidently he sent a private protest about such treatment to Hitchcock and Attorney General George W. Wickersham, both of whom were interested in Alaskan development and knew George Perkins, of Morgan and Company. Ballinger, already irritated by Pinchot's attempt to bypass his authority, was further vexed by these maneuverings.[5]

In June, Glavis reported to Pierce that he had seen Cunningham's private journal and that its entries proved that the claimants meant to consolidate their holdings after they were approved. He therefore asked for permission and additional time to press an investigation for fraud under the act of 1904. The Assistant Secretary, who shared his chief's impatience with the whole case by this time, showed little interest in Glavis' suggestions. Moreover, Lawler had just advised the department that the Cunningham claims qualified only under the Coal Act of 1908, not that of 1904. Wickersham offered to write an opinion on the matter, and Ballinger was consequently more interested in securing immediate judgment of the case than he was in gathering additional details. He directed Glavis to suspend further investigation until the Attorney General's opinion should be received. The agent, who was inordinately proud of his past work, which Ballinger himself had praised, was greatly dismayed by this order. He was reluctant to criticize the Secretary, Wickersham felt after talking with him, but was suspicious of Pierce and Dennett. Glavis assumed that they would denigrate his suggestions and perhaps try to damage his future work with the Department. Full of forebodings about anticipated wrongs, he took his problem to Garfield and later to Pinchot.[6]

Garfield accepted Glavis' belief that the Cunningham claims would be approved, because he was aware that Ballinger had unorthodox views about the administration of Alaskan resources. Pinchot, already alarmed by the Secretary's recent public statement about the national forests, heard Glavis' story in August and decided to intervene in Interior affairs for a second time. For several days Forest Service officials used their chief's authority to copy documents in the files of the Department. Among these they found evidence that Ballinger had terminated an agreement made between Pinchot and Secretary Garfield

whereby the Forest Service would bear the expense of administering
forests within Indian reservations—the domain of the Interior Department. Ballinger had acted upon Lawler's opinion that the arrangement
was illegal because only Congress could determine the use of appropriations. Surprisingly, he had not yet informed Secretary Wilson or the
Commissioner of Indian Affairs of his decision to terminate the agreement. Ballinger probably had taken this step as part of his determination to minimize Forest Service influence in his Department, but Pinchot interpreted it as further evidence of his undermining the policies
established during the Roosevelt years. The Chief Forester was not
anxious to enlarge the area of controversy, but he decided that these
several issues warranted a second appeal to the President. On August
12 he referred Glavis' complaint and the other points to Taft. Whatever
might result from this, he felt that the challenge would make it difficult for anyone thereafter to abandon or alter the Roosevelt policies.
Garfield expected Pinchot to succeed the discredited Ballinger as
Secretary.[7]

Still irritated by the seeming disloyalty of Newell and Davis in the
case of the power sites, the Secretary was incensed when he learned
of the Glavis story and of Pinchot's men rifling the Department files.
As a man with hypersensitive concern about honesty and loyalty in
public office, he found their suspicions intolerable, but he was at first
too stunned to know how to treat them. In a short time, however, he
decided to present the whole matter to the President, confident that
none of the accusations would reflect on his integrity.[8] Taft shared his
indignation and his view of official authority; he felt that Ballinger had
been wrongly subjected to insulting behavior by Moore and to undue
pressure by the Forest Service. Although Taft admired Pinchot's great
contribution to federal conservation, he had no patience with his over-
zealous methods. As Secretary of War he had been one of several Cabinet members who had experienced the adamant power of the Chief
Forester's influence over interdepartmental issues.[9] The President was
now determined to judge both sides of the disagreement. He sent copies
of Pinchot's charges to Ballinger with a request for full explanation
of each point. In reply, the Secretary professed that he was "deeply
wronged and incensed" by the way all of his critics had bypassed him
in presenting their complaints. He submitted a brief of more than six
hundred pages, compiled from statistics produced by his staff, and took
it up to the President's summer home in Beverly, Massachusetts. A little
more than a week later, Taft sent his decision to both officials. Actually,
he had not examined every detail of the lengthy explanation, but he

had read Lawler's summary arguments. He even incorporated some of the counselor's phraseology into his own conclusions about the Cunningham claims. Wickersham drew up a more detailed opinion, but Taft used only a few points from it, for revisions. In order to show that the full opinion had been taken into consideration, however, the Attorney General's statement was dated before the letter of judgment. Pinchot's adherents did not know of these proceedings until the subsequent congressional investigation, at which time they used them to discredit Ballinger and Taft.[10]

The President's letter to Pinchot, dated September 13, 1909, discarded the charges made by Glavis as inaccurate in several important details and wholly mistaken in the assumption that the Department had stifled the investigation of the Cunningham claims. Taft felt that Ballinger had not violated federal statutes by assisting in the submission of these entries after he left the Land Office because the restriction had been interpreted to apply only to money claims. He also upheld Lawler's opinion concerning the agreement on forests within Indian reservations. Pinchot's associates, he insisted, were condemning persons not because of any real wrongs committed, but merely because they differed in their interpretation of administrative methods. This idea was a repetition of a statement expressed by Lawler to Ballinger in July, and one which the Secretary's staff generally shared. Having put the charges in that perspective, Taft assured Pinchot that Ballinger was pursuing established policies and making as great a contribution as the Chief Forester.[11]

PREJUDICE AND PRIDE

In August, Pinchot and Garfield had expected Ballinger to resign; but after reading the President's letter of September 13 they were forced to conclude that he had been misled by the Secretary or was willing to whitewash him to save his own administration. Such a "fatal blunder" destroyed their hope that he might effectively adjudicate the controversy.[12] They had not, however, suspended their activities in anticipation of the decision. Pinchot did not doubt that Taft would uphold conservation, but he was convinced that a public exposition of the affair was essential. As head of a federal bureau which had agents scattered across the country, and as a symbol of Roosevelt's still substantial prestige, he was in a remarkably advantageous position to carry out a publicity campaign. By that time, his opportunity was further enhanced because of the public reaction to the Aldrich tariff and the fight of the Insurgents in Congress to overcome the power of Speaker of the House Joseph G. Cannon.

The men who were willing to prejudge Ballinger and Taft in the months that followed were responding to two considerations. Many of them hoped that the controversies would force the administration to embrace the Roosevelt policies. The Democrats naturally welcomed a good source of political ammunition. All of them relied upon the publicity which appeared in the newspapers and magazines that were already flourishing upon the sensational aspects of the reform movement. Like the conservationists themselves, the journalists seemed less interested in analyzing events than in provoking public response. Because the subject matter involved in the Ballinger controversy was technical and still only partly revealed, their coverage of the affair was necessarily inaccurate and often distorted. Before the issue was officially acknowledged, press copy was studded with rumors from the capital and the West. Forest Service releases originally distributed for public understanding of resource policy were now reprinted to fill the vacuum created by the silence of the men involved in the affair. With the reading public's curiosity thus whetted, anything became acceptable as news. Correspondents searched out disgruntled government employees, disgusted settlers, and habitués of congressional cloakrooms for statements about Pinchot, Ballinger, Taft, Roosevelt, or anyone remotely connected with the departments involved.

From August to October, the President, the Secretary, and the Chief Forester made the controversy front-page news by their separate travels through the states of the West. Whenever they were questioned by reporters, they smiled, chatted amiably, and denied the real extent of the disagreements. But their actions were belied by a startling verbal explosion that occurred in August at a meeting of the National Irrigation Congress in Spokane, Washington. Reclamation policy was the principal topic of interest there, and the delegates talked of little besides the promise and danger of Ballinger's administration. Tension quickly produced a division in their ranks: the supporters of Pinchot were led by his disciple George Pardee, former governor of California, while the defenders of Ballinger rallied around former Senator John Wilson, of Washington. When the Chief Forester arrived at the convention, he had a private conversation with Pardee and Glavis; together they decided that a scheduled address by the Secretary would doubtlessly be an attack on Garfield's policies. To offset that, and in order to publicize the critical nature of the controversy, Pardee altered his own speech and inserted the charge that Ballinger's attempt to restore the power sites was evidence that a national power trust was still insidiously active. Wilson replied with allusions to the tyranny of the Forest Service

and the Bureau of Reclamation, but the delegates were anxious to hear
the speeches of the two antagonists themselves. Pinchot took the rostrum
and repeated his belief that the public interest was paramount to the
law, but neither he nor Ballinger referred directly to the controversy.
The partisans of each tried to shape the resolutions issued by the assembly during the sessions that followed. By the time of adjournment
the Pinchot supporters were in the majority. To the disgust of Ballinger's friends, they also dominated the National Conservation Congress
which met at the Alaska-Yukon-Pacific Exposition in Seattle a few
weeks later.[13] In reporting these events the newspapers in the West
which were already critical of federal resource policy roundly condemned Pardee's speech. Yet when Pinchot went to Oregon and California after the conventions he drew large and enthusiastic audiences.
Significantly, the San Francisco *California Weekly,* an organ of the
local reformers, announced that it believed the Garfield-Pinchot interpretation of federal authority, not Ballinger's, was the proper one. Such
comments indicated that westerners were already willing to take sides
in the controversy over federal policy.[14]

It was also obvious that the conservation issue would eventually become inextricably bound to political alignments. As the Ballinger affair
began to appear in its full scope, the progressives in the Republican
party grew fearful that it might do more than discipline the Taft administration. Many of the Western admirers of Roosevelt still retained
their confidence in his hand-picked successor, Taft. During the late
summer months, these men were reluctant to join either side. Congressman Needham, of California, for example, discounted the exaggerations
of the press. In Needham's opinion, Pinchot's policy was a benefit to the
whole country, but that fact did not make the Chief Forester right about
every matter. In private correspondence he expressed full confidence
in the President's ability to adjust the differences amicably.[15] Chester H.
Rowell, another progressive Republican of California and editor of the
Fresno *Republican,* perceived that those differences would be more difficult to reconcile than the antagonists themselves. His letter to Taft
ominously alluded to the way in which the emotionalism stirred up by
the press was bringing about an oversimplification of the issue. The
Ballinger controversy, he advised the President, was assuming

a certain symbolic importance in the imagination of the people ... quite aside from
any question of strict analytic justice as between the two men. Both may be personally 'working for the same end' as you say, but their names have got attached to two
popular movements which are seeking opposite ends, and represent two fundamen-
tally contrary theories of government.[16]

The Western progressives could already observe that the divergence of opinion was taking on an unmistakable political cast. William S. U'Ren, a leader of the reform element in Oregon, confided to his state's Senator Jonathan Bourne that most of his acquaintances favored Pinchot as against the administration:

They condemn Mr. Ballinger without hesitation and speak as though they hoped the President is really standing in with the people; but, there is a lurking fear in their minds that he is not. . . . Comparatively few are as well satisfied now as they were last year that Mr. Taft really intends to support the Roosevelt policies.[17]

The growth of these doubts among the progressives in the Republican party would eventually strengthen Pinchot's publicity campaign.

Secretary Ballinger was as firm in his convictions as Pinchot, but he had none of his adversary's fighting ability. Like their chief, the men in the Department also underestimated Pinchot. Dennett, for example, described him as "a spoilt darling; a most dangerous man . . . a millionaire with a fad and the inclinations of an inquisition," who was provoked because he could not run Interior affairs as he had done in the past.[18] Ballinger said nothing, and, because he did not think such action was warranted by the dignity of his office, made no attempt to reply to his critics. He appreciated the way in which such friends as editor Erastus Brainerd, of the Seattle *Post-Intelligencer*, defended him in the press. When supporters offered to gather charges against the Forest Service, however, the Secretary merely acknowledged receipt of their suggestions and refrained from using the information. He did not want the assistance of those whose methods and character reminded him of his detractors. "I prefer the approval of people of conservatism and sound judgment," he told a well-wisher, "rather than those who are controlled by sentimentation."[19]

His first reception by the public after the controversy was revealed proved to be gratifying. Traveling through the West with Carter, of Montana, and Frank Flint, of California, both members of the Senate Irrigation Committee, he inspected reclamation projects and paused often to explain the Department's new policy to delegations of water users and newspapermen. He welcomed criticisms of the federal operations and even made a few petty remarks against them himself. When he reached California, however, he carefully avoided meeting agents of the Truckee Power Company. Instead, he joined Taft for a visit to the Yosemite area. The two officials met John Muir there and emerged from the park sharing that crusader's view of the undesirability of the Hetch Hetchy grant. No public reference was ever made to the charges then spilling from the press, but Ballinger invariably defended his belief in a government of laws when he spoke at meetings and banquets throughout the West.[20]

When he returned to his office after the President upheld him in September, he found a deluge of mail waiting for him. The letters were written by men who shared his views, including Mondell and Clark, of Wyoming, and Senator Charles Hughes, of Colorado. Another came from Senator Fulton, of Oregon, by his own description the first man to challenge the "tyranny" of Pinchot in 1907. Both Taft and Ballinger thought highly of the former senator but, because of his past connection with the timberland frauds, they could not favor him with a federal judicial post. All of these correspondents denounced the conservationists, who, they believed, were conspiring against the administration, and assured the Secretary that the responsible citizens and newspapers of their states supported him.[21] One of the most comforting letters came from a Democrat: Franklin K. Lane, of California, Roosevelt's choice as Interstate Commerce Commissioner, who was to be reappointed by Taft.

I hope you will not let loose newspaper talk distress or excite you [Lane wrote]. Remember that a wise man once said that "politics is gossip." No one thinks you are not entirely straight—I've talked with hundreds of people out west and [in Washington, D.C.]—they differ as to what the policy of the government should be but they take no stock in any idea you are not patriotic and honest. I'm not on your side of the fence politically so that I can get at sentiment better than you can and I want you to feel that men are not unfriendly or unjust. You will find that this thing will all wash out.[22]

Such assurances must have confirmed Ballinger's disdain for the clamor in the press and strengthened his resolve to remain aloof until cooler judgments prevailed. It was significant, however, that the total number of letters he received was less than a third of the amount going to Pinchot at the same time. Moreover, half of Pinchot's mail came from the West—from Colorado, Oregon, and even Washington—where most of Ballinger's partisans resided.[23]

The President's September letter was a source of great personal satisfaction for the Secretary, but its effect was immediately shattered by the comments which appeared in newspapers and mass-circulation magazines. The August issue of *Hampton's* fired the first shot against Ballinger's policy and integrity. The most offensive articles appeared in *Collier's Weekly* during the fall and winter months of 1909, under such titles as: "Are the Guggenheims in charge of the Interior Department?" and "Ballinger—Shyster Lawyer." The subject matter of these exposés was based upon information furnished by Glavis, recently dismissed from the Interior Department after Taft's letter, but the prose and titles were written by imaginative journalists. The text often consisted of alleged conversations, but it was usually sprinkled with enough technical detail and official correspondence to lend an air of credibility to the story. The writers made no effort to inform readers of the legitimate differences in administrative procedures, or to distinguish between official intentions and active events. In some instances the articles were almost slanderous in implication, a fact which caused Pinchot to post bond with the publishers against possible legal action. These issues of *Collier's* naturally aroused further public interest and elicited comment on the charges by more responsible magazines. One of these, the *Outlook*, at first decided upon judging Ballinger separately from the acts of his administration. The Secretary was above criticism; his proposed changes in former policies, however, were open to objections. This split decision may have represented the personal sympathies of the editor, Lyman Abbott, a friend of Roosevelt and Pinchot, and E. L. Baldwin, Ballinger's friend. In the course of several months the sheer volume of opinion in print—apart from its substance—seemed to belie Taft's dismissal of the charges as mere "shreds of suspicion."[24]

Of all the accusations being made, references to Ballinger's past connection with the Alaska claimants were the most persistent. The Secretary was particularly hurt by Garfield's statement that he had not approved of his former Commissioner's serving these investors—a feeling he never expressed to Ballinger.[25] In a quiet effort to halt the "outrageous slander," Ballinger asked Judge Ronald, his former law partner, to assure Abbott that the firm had had no substantial relations with land development corporations while he was in charge of the Land Office. Ronald thereupon wrote a lengthy disquisition which was based upon the records of the partnership, but unfortunately was not clear about several details. The author was later to be discomfited when his veracity was questioned by Ballinger's critics. Judge Hanford, who was also asked to write a personal endorsement, wisely declined to do so. He was at that moment delivering anti-conservation harangues in the Northwest and, although proud of the fact that his name was odious to conservationists, realized that a letter from him would serve to arouse new slanders against his former protégé. Judge Thomas Burke and other prominent Seattleans agreed to write to friends of Taft and Pinchot. One of them, former Governor John McGraw, who was now associated with the Cunningham group, swore from his personal knowledge that Ballinger had not halted the Glavis investigation of the claims. Another, lumberman J. J. Donavan, wrote to *Collier's* to say that the magazine had "descended into the gutter." The effectiveness of all of these letters was obviously marred by the backgrounds of their authors. Even if they had been printed and distributed to the public, they could not have offset the volume of accusations.[26]

By November the Secretary seemed to be more attentive to charges against the Forest Service which were sent to him by Heyburn, Patterson, and other Western senators. Still, he refused to sanction a mass meeting on his behalf to be held in Seattle, fearing that it would not seem proper and would probably be exploited by his critics. At the end of the month, however, he heeded the advice of Baldwin and Charles L. Pack, of the National Conservation Association, and tried to take the public into his confidence. At a meeting with reporters Ballinger dismissed the sensational magazines as "literary apostles of vomit" who hoped to invent calumnies "so rapidly as to preclude reply." He denied that he had been the Cunningham group's attorney, and he defended his actions as Secretary of the Interior. "I have not only been consistently in the vanguard of the conservation movement," he asserted, "but have sought to give it permanence along lines reasonably within the spirit of present law and to secure adequate additional laws."[27] Because many of the press services were already discounting information coming from the Department, these statements were ignored or were buried on the inside pages of most newspapers. By that time Ballinger was so desperate for public vindication that he considered bringing a lawsuit against *Collier's*. Several close friends advised against it, however, and Wickersham told him that it would not be legally warranted.[28] It seems unlikely that he would have instituted any such action without Presidential sanction.

The reticent course taken by the Secretary during these trying months disclosed much about his character and about the way in which he would be overwhelmed in the fight with Pinchot. Privately, he confessed that he had at first refrained from public discussion of the affair because he did not want to bring "any unnecessary disparagement" upon Garfield.[29] In view of Garfield's sudden turn against his onetime friend, this courtesy was sadly misplaced. Ballinger's primary reason for remaining quiet was his confidence that the President stood with him on the immediate issue of reclamation policy. Early in August, Taft had urged him to "put the brake down until Congress shall meet and then we will present the situation to Congress exactly as it is and make such recommendations as you believe ought to be made in regard to it. We must be very accurate in our statements as to the conditions that exist," he added significantly, "because our motives may be misconstrued, as they have already been and we shall encounter bitter criticism and judgment from those who are left in an embarrassed condition," meaning the authors of former policies.[30]

From the time that his administration was first challenged, in April, Ballinger grew increasingly dependent upon the President. Memoranda of Cabinet meetings indicate that he discussed every controversial subject with Taft and abided by his chief's opinions about details which, under normal circumstances, would quite properly have been decided by the Interior Department.[31] Thus assured of the highest approval, he was understandably less anxious to cultivate public support. The President well knew that his Secretary was relying upon him and taking slight means to defend himself,[32] but Taft's own reticent character proved to be a weak reed to lean upon.

CLIMAX AND ANTICLIMAX

In September, Pinchot had a private conversation with the President in Salt Lake City, while they were in the midst of their tour through the West. On that occasion Taft reiterated his belief that the subjects of dispute were more anticipated than real, and he again assured Pinchot that Ballinger was equally sincere as a conservationist. The Chief Forester was, undoubtedly, disappointed to learn that the significant events of the preceding months had made no impression on the President, but he did not mention this feeling. Courteously, but frankly, he stated that he could not change his opinion about these matters. Taft's heartiness became subdued. Quietly, he said that he would not like to lose Pinchot's valuable services to the nation. The latter was not quite sure whether this was a warning or an ultimatum. Just as quietly, he replied that he did not wish to resign, but believed that the issue was paramount even to his post in the government.[33] When he left the President, Pinchot's feelings must have been a mixture of regret and exhilaration. He was surely saddened to see the end of his close relationship with the White House. The successes of the past years had been the source of great pride and greater ambitions, but he was never a man to be satisfied with past accomplishments. Pinchot was always the White Knight—righteous, audacious, restless. The statement he made during that brief conversation with Taft was the most ambitious stand he had ever assumed. It was also the greatest gamble he ever undertook. In the contest that would inevitably follow, he was armed not with evidence, but with the force of public opinion—a force which he and Roosevelt, and their co-workers, had built in part by the conservation crusade. The enormity of the gamble was exceeded only by the size of the victory that was possible. Such a challenge was irresistible to a man like Pinchot.

If he had any initial doubts about his decision, the mass of letters, telegrams, and resolutions from East and West put him in high spirits. Revising his original strategy, he abandoned plans for a history of the conservation movement under Roosevelt, which he had intended to write with Garfield, and decided that a nationwide press and speaking campaign would be a thousand times more valuable as publicity. A host of friends confirmed the wisdom of that campaign. Stewart Edward White wrote to describe the way the controversy was rousing the indifferent, "the fence-sitters," into "a vigorous partisanship." Whatever the disappointments or losses involved, the affair would be a "bully good investment" in the great asset of public opinion. "You remember," the author reminded Pinchot, "we were saying ... that a really *hard* setback [in conservation] would not be a bad thing? Well, in my opinion, this is it."[34]

Encouraged by these responses, Pinchot sent a second letter to the President in November to demonstrate Ballinger's "unfriendly attitude toward conservation."[35] By then, Taft and his advisers had agreed upon the need for a congressional investigation of the whole controversy. In so deciding, the President and his Secretary of the Interior meant to imply that, from their own knowledge, there was nothing in the documentary evidence which would sustain any of the charges. They also hoped that a trial before a prestigious and influential forum would offset the distortions of the press. Ballinger particularly welcomed vindication at the hands of men who shared his emphasis upon strict adherence to the law. In December, he asked Senator Jones to introduce a resolution calling for an investigation of the Interior Department, but insisted that it would do no good unless the Forest Service were also subjected to official inquiry. "I assure you," the Secretary wrote, "it can not be made too broad in its scope to suit me and those under me."[36] His critics eagerly agreed to the larger investigation. Pinchot was happy to use the occasion to reach a greater public audience for the defense of his policy and his bureau. The Insurgents in Congress supported inclusion of the Forest Service in the resolution so that the investigation should not result in a one-sided verdict.[37]

Pinchot correctly assumed that the majority of the investigating committee would reflect the administration's view of his conduct in the affair. Uncertain whether he could effectively discredit Ballinger under their scrutiny, he refused to suspend his publicity campaign to await the dubious outcome of an extended inquiry. When several solicitous

Republican leaders pointed to the substance of the Secretary's annual report in late November, Pinchot and Garfield were not impressed. The conservationists noted that Ballinger defined his policy there with statements that, considering the tendencies of the preceding months, were suspiciously qualified: "While development is the keynote," he announced, "the best thought of the day is not that development shall be by national agencies, but that wise utilization shall be secured through private enterprise under national supervision and control." He went on to say that the Reclamation Service had been subjected to "much unjust and to some just criticism." In the opinion of the Pinchot men, the report contained nothing really original. If that document showed Ballinger standing by federal resource policy, Garfield decided, it was because the controversy had scared him into signing it.[38] Moreover, Pinchot's thoughts were far removed from such empty gestures. On December 31 he wrote to Roosevelt for the first time since the former President had left on his African safari. Asserting that the Taft administration was taking a course directly away from Roosevelt's policies, Pinchot reported that the federal appropriation for the newly organized National Conservation Association had been lost because of insufficient interest at the White House. Secondly, he charged that the appointment of Ballinger brought about the "most dangerous attack yet made upon the conservation policies—an attack now happily checked, at least for the time."[39] Roosevelt had received reports of discontent before this, but these grim sentences from an old comrade made a profound impression upon him.

In that same month of December, Pinchot wrote another letter: a defense of Overton Price and Albert Shaw, members of his staff who had aided Glavis in the publication of the charges against Ballinger. At the request of the Secretary, the President was considering their dismissal. Pinchot was aware that Taft had included him in a recent order prohibiting any member of the Forest Service from discussing the interdepartmental controversy in public. He therefore took a copy of the letter to his superior, Secretary Wilson, and asked permission to issue it. Pinchot explained the contents, but Wilson did not read the letter. Evidently uneasy about the matter, he suggested that Pinchot submit it directly to Taft. In the course of the conversation that followed, Wilson expressed his hope that the harmful controversy could be ended, then gave his assent to some minor Forest Service business. Pinchot left the office with the thought that Wilson had not specifically opposed issuance of the letter, but Wilson later testified that he had not consented to it. Realizing then that there was an even chance of his being dismissed for insubordination, the Chief Forester decided that his purpose was more important than his office. The letter was delivered to Senator Jonathan Dolliver, of Iowa, chairman of the Committee on Agriculture and Forestry and a personal friend. Dolliver read it from the floor of the Senate and Pinchot waited for the explosion that he believed would be necessary and beneficial.[40]

When Taft talked with Pinchot in September, he had maintained that he was not concerned with reëlection, but was going to do the right thing in the controversy "whether the people liked it or not."[41] Generally, he admired the contribution of the Chief Forester during the preceding years, but was now painfully familiar with Pinchot's egocentric view of federal resource policy. Seeking to settle the dispute, he had already obtained Ballinger's full coöperation, but, in spite of private interviews and extended correspondence, he could not restrain the Chief Forester. By the time he received Pinchot's second criticism of Ballinger, in November, he was beginning to detest him. In private letters he referred to Pinchot as a man with a "swelled head" full of Roosevelt's "socialist tendencies." It was obvious to him that Pinchot, with "Jesuit guile," was planning a coup to bring about his own dismissal in order to wreck the administration.[42] The Dolliver letter was the last straw on the broad back of the President's patience. Early in January, 1910, he discussed the matter with his Cabinet, whose members naturally upheld their colleague, and then asked Wilson to dismiss the Chief Forester from his office. In a personal communication which omitted the customary "My Dear Gifford," Taft charged Pinchot with acting upon subjects which were distorted by muckrakers, and with insubordination which impaired his further usefulness to the administration.[43] Technically, the President's decision was justified, but it was a profound shock to the public. Perhaps, as Editor Brainerd told Ballinger, it should have been made immediately after the incident at the Spokane congress.[44] Certainly, he should have given greater heed to "whether the people liked it or not." If it had happened before the storm of publicity over Taft's departure from his predecessor's practices, the consequences might have been less significant. Instead, the press campaign had led newspaper readers to expect the dismissal of Ballinger, not the defender of Roosevelt's policies. The President's action appeared to confirm every doubt raised by his critics.

The dismissal of Pinchot also made the congressional investigation look like a needless hypocrisy. Many newspapermen covered the sessions, not to report fairly, but to find sensational news copy. From the first, there seemed little reason to expect an impartial examination of the dispute. Just as Pinchot had anticipated, the majority of the members appointed to the committee guaranteed a decision in Ballinger's favor. The chairman was Senator Knute Nelson, of Minnesota, one of the President's chief legislative lieutenants, who fully sympathized with the emphases of the Secretary's new policies. Only two other senators were from the West. George Sutherland, of Utah, did not share Governor Wells's interest in resource conservation, and he invariably defended a strictly legalistic view of administrative authority. In the course of the hearings he was particularly solicitous about evidence concerning abuses by the Forest Service and indignant over alleged mistreatment of settlers on the public domain. At home his political opponents referred to him as a "willing tool of the Guggenheim interests," but it was political orthodoxy that shaped his judgment of the case. When, for example, one attorney suggested that there was something questionable about Republicans' appointing their own party members to office rather than Democrats, the senator quipped that if such an attitude ever prevailed generally he would get out of politics.[45] His colleague, Frank Flint, of California, represented a more moderate Western view of federal policy, but took little part in the sessions and was content to vote with the administration men whenever a decision was made. On several occasions both senators agreed to restrict testimony which favored Pinchot and the Forest Service.[46] There were no westerners among the Democratic minority of the committee; their criticisms of Ballinger's actions were denounced by some members of the party—for instance, Governor Shafroth of Colorado.[47]

Understandably, Secretary Ballinger put his entire trust in the investigation, yet he did not make the most of these advantages. He had been warned by his friend Ormsby McHarg to get the best legal counsel for the ordeal. "You have the battle of your life on, and you want to get the biggest lawyers that you know to go into this case and fight like hell. If you don't," McHarg added prophetically, "your reputation will be shot and cut at and it will take a fortune and history to restore it to you."[48] Ballinger decided not to select government-appointed attorneys, as he might legally have done. Instead, he took the advice of the President's friends and retained John J. Vertrees, of Tennessee. It took him many months to compensate the lawyer from his personal finances, but Ballinger insisted upon paying the greater part of the $17,600 fee for Vertrees' services.[49] Unfortunately, the Secretary did not get the best assistance for his money.

The hearings of the investigating committee began with an opening statement by Vertrees which described Ballinger as the victim of a conspiracy. But the Secretary was not immediately called to the stand—as the purpose of the inquiry warranted and as Chairman Nelson would certainly have permitted. Instead, Vertrees called on Pierce, Dennett, and other subordinates to testify first. These men were obviously limited in their personal knowledge of many events and were therefore ineffectual as spokesmen for the Secretary's opinions and actions. Louis Brandeis, counsel for Glavis, later confessed that he and his staff were caught unready by the opening session and had not then gleaned their evidence from the mass of documents pertaining to the controversy. If Vertrees had called Ballinger first, their opponents might have been forced to construct a defense along lines determined by his testimony. Of equal significance was Vertrees' failure to exploit the most important aspect of the controversy: the problem of administration of conservation in the West. Personally unfamiliar with conditions in that region, he failed to acquaint himself with the basic subject of Forest Service procedures and tried unsuccessfully to get Pinchot to give a brief summary of the complex problems involved in regulated resource use.[50] The attorney also proved to be inept at the art of cross-examination. While questioning witnesses, he upset himself and the committee, could not force Pinchot to admit that he wanted revenge, and even tried the classical maneuver: "When did you form the purpose to assault and attack Mr. Ballinger."[51] As part of his defense, Vertrees insisted upon the difference between knowledge and belief, yet he tried to expose the personal opinions of Newell and others. Finally, he missed his best opportunity by allowing Pinchot to leave the stand just as the subject of Roosevelt's sweeping withdrawals of 1907 was brought up.[52]

By the time Ballinger took the stand, in March, the testimony of a score of witnesses made it necessary for him to spend hours in explanation and denial. He was thus not only burdened with his own defense, but also subjected to the probing tactics of Brandeis and Pinchot's attorney, George W. Pepper. It was Pepper whose examination revealed the Secretary's lack of faith in the efficacy of reforestation and his slight acquaintance with details of Forest Service regulation. At one point Ballinger described the leasing of forest areas to cattle and sheep raisers as a selfish policy. In that astonishing opinion he certainly did not speak for many thousands of westerners. Neither he nor his counsel offered adequate explanations of the differing views toward resource administration. They had letters from disgruntled settlers inserted into the record, but such evidence could not enlighten the committee or make any impression on the public. Considering Ballinger's long silence about his policies and his hopes concerning the official investigation, his failure to deliver any lengthy exposition from the stand is puzzling. Perhaps he was aware that the Taft men were hoping he would "keep his head level" during the ordeal and his characteristic reticence was increased by that knowledge.[53] He limited his answers almost entirely to the information asked for by the attorneys, offering very few comments of his own. More than once, Nelson and other members of the committee had to prompt him to state his opinion of federal authority. Brandeis, who was by that time well informed about the details of the controversy, was unable to get Ballinger to admit to having halted the investigation of the Cunningham claims, but he made the most of the Secretary's reluctant behavior. The committeemen often objected to these tactics, but Ballinger coldly declined to be intimidated by them. "I have given you all the reasons you are going to get," he announced at one point. "You may pursue it as long as you please." Even when he did respond to extraneous questions, the answers were later used to reflect upon his veracity. He denied, for example, that he had ever consulted Hitchcock about patronage matters, when no one familiar with the practices of traditional party politics could believe this. Consequently, when he denied that certain conversations with Glavis had ever occurred, his statement seemed equally untrustworthy. Satisfied with what he had said, he finally excused himself from further testimony because of the press of Department business.[54] Ballinger's performance on the stand left a decidedly negative impression on an expectant public and confirmed the growing feeling that he was hiding something.

Compared to the course pursued by their adversaries, the Pinchot men successfully exploited their self-assumed role as prosecutors for the people. Glavis offered many documents relating to the erratic—and therefore suspicious—handling of the Cunningham claims. In demeanor Glavis seemed to be an earnest, courageous young man who retained his calm assurance in spite of the pressures used by Vertrees and several committee members. Garfield and Newell emphasized their former propinquity to Roosevelt, thereby introducing a touchy subject. Throughout their testimony, the majority of the committee found many occasions to praise President Taft, but political wariness made them reluctant to comment on the contrasting policies of his predecessor.[55] Next, a surprise witness took the stand. Frederick Kerby, a stenographer in Ballinger's office, had participated in preparing the lengthy defense which the Secretary submitted to Taft at Beverly. His description of the way that compilation had been completed, in secrecy and at midnight, and his admission that the notes were afterwards burned made newspaper headlines across the country. Kerby also disclosed that

Wickersham's detailed opinion had been predated. Taft dispatched a letter to the committee to explain that his letter of September 13 corresponded in many but not all of its points to the memorandum written by Lawler, but nothing could erase the fact that the President's exoneration of Ballinger had not been based upon his personal examination of the controverted evidence. Pinchot described the subterfuge as terrible enough to make "every decent American squirm in his skin."[56] Kerby, like Glavis and Newell, was immediately hailed by many observers as a brave young man who, risking his own position, had put the country's interest before loyalty to his superior.

Pinchot's appearance before the committee was a dramatic contrast to that of his adversary. When he took the stand, late in February, he began his testimony with a prepared statement which defined his beliefs and immediate purpose in unmistakable language. Ballinger, he asserted, had accepted the post of Secretary with the clear determination of wrecking established water power policy and had replied to protests with explanations that were "essentially false." The text concluded with a point implied by earlier testimony and still unshaken by the defense: "... the interests of the people are not safe in Mr. Ballinger's hands ... The Secretary of the Interior has been unfaithful both to the public, whose property he has endangered, and to the President, whom he has deceived."[57] The charges which had been discussed in the press for more than six months seemed to be sustained as much by the boldness of Pinchot as by the blandness of Ballinger.

The last of the witnesses left the stand in May, 1910, and the committee turned to the unenviable task of handing down a judgment. A few months later, the majority published its report, asserting that the charges against the Secretary had their origin in a "strong feeling of animosity created by a supposed difference in policy respecting the conservation of natural resources." They found no wrongdoing involved in Ballinger's strict interpretation of the laws and none revealed by the mass of evidence presented by both sides. Pinchot and his partisans, the report concluded, had raised matters of mere doubt, not error.[58] A second and dissenting report was issued by the minority consisting of the Democratic members and one Insurgent congressman, E. H. Madison, of Kansas, who agreed with them in a separate statement. The mass of documents entered as evidence, they announced, "clearly indicated duplicity" on the part of Ballinger and Pierce in the matter of the Cunningham claims. The report bristled with various journalistic devices: an insinuating reference to the Secretary's acquaintance with Perkins of J. P. Morgan and Company, noting that he used the term

"exploiting" when discussing resource use, and—bending even further—pointing to Moore's habit of addressing his letters to "Dear
Ballinger." On firmer grounds, the minority report argued that Pierce's
knowledge of his chief's intentions was as limited as Taft's had been;
attestations to Ballinger's integrity by these two could therefore be
discounted. The conclusion was a restatement of Pinchot's opening
charge: "Mr. Ballinger has not been true to the trust reposed in him
as Secretary of the Interior[,] is not deserving of public confidence,
[and] should be requested by the proper authority to resign his office."[59]
Neither report took cognizance of the way in which the Pinchot men had
initiated their criticism of the Secretary months before the Glavis
charges were made.

Ballinger thus received an official exoneration which impressed few
observers and converted none. Privately, he admitted that he had hoped
for a nearly unanimous verdict and was profoundly upset by the strong
minority report. The committee, he grumbled, had been duped by "a
gang of dishonest troublemakers."[60] Publicly, he announced his intention of "giving the American people some idea of the purity of the
knives of my traducers" as soon as he was out of office. For a second
time he considered a libel suit against such "scoundrels" as *Collier's,*
but this time his friends advised him that the editors could not be
extradited to be tried in a Seattle court.[61] Even if the suit had been
pressed, it might have underscored the painful fact that Ballinger had
failed to get effective vindication at the hands of the administration.
Instead, as McHarg had warned, his reputation was destroyed—but
neither a fortune or half a century of history has restored it to him.*

---

* The historiography of the Ballinger-Pinchot affair, like the controversy itself,
was determined by the contrasting effectiveness of the antagonists. When a textbook
in American history was published in 1915, Ballinger was greatly upset to find that
it described him as a tool of the corporate interests, and once again he contemplated
bringing a libel suit. When he consulted Wickersham, however, he was advised that
the case would merely resolve itself into a new prosecution "of the same character
as that conducted by Pinchot and his friends in 1910." (R. A. Ballinger to W. A.
White, May 3, and to G. Wickersham, April 1, and Wickersham to Ballinger, April
5, 1915, Ballinger Papers.) By the time of his death, in 1922, he had made no effort
to reopen the controversy or to seek public exoneration.

Because Pinchot remained active in politics during the subsequent decade, he did
not have time to publish an account of the affair, but he was pleased to note that the
first essay on it, Rose M. Stahl's *The Ballinger-Pinchot Controversy* (1926), completely upheld his actions and those of his associates. Apart from the fact that it
did allude to the former Chief Forester's unusual influence over the Department of
the Interior, the work was limited in objectivity and in its use of primary sources.
After Pinchot retired as governor of Pennsylvania, in 1935, he compiled two
volumes of typescript from material in his own papers and from notes submitted by
his disciples. Before he was ready to issue this comprehensive account of the conser-

vation controversy, Henry F. Pringle published *The Life and Times of William Howard Taft* (1939). That study tried to redress the balance of opinion that had been upset by the triumphs of the progressives, but it failed to emphasize the actual difference between Taft's and Ballinger's views of resource policy, and naturally it did not criticize the President's inconsistent handling of the controversy. After reading Pringle, Secretary of the Interior Harold L. Ickes, a former Theodore Roosevelt Progressive, reëxamined the documents of the investigation and, writing in the *Saturday Evening Post* (May 25, 1940), concluded that Ballinger had been an "American Dreyfus." In a lengthier tract, published by the government the same year, he correctly pointed out that there was no evidence of a wrongful act by his predecessor, but he did not examine the administrative problems involved in the issue. Generally, Ickes hoped to use these expositions to discredit his erstwhile friend Pinchot, who was then publicly opposing the proposal to bring the Forest Service back into his Department, which was to be renamed the Department of Conservation. By this plan, he hoped to clear away the shadows of suspicions cast upon the Department of the Interior by the irresponsibilities of former Secretaries.

The dispute with Ickes prompted Pinchot to make his manuscript account available to Alpheus T. Mason, the biographer of Brandeis; in 1941, Mason published *Bureaucracy Convicts Itself.* The author carefully selected documents from the records of the investigation, placed them in a setting of black-and-white characterization reminiscent of the journalism of the period of controversy, and produced a readable but incomplete case for Glavis and Pinchot. Near the end of his book (p. 181), Mason admitted that Ballinger was not technically guilty or unfaithful to his official trust, but this statement was practically suffocated by the implications on almost every other page. Moreover, he chose a particularly unfortunate title in view of the fact that "bureaucracy" was the term commonly applied to Pinchot and his policy. Writing his autobiography, *Breaking New Ground* (1946), Pinchot clearly indicated that he had acted to prevent the initiation of administrative changes which differed from the procedures of the Roosevelt men. It is obvious throughout his account that he always believed the whole conservation movement to be dependent upon his personal actions.

By that time historians were examining the controversy from several points of view. George E. Mowry's *Theodore Roosevelt and the Progressive Movement* (1947) put the event in the context of the doubts and determinations of the Insurgents. But, from the surveys of Charles A. Beard to current publications, American history textbooks have usually celebrated Pinchot's sacrifice and repeated the description of Ballinger as a corporation lawyer whose opinions reflected the West's hostility to resource regulation. Only a few of these widely used volumes have modified this erroneous oversimplification by noting the basic problems of administrative jurisdiction and procedure. For the most part, such accounts have not been prepared with reference to the papers of Pinchot or the published documents of the investigation. Both these sources clearly reveal that the Chief Forester took a great gamble when he sought to discredit Ballinger. M. Nelson McGeary's *Gifford Pinchot: Forester —Politician* (1960) provides a useful account of the affair from the viewpoint of the Pinchot men, but it does not examine the administrative or Western aspects of the controversy. Recently, Samuel P. Hays's *Conservation and the Gospel of Efficiency* (1959) did yeoman service in analyzing the complex problems involved in the regulated use of resources. The present discussion, based upon manuscript sources which include the newly opened Ballinger Papers, has placed the controversy in the essential context of Western attitudes toward federal conservation policy.

CHAPTER V

THE CRITICS' CAMPAIGN

THE TWO CITADELS

THE CRITICS of conservation were pleased by the eruption of the Ballinger-Pinchot controversy. They hoped that it would expose the tangle of federal resource administration and damage the prestige enjoyed by the Chief Forester. They had not, however, waited until the appearance of that fortuitous affair before organizing campaigns to discredit the federal policy in the West. During the first months of 1909 traditions of politics and protest had joined in notable combination in at least two states. In Colorado, a militant Democratic majority took up the critics' cause. When the party held its national convention in Denver the summer before, the followers of William Jennings Bryan had nominated their favorite on a platform that included a denunciation of monopolies, both private and governmental. In the subsequent campaign, Colorado Democrats used references to that unholy alliance to wound their opponents, who were already weakened by an internecine war involving the followers of Senator Guggenheim. The "Smelting Trust and the Federal Forest Department," they charged without regard for logic, were plotting together to erect a "Pinchot-Guggenheim Domain" in the state. Farmers and stockmen were warned that the party of Roosevelt and Taft would continue to retard the development of the West and mistreat its citizens. In the face of such publicity few Republicans were willing to defend the policy or criticize the work of their administration. At the election in November, 1908, Bryan carried only Colorado and Nevada in the West, and these two only by narrow margins. The Denver *Record-Stockman* nevertheless insisted that the victory of state Democrats represented an "undoubted revolt of the West against Pinchotism." Rueful Republicans there advised Taft and Pinchot that their state was lost partly because of the reaction against conservation policies.[1]

The election of former Congressman John A. Shafroth as governor of Colorado seemed to confirm the boast of the Denver newspaper. Long an active opponent of federal resource regulation, Shafroth had promised a reversal of the policy during his campaign, and just before his inauguration, in January, 1909, he consulted with several advisers in order to outline a plan. Together with J. Arthur Eddy and D. C. Beaman—organizers of the Public Lands Convention of 1907—the governor-elect formulated a scheme of counteraction and, a few days later, announced his intentions in his inaugural address. After securing modification of national forest boundaries, Colorado was to take a leading role in establishing state control over all lands and resources. "In view of local conditions," he asserted, "we believe the State should adopt and execute its own policy of conservation and rules for the regulation and disposition of public lands and other natural resources." He asked the new legislature to adopt measures by which these holdings could be acquired.[2] Dozens of Coloradans responded to the address during the following weeks. One of them, Eddy, hailed the speech for showing Pinchotism in its "true" light. Another, however, wrote a warning. Describing himself as a Democrat, J. B. Killian, of the Delta County Livestock Association, urged Shafroth not to force conservation into the realm of politics. It was not, he believed, a party matter—the proposal would certainly wreck the new administration if it were attempted.[3]

Confident about sentiment in his state, the governor considered his project as a positive source of support for his administration. He was immediately gratified when the legislature responded with a resolution that demanded revision of Forest Service regulations. In the state executive branch, however, the Conservation Commission established by his predecessor was still the most influential body of policy makers. Obviously intending to pack it with his own sympathizers, Shafroth appointed both Eddy and Beaman as members, as well as state Senator Elias Ammons and former Senator Thomas Patterson. The views shared by all of these men were summed up in Eddy's letter of acceptance. Promising to support any conservation proposition that was "safe and sane," Eddy reiterated that he was "utterly opposed to proceeding upon those theories that would serve to rob our State and its people of the customary and usual opportunities afforded all of our States heretofore," through the disposal of the public domain. Holding that traditional bias, he could not subscribe to the idea of sacrificing "individualism" for methods that would "save to provide for the future at the expense of the present."[4] The governor, however, had not decided to replace conservationist F. C. Goudy as chairman of the Conservation Commission, perhaps because he had no sudden coup in mind and did not want to arouse his enemies prematurely.

Regardless of political loyalties, other citizens in the state responded enthusiastically to the spirit of Shafroth's actions. One newspaper—which customarily referred to Guggenheim as "$enator $imon"—complimented the governor on his attacks against Pinchot's policies. Another referred to a prominent Republican who threatened to leave his party if Taft retained the Chief Forester. The forces of opposition to conservation were ready, according to the *Rocky Mountain News,* to join in a "final rout of this accursed Pinchotism from the West forever."[5] In anticipation of such a victory, many Colorado stockmen boldly trespassed into the national forests or donated funds to assist in the defense of Fred Light's case before the United States Supreme Court. One of the centers of defiance was Pike National Forest, near Colorado Springs, the site of a ranch owned by Elias Ammons. For months the residents of the area refused to associate with forest rangers and spoke to them only to insult and belittle their work. As one officer remembered it, the Forest Service was "cussed up one side and down the other" whenever the rangers convened meetings to settle local grazing problems. The air of irresponsibility encouraged by Shafroth's policy was also conducive to unlawful timber cutting. In the southwestern part of the state, depredations in the San Juan National Forest were so common that the citizens of near-by Silverton sent delegates to the Conservation Commission to have the cutting stopped.[6]

In the midst of these ominous rumblings, Gifford Pinchot announced that he was coming to Colorado for a public debate on conservation. The Denver *Republican,* an organ of the Taft administration, hopefully maintained that opposition to the policy would melt away when the people were thus informed. The Democratic critics, however, eagerly prepared for the occasion by selecting state Senator Ammons to meet Pinchot in debate before the legislature in March, 1909. Once again the Chief Forester shattered local illusions by displaying his intimate, practical knowledge of resource problems. Ammons' remarks wrapped traditional objections in the rhetoric of political oratory and followed a straight line of constitutional interpretation to state control as the only proper alternative. When the meeting was over, the *Republican* decided that Pinchot had satisfied all but the "chronic kickers." The *Rocky Mountain News* called him a plain liar, however, and did not bother to tell its readers that he had subsequently met with local users of water and range to learn of needed adjustments in boundaries and regulations. Generally, whenever such adjustments were announced, the hostile press ascribed them to the influence of the President or Secretary Wilson and solemnly described them as "a deathblow to Pinchotism." Whatever effect the debate may have had on public opinion in the state, it evidently encouraged the supporters of Shafroth in the legislature; they promptly brought forward a resolution of censure against Pinchot and the Forest Service.[7]

Riding the crest of the wave of opposition, Governor Shafroth and his adviser Eddy organized a National Public Domain League in June. In reality, the League was merely a publicity office for the dissemination of anti-conservation propaganda. Three months later, it had sent out 75,000 pieces of printed material, most of them copies of eleven "bulletins" written by Eddy. By the end of the year, these messages were being mailed to westerners in Congress. In addition, Eddy's personal correspondence, bearing supplementary protests, went to members of the Taft administration and to prominent critics of federal policy. One of these, Senator Carter, of Montana, responded with predictable enthusiasm. The League, he wrote, constituted the only opposition "by the people to Mr. Pinchot's 'course of empire.' " Equipped with pamphlets and bulletins, Shafroth's adherents appeared at various conventions throughout the West. Former Senators Teller and Patterson, as well as Eddy and Ammons, served as delegates to the Twentieth Trans Mississippi Commercial Congress, held in Denver in August, 1910. There they sponsored resolutions endorsing the League, favoring private development of water power, and criticizing the Forest Service for imposing hardships on farmers, prospectors, and investors. D. C. Beaman repeated these ideas at the first National Conservation Congress, in Seattle, during the same month.[8]

The dismissal of Pinchot early in the year gave great impetus to the critics' campaign and specifically encouraged the governor's coterie to make an open attack upon the Colorado Conservation Commission. At first they monopolized the deliberations of that body by forcing through resolutions defending private development of resources. These resolves were immediately dispatched to their spokesman in Congress, Representative Edward Taylor, who had them inserted into the *Congressional Record*. Then the Shafroth appointees tried to obstruct the influence of those whom they referred to as "crazy conservationists." The maneuvering involved in this effort became so exasperating that Beaman dramatically resigned from the Commission, and then was easily persuaded to reassume his membership. After a few weeks of such futile theatricals, Eddy decided that the only effective way to control the organization would be for the governor to appoint seven more "Stalwarts"—men who would be willing to fight for the principle that "the public domain belongs to all of the people, strictly in the sense that any or all of [them] may come to take & use it as their own, upon equitable apportionment." Unless these appointments were made, he warned Shafroth, the Commission would be crippled by endless ties in voting. Four vacancies were filled in the next few months, but the governor seems to have chosen men for their political loyalty rather than because of their views on conservation. Although the critics had not fully or lastingly undermined the work of the Commission, their efforts were praised by these men as the nearest thing to a "real opposition fight by the people of the West." When Carter sent his congratulations to them for pointing the way for state action, his statement was printed in the official proceedings. The conservationists remained undisturbed, however, and refused to be intimidated by men whom they described as "howling coyotes."[9]

The Colorado critics could attack the policy of Republican administrations with impunity, but mere irritation with federal regulations could not overcome political loyalties in other parts of the West. The single exception was Washington State, traditionally a Republican stronghold. There, as in Colorado, a handful of state officials and private citizens sponsored a publicity campaign against the policy and on behalf of state control. Governor Marion E. Hay proved to be the most important source of ideas and actions for the movement during his four years as chief executive. His views on conservation were not widely known when he assumed office after the death of the incumbent governor. Conservationists knew only that he was not a friend of Land Commissioner E. W. Ross, but Hay soon revealed that he had no sympathy with federal resource regulation, either. During the Conservation Congress in Seattle he joined Ballinger's mentor, Judge Hanford, in an effort to have the resolutions committee endorse state control. When that failed, he vigorously opposed the adoption of a statement praising federal administration. Hay's personal convictions were reinforced by his friendship for Senator Jones and editor Erastus Brainerd of the *Post-Intelligencer,* and by his association with Albert Mead's former secretary, Ashmun N. Brown, who had been a newspaperman in Seattle and Olympia for twenty years.[10]

The critics were more numerous in western Washington, but they had an effective sympathizer in Spokane. That community, the home of Pinchot's admirer Will Cowles, of the *Spokesman-Review,* was the center of mining enterprise on the eastern slope and in near-by northern Idaho. In the fall of 1909, L. K. Armstrong, the editor of the *Northwest Mining News,* of that city, organized a Western Conservation League along the lines of the Colorado organization. According to the terms of its constitution, the League was established in order to obtain justice for the West by securing state control of resources. It was opposed to federal tenantry, favored proper use of resources without undue charge, and agreed to coöperate with federal agencies only when such action would benefit the state. The document also called for an "early emphatic protest" to halt the alleged loss of revenue which the West suffered under existing policy. Armstrong also published bulletins—fewer in number than Eddy's—to carry these ideas throughout the region. Although these efforts received some attention at the height of the Ballinger affair, the increasing political implications of that issue made the Washington critics more cautious. Hay consequently declined to endorse the League publicly, although in private he told Armstrong that he was convinced of the necessity for state control. Several prominent Republicans openly supported the organization, however, including Representative William Humphrey and Senator Jones. The latter regretfully admitted his belief that the public would eventually reject state control as an alternative, but he was nevertheless willing to fight for modification of the federal policy. Carter and Mondell also welcomed the work of the League, and Shafroth found it to be evidence that his own campaign was taking hold all over the region. With Carter, all of these men could agree that the time had come for the people of the West to "rise up as one man and demand their rights [and] to talk true conservation and proclaim it everywhere." Armstrong's immediate aims were less ambitious. He particularly hoped that his supporters would confuse and disrupt the state branch of the National Conservation Association. Jones, Cornelius Hanford, and Miles Moore, dissenting members of that organization, and Brainerd, as a member of the Washington Forestry Association, were consistently obliging in that respect. In addition, Armstrong sponsored more distant machinations when he sent J. J. Browne, a wealthy investor of Coeur d'Alene, Idaho, to Washington, D.C., to publicize the cause of state control.[11] All things considered, however, the Western Conservation League did not arouse as much interest within its home state or beyond as did its Colorado counterpart. Neither of these organizations was notably successful as a publicity bureau. Both lacked enough active participants and were limited in finances and facilities. Their intermittent communications must have converted very few people who were not already in the ranks of the critics.

SOUND AND FURY

Numerous speeches and articles were heard and read in the West during these years of controversy, but their number and impassioned tones belied the weaknesses of organized opposition and gave a distorted impression of Western sentiment. With very few exceptions, they reflected provincial economic or political interests, or various combinations of both. Editorials in the *Post-Intelligencer* and the *Rocky Mountain*

News, for example, defended specific economic investments and burned with vehement partisanship. The *Herald,* of the lumbering center of Bellingham, Washington, could concentrate on a single point of view; but the *Oregonian,* which dominated a large stretch of country supporting many economic pursuits, confirmed some aspects of conservation and complained about others. The complex of politics similarly accounted for the statements of the Western press. Many editors of the Northwest made no distinction between conservation and "Pinchotism," and willingly damned both along with "insurgency, disruption of the good old party that maintains prosperity and a tariff on lumber, and hostility to Taft and his cabinet." The Denver *Republican* supported the President and the Chief Forester as long as Pinchot was a member of the administration, but joined their Democratic competitors in denouncing him after he was dismissed. In those parts of the West where criticism of conservation had always been pronounced, Republican editors eagerly equated support of Ballinger with party loyalty and devotion to the interests of their region. In the midst of the soul searching caused by the course of the controversy, the Denver *Post* went so far as to dismiss an anti-Ballinger editorial writer and replace him with a journalist who helped transform that paper into one of the most outspoken critics of federal policy.[12]

Newspaper opinion was, in turn, modified by the changing realities of political life. In Arizona, for example, George Young, secretary of the territory and a friend of Ballinger, personally intercepted anti-administration or pro-Pinchot news copy and kept it out of the newspapers of Phoenix. As owner of a newspaper in Coconino County, long a center of criticism, Young believed that he could also effectively change popular support of conservation in the territorial capital. Yet he feared that such a change might increase the schism in the Republican party locally.[13] Similarly, in Montana, an agent of the Interior Department distributed form letters containing "correct" versions of the Ballinger affair so that local newspapers would not have to reprint information issued by the Forest Service. He also asked editors to scrutinize any news copy originating from the East and eliminate all suspicious statements which might reflect upon the Taft administration.[14] At the apogee of public excitement, the emphasis upon political loyalty seemed to be effective in some instances. The most striking example of such an influence was the case of Calvin Cobb, an editorial writer for the *Idaho Statesman,* of Boise. As late as August, 1909, he had served as Pinchot's confidant on the subjects of conservation and politics in the state. Shortly thereafter he was apologizing for statements critical of his friend which appeared in the *Statesman;* within another half-dozen months he was himself writing tirades against the man and the policy. While doing so, Cobb was complaining that Eastern magazines were ignoring Ballinger's side of the controversy. Conservationists who were aware that the *Statesman* dominated Idaho were sorry to see Cobb's "poison" spread to smaller newspapers.[15]

The dismissal of Chief Forester Pinchot provoked the greatest outpouring of condemnation ever directed against the federal resource policy. His most implacable foes celebrated the event with cries of joy and with vivid imaginings. The elated *Post-Intelligencer* gave its readers a page-high picture of the "Discharged and Discredited Forester," a cartoon of him as a dead tree struck by lightning, and a savage article by Miles C. Moore. The cartoonist of the *Oregonian* conceived of the dismissal as the removal of a burdensome lock from the gate of the West. When the news was announced to the National Woolgrowers Association, then meeting in Ogden, Utah, it was greeted with spontaneous cheers. In the Southwest, editors agreed that the punishment was deserved, should have been administered long before, and was the best possible thing for their region. Perhaps the most vengeful tirade came from the *Owens Valley Herald,* of Big Pine, California, recently embittered by federal confirmation of the use of a local lake as a city reservoir for Los Angeles. "Pinchot has fallen," the editor crowed, "a false prophet and a wooden idol [who] could no longer endure." He had acted "not wisely but arrogantly . . . to us he was a tyrant. . . . Under Roosevelt, Pinchot's power was absolute. Petitions from the people here, objecting to the wrongs . . . were thrown into the official waste basket. . . . The people may now appeal to President Taft's justice, for justice has never reigned more openly in the White House." The *Rocky Mountain News* hastened to give Shafroth's campaign credit for the dismissal. Anxious to avoid being identified with the unpopular trusts, however, that journal added that the removal must not be interpreted as a "letter of marque" for preyers upon the public interest. Rather, the event marked the beginning of a rational and lawful conservation policy. Finally, with mock dismay, the Boise *Capital News* asked editorially: "Pinchot having received the official axe, what will we anti-forestry fellows have to croak about now."[16] These press comments, naturally, did not represent the attitude of all westerners, but they did reveal a general expectation that a new era was at hand. Of equal significance, the editorials also documented a widespread feeling of regret over the nature of the decision. Several newspapers that distrusted Pinchot's policies observed nevertheless that there were other considerations involved in the case. The *Boomerang,* of Laramie, Wyoming, admitted it had wanted "Dude Pinchot" fired, but believed that, under the circumstances, he was guilty of no other crime than "honesty." The Denver *Republican* denounced his insubordination, but acknowledged that the nation had lost its defender of the forests. In Reno, Nevada, the *Gazette* agreed that Pinchot had usurped executive prerogative, but estimated that he was second only to Roosevelt in public esteem.[17]

A second subject of satisfaction for westerners was the possibility that Pinchot's successor would be a native of their region. At the Ogden woolgrowers' convention, the Utah delegation offered a motion which demanded the appointment of a practical man of the West, and the resolution was passed with acclaim. Governor Spry sent a telegram to Senator Smoot endorsing the idea, although he recommended no person in particular. Several editors suggested the names of men who they felt would not be "cranks" on the subject of conservation. The Butte *Miner,* in Montana, mentioned Senators Thomas Carter and Joseph Dixon, former Senator Lee Mantle, and Congressman Charles Pray. These nominations drew favorable comments from readers, but they also revealed a lack of understanding about the technical character of the office in question.[18] When Albert E. Potter was appointed by the President to be Acting Chief Forester, westerners were elated. An Arizona stockman who was then in charge of the Grazing Division in the Forest Service, Potter was thoroughly familiar with problems of grazing, especially in the Southwest. One of the citizens of his territory who naturally considered the selection a "high compliment" was Will C. Barnes, his assistant and long-time friend. When Barnes was interviewed by the Phoenix *Arizona Gazette,* he asserted that the event complimented both the West and Pinchot. Privately, he wrote to Pinchot to express his admiration, and to Potter to confide his hopes:

My feeling of regret at seeing G. P. go out was naturally much softened by the knowledge as to who his successor would be. . . . In fact, I believe your appointment is going to smooth over many of the little causes for friction which have existed between the Western people and the Forest Service in the past. I can say this without any disparagement for Mr. Pinchot because it is absolutely impossible for the average Western man to realize that an Eastern born and bred man can understand the feelings and appreciate the surrounds [*sic*] of the Western man.[19]

All over the region, the news was greeted by "hats in the air." The stockman's *Optic,* of Las Vegas, New Mexico, gladly quoted a statement made by Potter in Cheyenne, Wyoming: "I expect my relations with western interests to be most congenial. I desire to work in harmony with the livestock associations to permit the fullest use of the national forest ranges, to foster the stock interests and promote the general welfare of the west." The New Mexico editor agreed that Potter's influence would convert the enemies which Pinchot had made for the federal policy. He would be the harbinger of the new era.[20]

Unknown to the celebrants in the West, the permanent retention of Potter was immediately opposed by the conservationist advisers to the Taft administration. They noted that he was not a trained forester and that his selection was endorsed by some of the most unrestrained opponents of Forest Service policy. Indeed, the conservationists believed that he could not stand up against Ballinger's "revolutionary proceedings" under any circumstances. Mindful of these objections, Potter decided to step aside after endorsing the appointment of Henry S. Graves. As a former director of the Yale Forestry School and dedicated disciple of Pinchot, Graves would be wholly acceptable, but even he would have a "difficult row to hoe" until the Secretary of the Interior could be checked. After he took over the Forest Service, Graves was confronted with pressures, not only from Ballinger, but from his own superior, Secretary Wilson. The latter carefully informed him that he could expect none of the privileges and influence which his predecessor had enjoyed. By August, 1910, feelings within the Department had become so strained that Graves lodged formal protest with the President and privately feared he might have to resign.[21] Beyond the fact that he was a Pinchot man, the West knew nothing about him, and the announcement of his selection deflated high hopes all over the region. Barnes was especially disappointed, but he blamed his fellow westerners for the outcome. No man from their part of the country, he reasoned, would ever be allowed to direct the Forest Service until the sentiments expressed by their delegates in Congress changed substantially.[22] Reference might also have been made to many political leaders in the states and their spokesmen in the press as well.

The storm of publicity raised by the Ballinger-Pinchot controversy furnished a congenial atmosphere for criticism during the next two years. Because the affair made anybody's opinion good news copy, the opponents of federal resource policy attracted greater public notice during this period than they had at any other time. Senator Carter had told L. K. Armstrong that the people should "rise up as one man [and] begin to talk true conservation and proclaim it everywhere." Those who did rise up, however, were hardly the "people" of the West, nor did they talk "true" conservation. By occupation they were state officials, journalists, lawyers, and investors—men whose power and security rested upon a strict interpretation of federal authority.

Of the state officials, Governor Edwin Norris of Montana was perhaps the most widely known because of his success in obtaining laws from his legislature for systematic resource use. Conservation, he told the Land and Irrigation Congress at Chicago in 1910, was a "practical business problem" for which emotional enthusiasm might serve to spur action, but could not "point the way." In the following year he reminded his legislators that the states could best conserve their own resources. Reprinted as a pamphlet, his address became one of the most widely distributed tracts of the critics' campaign.[23]

Most prominent among the journalists who participated in that project was A. N. Brown, a friend of Ballinger and editor Brainerd. Far more courageous in his convictions than many other critics, Brown's penchant for ridicule sometimes reflected upon himself; one piece he wrote as a filler for Washington State newspapers was entitled "Silly Teddy and Shifty Pinchot." Another prolific essayist was J. J. Underwood, a former reporter in Alaska, whose writings exposed the "crime" of conservation for readers of the Seattle *Times* and *Leslie's Illustrated Weekly,* a national magazine. George L. Knapp, an editorial writer for the *Rocky Mountain News,* explained "the other side" of conservation in the *North American Review.* He denied that the federal government had any right to interfere with the lumbering industry, and described its regulations as ruinous, its propaganda insidious. "Our natural resources have been used," he insisted. "The Pine woods of Michigan have vanished to make the homes of Kansas. . . . We have turned forests into villages, mines into ships and skyscrapers, scenery into work."[24]

No lawyer in the ranks of the critics was more outspoken than Frank H. Short, an attorney for several water power companies in California. One of the pamphlets he wrote was entitled "An Open Letter to Mr. Gifford Pinchot," which denounced the alleged monopoly held by the Forest Service over potential power sites. In a speech before the Los Angeles Chamber of Commerce, Short asserted that the people's right of self-government was being taken from them under the guise of paternalism and was being vested in centralized federal bureaus. The *Times* of that city commended these opinions as the only really "American" view and held them to be far more proper than the "dreamy conservationist policy of obstruction" pursued by "self-conceited reformers."[25] Frederick S. Titsworth, of the Colorado Scientific Society, also explored the legal implications of conservation. In an address before that organization he defended state sovereignty and private enterprise, agreeing with Governor Norris of Montana that resource use was a "purely business question."[26]

Westerners closely connected with specific economic interests were usually reluctant to speak against the federal policy in public, perhaps because their motives would be questioned by the trust-conscious press. Lumberman J. J. Donavan, of Bellingham, Washington, had no qualms about entering the lists of the critics, however. As owner of the *Herald* in that community, he was determined to wage a one-man campaign in leading the "Rebel West" in its "Warfare on Conservation." A long-time resident of the forested northwestern part of the state, he believed that federal administration was a failure. "Our country has suffered from it for eighteen years," he reminded his friend Governor Hay, "[and] two thirds of the county [is] inside the reserve.... The government has done a little trail building during the last two years, but lumbering has stopped because only the strongest companies can afford to build the railroads and pay the price the national government asks.... The theory is beautiful, the practice wretched." In California the unsettled state of the new oil industry and the absence of adequate federal legislation accounted for the complaints of eager investors. Curtis H. Lindley, a specialist in mining law at the University of California and a speculator in several oil companies, spoke for many colleagues when he told the San Francisco Bar Association that the selfishness of existing federal regulations was jeopardizing the entire oil industry in the state.[27]

The critics' campaign aroused the interest of several citizens who seem to have been moved by personal convictions within a private area of activity. Former Governor Hagerman of New Mexico, for example, renounced his earlier admiration for Roosevelt, the man who had removed him from office in 1907, and composed articles critical of Pinchot and the Forest Service. The memory of Roosevelt was fresh in the mind of another westerner who published a small pamphlet which included the assertion that his region would not tolerate a federal resource policy based upon the "methods used to seize Panama." One citizen of the Northwest volunteered to distribute "quite a collection of brief pungent articles" against conservation "for the eddification [*sic*] of the ignorant" while traveling through the lumber camps of the Pacific Coast states.[28] Unfortunately for the critics, there were not many men of this type who would carry the campaign to the "grass roots."

The activities of the Seattle Chamber of Commerce exemplified the contributions made by a few civic organizations in the West. Early in 1910 that body appointed a special committee to report on the problem of proper conservation. With Thomas Burke as chairman and Judge Hanford and former Governor McGraw as members, the group naturally endorsed the interpretations of Taft and Ballinger. Their report defended state control as the only possible means for resource development without government ownership and bureaucracy. It was subsequently reprinted as a pamphlet and distributed to commercial and political organizations all over the region. As the contest grew hotter, the Chamber planned to issue a series of "Municipal Monographs" on this and other subjects. Only the first was ever published. *The Neglected West* was a plea to keep government from interfering in private property. If there was a danger of possible legislative corruption in a program of state control, the pamphlet maintained, the honesty inherent in private enterprise would hold it in check.[29] Similar arguments were included in tracts on other commercial subjects issued by Chambers in Denver, Los Angeles, and Portland.

Almost without exception, the speeches and writings directed against federal conservation consisted of empty rhetoric which served only to confuse local understanding of the vital issue. The habitual play on words often produced barren ideas. The *Owens Valley Herald*, for example, declared itself opposed to "mere conservation conversation, such as Pinchot practices." The Oregon City *Enterprise* pouted that Roosevelt, then hunting big game in Africa, was hardly "conserving the lives of those who inherit the forests." What Oregon really needed, the director of a land development company announced, was "more transportation and less conservation." In the same state, John Minto thought he saw a historical precedent: Roosevelt had given Pinchot greater power than the King of England had exercised over the American colonies. The governors' conference at the White House, he added, was called merely to distract attention from what Pinchot was doing, and by defining their policy to mean anything salable by the Forest Service the two executives had beaten the word "freedom" to a frazzle.[30] Perhaps the saddest case of the critics' irrationalities occurred in the summer of 1910. During July and August fires swept across millions of acres of forest lands in northern Idaho, destroying an estimated three billion board feet of lumber and taking scores of lives. For weeks the holocaust resisted the combined efforts of ten thousand federal and state troops before it was brought under control. Senator Heyburn did not wait for the smoldering stumps to cool around his home town of Wallace before he publicly accused Pinchot of being responsible for the fire. By prohibiting the burning of dead underbrush and by barring prospectors who, the statesman asserted, might have acted as fire wardens, the Forest Service had made the disaster possible. His tortured explanations were immediately endorsed by Carter and Mondell and printed in several Western newspapers without comment on the enormity of their content.[31] Yet, if the fire revealed anything about conservation, it emphatically proved the inadequacies of state control over problems that were obviously interstate in scope.

THE FIRST BATTLE

The responsible leaders of the critics' campaign were politically experienced enough to realize that scattered publicity could not attract public attention to their cause. Governor Hay of Washington was particularly interested in getting representatives of the West to present a unified front on the issue and, in the summer of 1910, decided to organize such a stand at the second National Conservation Congress, in St. Paul, Minnesota. Recalling the way in which westerners had been "very shabbily" treated the year before at the first Conservation Congress, he asked the secretary of the sponsoring body, the National Conservation Association, for an assurance that the delegates from Washington State would be given a prominent place on the program and the courtesy of the floor for one hour. The request was denied. When Hay learned that other Western governors had received similar replies, he drew up a call for a meeting to be held at Salt Lake City a few days before the convention. This conference, he hoped, would serve to bring about a unity of expression for the present, and might devise a single aim for future action. The immediate purpose was to outline some plan to oppose an endorsement of Pinchot by another "packed" meeting. Hay solemnly denied any intention of raising a sectional controversy, but he reminded his fellow executives that Eastern-dominated policies were subverting the interests of the West. Recent events, he added pointedly, had disclosed the true character and aims of federal administrators. Because efforts were being made to force candidates for Congress to ally themselves with the conservationists, Hay claimed that the policy was thereby subversive to the interests of the nation as well. It was imperative, he concluded, for the governors to formulate "a legitimate concert of action" before they appointed delegates to the Conservation Congress.[32]

Hay must have been encouraged by the responses to his invitation. Governor James Brady of Idaho concurred with its sentiments wholeheartedly and believed that his colleagues would endorse the ideas when they met. Governor Brooks of Wyoming promised to publicize the proposal in his state. In Oregon, Acting Governor Jay Bowerman welcomed the opportunity to express his opposition to conservation. Although he was committed to remain in his state for the primary elections, he selected delegates who were above any suspicion of sharing "the fads and theories" of Pinchotism. Shafroth of Colorado also sent a proxy, but pledged himself to active support of any recommendations made at Salt Lake City. Governor Spry of Utah, however, found himself in an anomalous position. Although he agreed with Hay that the West's real interests were being ignored or distorted, he did not share the implacable hostility of the other governors. Yet his basically conservative nature had been profoundly disturbed by the Ballinger-Pinchot affair. When the executives convened, however, Spry's longtime trust in federal conservation caused him to moderate the tone of discussions and resolutions. Although it was Hay who claimed that Roosevelt's policy had been made possible because of the adherence of many westerners, Spry might more justly have pointed out that fact. Before adjourning, the governors issued a moderate public statement which merely defended the West's integrity, objected to the sensationalism of the conservation crusade, and demanded proper recognition at the Conservation Congress. Eddy of Colorado nevertheless leaped to the conclusion that the meeting marked "the beginning of the end" for Roosevelt and his policy. Actually, the whole affair aroused slight attention in the region. Western conservationists dismissed it as "a lot of cheap publicity."[33]

At St. Paul, meanwhile, the supporters of both Hay and Pinchot were preparing for the coming struggle. While members of Ballinger's staff gathered information for the governor of Washington,[34] Pinchot's lieutenants were laying groundwork for the convention's endorsement of sustained federal resource administration. When Governor A. O. Eberhart of Minnesota asked the program committee to give the representatives of the West an important place in the proceedings, Pinchot insisted that these men would turn the meeting into an anti-conservation congress. The former Chief Forester agreed with Roosevelt that a full range of opinion should be permitted, but he intended to make sure that the principal speakers were men who shared his own views. He remained in constant contact with Thomas R. Shipp, secretary of the sponsoring organization, who informed him of the previous maneuvers of the opposition in St. Paul. Weeks before the convention opened, Shipp reported that the Western governors were plotting to capture it for the cause of state control of resources, and asserted that the Minnesotans in charge of local arrangements were aiding this conspiracy. The real source of such machinations proved to be Louis Hill, the president of the Northern Pacific Railroad and son of its builder, James J. Hill. The Hills' transportation empire and land holdings were vital to the economy of the Northwest and their influence was accordingly substantial. The younger Hill not only endorsed Ballinger's view of reclamation by private enterprise, but also spent his own funds to distribute the bulletins of the National Public Domain League. Moreover, as a conservative Republican, he feared that Pinchot might turn the Conservation Congress into a demonstration against the Taft administration. Working behind the scenes at St. Paul, he spread such false rumors as the statement that the President favored state control and was anxious to discuss that alternative with the Western governors. It was Hill who persuaded the local committee to send invitations to those who would not be afraid to "get up and state . . . the actual conditions" that existed in the West because of Pinchot's policies. When the meeting convened, he proudly assured Ballinger, those advocates of a new political party would be effectively thwarted.[35] In the last analysis, the conservationists wielded what Shipp called the "Big Stick" of publicity; even in the West, few newspapers believed that the critics would triumph at the convention.

Hay's coterie at St. Paul included Ross and Armstrong of his own state, Governors Norris of Montana and Brooks of Wyoming, and Shafroth's indefatigable guardsmen, Eddy, Beaman, and Ammons. Waterpower attorney Frank Short represented Governor James Gillett of California. It was Ross who used Ballinger's name in his opening speech from the floor—and was hissed by the assembled delegates. The critics ignored this sign, however, and persisted in their plan. Short spoke against federal landlordism; Brooks read the resolutions of the Salt Lake City conference; and Norris, who had earlier despaired of offsetting the conservationists, made an appeal for confidence in the ability of the states to handle their own resources. In every instance, the speakers failed to arouse the interest of the assembly. Within the first two days of the congress their scheme was totally frustrated, and they finally stalked out of the meeting in anger.[36]

It was obvious that the dissenters did not speak for a solid West. Indeed, every state of that region sent other representatives who were loyal supporters of federal conservation. Among the most prominent westerners were Francis Heney of California, and Judge Benjamin B. Lindsey of Colorado. Members of the conservation commissions of Oregon, New Mexico, and Washington served on the committee which wrote an unequivocal endorsement of Pinchot's policy. The view of these men was well expressed by the delegate from Utah. Because Spry was unable to attend, he had appointed E. T. Merritt, of the state resources agency, to carry to the convention a formal statement which attested to Utah's continuing support of federal administration. If the state suffered from mistakes made by the government, this document pointed out, it had also suffered from its own past mishandling of natural wealth; there was reason to hope that the errors of both origins would not be repeated in the future. Pinchot was immensely pleased by such support from the West, and he duly acknowledged its contribution when he address the congress.[37]

As the critics had feared, the specter of politics haunted the sessions at St. Paul. Roosevelt's dynamic speechmaking tour into the West was the cynosure of all eyes, even to the exclusion of gossip about the alleged Hay conspiracy. Late in August, the former President reviewed a parade in Denver while standing on a platform with Shafroth on one side of him and Pinchot on the other. Later in the day, he praised Colorado's support of conservation, but pointedly remarked that no good could possibly come from a system of state control of resources. Shortly after the Conservation Congress met in September, he delivered his call for a progressive crusade at Osawatomie, Kansas, in a speech drafted by Pinchot. His disciples throughout the country were electrified by the implied promise of his leadership, and those attending the convention were stimulated to give a political cast to its deliberations. Pardee of California, a member of the resolutions committee, vigorously opposed inclusion of Taft's name in a statement concerning the fulfillment of the Roosevelt policy. At the final session, the President himself delivered a defense of his administration's record and declared significantly, "the time has come for a halt in the general rhapsodies over conservation." Otherwise, his performance was unimpressive; he admitted to Ballinger that it had been a "very stupid speech."[38] The appearance of Roosevelt at St. Paul, and the appeal of the progressive revolt, contributed to the preparations and support of the conservationists to insure their ultimate victory at the Second National Conservation Congress.

The best measure of their success was the disorganization of Hay's coterie during the subsequent months. The governors "might as well have sent . . . rag dolls" instead of delegates, Hay complained to Shafroth. To lumberman J. J. Donavan, he reported that the meeting was overwhelmed with a lot of "tommy-rot and twaddle" about the resources of the West. If the states of that region did not stand together in the future, he warned darkly, they would find themselves "completely bound to a hard and fast policy that will turn the wealth of this country over to the Federal Treasury." About the same time, Senator Borah interrupted a speech he was delivering in the East to denounce the

Conservation Congress as a "cruel and brutal farce." He found it especially despicable because some delegates there were "watching and spying on one another for political advantage" while "suspicion and misrepresentation went on and academic discussion proceeded." Several western editors joined in these lamentations and agreed that if the citizens of their region failed to stand together, they would be tricked again by the East. Their plans frustrated, their pride bruised, the critics decided that they would hold their own meeting. Brooks and Norris suggested that another Denver convention be held. Gillett hoped that they could meet in San Francisco the following summer, and was particularly anxious that "every interest" be represented—he listed these as "mining, coal, oil, timber, and power companies." No action was taken on these suggestions, however, perhaps because several of the governors were too preoccupied with the approaching November elections. When the critics were able to hold their convention the following year, political fortune had removed several of these executives from office.[39]

In fact, the opponents of federal policy had their day at a meeting of the American Mining Congress, in Los Angeles, a few weeks after St. Paul. That organization was composed of investors and operators who were wholly dissatisfied with the federal regulatory program for use of the public domain. Although their sessions were concerned with the technological and commercial problems of mineral development, they attracted much public notice because of the publicity given to the events of the Second National Conservation Congress. Many observers wondered whether this meeting would also crumble under the force of Pinchot's influence. The critics prophesied, however, that the attitudes of oilmen and mining speculators from California and Nevada, the states sending most of the delegates, would prevail. The Los Angeles *Times* proudly gave the meeting generous coverage in its pages. Every day its editorials ridiculed "Monsieur Pinchot"—evidently a reference to his European education, but also an implication of effeteness or un-Americanism. He was portrayed by staff cartoonists in a variety of roles: the dog in the manger of industry, the crippler of pioneers, and the reason why the younger generation was attracted to anarchism. When the newspaper reported that its victim was then in the state examining oil fields, it hoped that he would have his eyes "opened to his fallacies." After completing that tour, Pinchot came to the convention to defend his policy. Although the delegates treated him as a good, if impractical, fellow, they saved their applause for a letter from Ballinger which favored the disposition of oil lands for private entry, and for Congressman Sylvester Smith, of California, who promised to initiate legislation for that purpose. The Mining Congress then adopted resolutions which were almost the exact opposites of those issued by the Conservation Congress. They demanded the opening of mines of every type within the national forests, and denounced the use of leases or the application of royalties in the working of these mines. Because miners had pioneered in the settlement of the West, they concluded, any policy which interfered with mining development was, therefore, detrimental to the real interests of the region. To report the nature of these resolutions, the *Times* used an exultant headline: MINING CONGRESS DELIVERS KNOCKOUT BLOW TO PINCHOTISM. One delegate, who was a friend of Shafroth, testified that he had personally witnessed "Pinchotism knocked over the rope, & punctured with bruises. We had our inning this time."[40]

The ball game, however, was far from over.

CHAPTER VI

THE LIMITS OF REACTION

PLANS FOR STATE CONTROL

BY THE SUMMER of 1910, the critics of federal conservation realized that a publicity campaign was no more than a means to the paramount aim of securing changes in resource administration. Existing policy could be modified either by state action or by the decisions of a sympathetic Congress and administration. In both cases, a more unified plan of publicity and procedure would be essential. As Governor Hay saw it, an alternative policy of state conservation could not be adopted until the hypocritical myth about the untrustworthiness of the West was destroyed. "The eastern people seem to have the idea that this is a great big gold mine out here [Hay observed somewhat bitterly] and if they don't get in and protect us from ourselves all of these great resources will be swallowed up. They seem to think the Western people haven't the brains or capacity to attend to their own affairs." When he learned that Pinchot had publicly endorsed state-federal coöperation in resource administration, he wrote to that adversary and repeated the point frankly and firmly: "All we desire is that we have an equal show, and if we are wrong and our ideas are bad we are willing to submit to what is for the best, but until it is shown to us that we are not competent and qualified to say how our [resources] shall be handled, I am not in a position to change my present views. . . . I have an idea that the people of the States where seventy-five per cent of these natural resources are located are fully competent and qualified to administer them.'" Such assurances, however, were lost upon conservationists who were mindful of the indifference, waste, and frauds of the preceding years.

Hay's own state of Washington was the best example of a "home conservation" policy, as he called it. There, the State Forester was given power to set aside lands suitable for reforestation, and funds were allocated for fire protection in all forests, whether federal, state, or private. More recently, the legislature had carefully made statutory distinction between surface rights and title to minerals beneath the ground, thereby increasing the amount of agricultural lands open to entry and regulating exploitation of resources in the same areas. The state was one of the first to establish a system of fish hatcheries and to plan for the protection of orchards against insects and disease. Hay was particularly interested in expanding the use of the water sources in Washington. Pending action by the legislature, he appointed a Water Commission, personally corresponded with land developers and business-men, and then urged the passage of a bill which, he said, would take care of future needs without interfering with "vested rights or the rights our people have already obtained." Obviously, the governor was genuinely concerned with applying adequate conservation methods in his state, but he deeply distrusted the methods used by the leaders of the conservation crusade. After the treatment his adherents had received at St. Paul, he was unable to decide whether Pinchot was a great humanitarian or an ambitious egotist. "The importance of this great problem is too vital to the interests of the entire country," he chided the former Chief Forester, "to permit the difference or pique of individuals to interfere in any way with the consummation that we all desire. The question of methods, after all, is secondary. We are all aiming at the same end. . . . Above all, it should not be . . . made the football of politics or politicians either in the nation or the states," which was "a danger that would be fatal [for] the entire program of conservationists."[2] Hay was not above putting politics before his interest in resources, however, as events would prove.

The West could not stand idle until the East came round to the point of trusting it. If the legislatures of all the Western states would pass "reasonable" conservation bills during the winter of 1910–1911, Hay believed, then most easterners would be satisfied that the region was fully competent to act wisely and was not under the control of corporate interests. In his own state, he tried to arouse public attention to such a plan by asking newspaper editors to publicize the need for legislative action. When he addressed a meeting of the State Press Association, in September, 1910, however, he made slight reference to the state's interest in conservation; most of his remarks were attacks on Pinchot's "faithful satellites" in the West. Moreover, the occasion of the governor's annual message could have afforded another excellent opportunity to impress observers everywhere with the sincerity of a state program. But again, Hay's remarks there were far more emotional and critical of conservation than his private correspondence. He told the legislators that the choice between federal and state control of resources was a matter of principle "vital to our form of government." If the states, he declared, "supinely give over complete control of our natural resources to the National government, we acquiesce in and become accessories to the immolation of local self government. Federal control . . . means the weakening of state governments, the curtailment of their activities and the deprivation of a big source of state and local revenue." It was this last consideration that provoked Hay into referring to the movement without the sweet reasonableness used in his correspondence with Pinchot: "National conservation is designed less to benefit the consumer of the products of those resources than as a new means of obtaining revenue for the National treasury. This . . . is the acme of injustice." Instead of recommending the needed resource legislation he had already publicized, the governor created a committee to study the problem of use fees and royalties, and reminded Washingtonians that the state would be "inexcusably derelict" if it failed to protest against the continuation of these charges. Finally, as if to convince conservationists that their suspicions about the critics were correct, he declared that the timber in the national forests ought to be sold and the acreage opened to homestead entry.[3]

Elsewhere in the West, governors and legislatures behaved as if they too were lining up to "take a poke" at conservation.[4] The boldest act of defiance was made by Governor Jay Bowerman of Oregon in January, 1911. Devoting most of his annual message to an attack on federal policy and state coöperation, he asserted that "officious and unwarranted conduct" by "some of these petty federal employees" had in part exterminated the livestock industry in the state. Although the timber in the national forests was "ripe and should be manufactured," he maintained that the government permitted it to stand until it had been burned over and then sold it in large lots. Turning a baleful eye upon local conservationists, he denounced the Oregon Conservation Commission as the real source of these harmful conditions. Bowerman was particularly alarmed by the progressive political sentiments held by the members of the agency. Because these men had participated in the controversies over forest use policies in Oregon and the nation, he decided that they had destroyed their usefulness—an echo of Taft's statement to Pinchot—and asked the legislature to abolish the commission. Although the lawmakers did nothing about resource regulation, they eagerly repealed the Conservation Commission Act and, carried away by their perverse enthusiasm, even defeated a bill for the observation of a Conservation Day in the state. Then they ended the fruitless session by sending a memorial to Congress containing yet another protest against the national forests. Observing these events, the *Oregonian* praised the governor and agreed that the commission had reflected the Pinchot view of resources instead of upholding the interests of the state. The services of its members, the editor concluded without regret, had been "voluntary and unappreciated."[5] Resolutions favoring state control—but no proposed bills—were issued by the Colorado legislature under the Shafroth administration. Only Governor Norris of Montana made an effort to find a rational advantage in the alternative policy. State control of water power sites, he argued, might end the confusion and abuse arising out of federal administration of the lieu land laws.[6] The winter of legislative deliberation in the Western states proved to be impoverished in ideas, barren of action, and totally marred by the "pique of individuals" which Hay himself had decried a few months before.

There was a sufficient number of spokesmen for the critics in Congress to initiate some legislation for state administration of resources. Senators Jones, Borah, Carter, and Heyburn doggedly continued to attack every comment or suggestion favoring federal conservation. Yet they failed to devise any plan to give their region some measure of jurisdiction over the policy. Compared to the total membership, their votes were a mere handful, and their influence was further reduced when a Democratic–progressive Republican majority was elected in November, 1910. Moreover, it seems clear that none of them had a very profound understanding of effective resource regulations. Even such critics as the newspaperman A. N. Brown became exasperated by their ignorance of basic problems. Finally, they could not depend upon the support of members from their own region. When, for example, Heyburn introduced an amendment to exclude from the national forests all land containing less than a specified amount of timber, a majority of Western senators heeded protests from their constituents and voted against the measure.[7]

Out of the tumult of oratory and debate heard in the halls of Congress from 1910 to 1912, only two concrete plans for state control of resources were submitted by Western members. In April, 1911, Representative Abraham W. Lafferty, of Oregon, a man who tried to straddle the division in public sentiment at home, proposed a bill which would return all proceeds from the national forests to the states in which they were located. These funds would be applied to the gradual reduction of use fees, maintenance costs, and state indebtedness. In exchange, the states would provide regulations for water distribution and mining. It is not surprising that Lafferty's bill was stillborn. It could not command the approval of the conservationists or appeal to those who sought full control of all resources. The congressman later offered another plan, whereby a United States Forest Commission would be established, composed of the Secretary of the Interior, the Secretary of Agriculture, and the Chief Forester. This board would be empowered to distribute the proceeds from grazing and lumbering to the states, and the states' own forest commissions would enforce use regulations. In these vague outlines, the suggestion merely reproduced the existing organization of federal administration, and, as Pinchot pointed out, there was no advantage in abolishing what was already successful.[8] A year later, Albert B. Fall, senator from the newly admitted state of New Mexico, submitted a similar plan. Fall was a stockman whose ranch in the southeastern part of the state was hedged by national forests and Indian reservations. His maiden speech in the Senate had been a harangue against the Interior Department and the Forest Service that consumed parts of four days of the session, and ended with the statement that he hoped to see the Department abolished in the near future. During this address he proposed an alternative to federal conservation which would place all resources in reserves that would be managed and supervised by the governors of the states. The Secretary of Agriculture, and perhaps the Secretary of the Interior, would choose agents from among the residents to insure the execution of regulations. The state governments would determine the character and tenure of these officials and would pay all administrative costs.[9] In this way, federal standards would be enforced by men who best understood local conditions. In this way, also, every resource user would be at the mercy of state politics. The senator did not expand on his proposal thereafter, perhaps because he really had no faith in it. Subsequently, he continued to reveal his deep hostility to federal conservation while in the Senate and after being appointed Secretary of the very Department that he had hoped would be abolished.

Several private citizens in the West devised schemes for state control over resources. John S. Brady, a former governor of Alaska, based his idea upon the premise that the government should relinquish the power wielded by the Land Office and grant it to the states because they were better organized to apply policy locally. Legislation would be passed and confirmed by a referendum which would enable the states to buy all of their public domain for $11.25 an acre and pay for it by a bond issue of 1.5 per cent over a period of fifty years. The interests of the people would thereby be satisfied, and the government would receive substantial revenue. Each state could handle its lands "as it deems best and no doubt at a considerable profit," the author added.[10] Editorial writer George Knapp, of the *Rocky Mountain News*, believed that the states must first give up "federal pap" before they could dispense with federal interference. He believed that such agencies as the Reclamation Service were "keeping out private capital, fattening the reputations of a few local politicians and furnishing a peg on which to hang the federal bureaucracy we all want thrown away." Fervently, Knapp wanted to "get rid of the whole damned business; and give private initiative a chance in ditchdigging as well as in everything else.'"[11] Like the empty promises of the governors and the rickety proposals of the congressmen, these ideas were the thin mice brought forth by the mountain of criticism after two years of labor.

BALLINGER'S FINAL FRUSTRATIONS

Before January, 1910, the Taft administration wielded enough power and prestige to effect modification of federal resource policy, if it had been so inclined. A few days after the President dismissed Pinchot, he sent a special message to Congress, an attestation of his belief in federal conservation and a request for the enactment of several programs which theretofore had been handled only by executive orders. The uproar over the dismissal, however, completely overshadowed the message; Taft might just as well have said nothing on the subject then or thereafter. Privately, the Pinchot men were pleased with the President's suggestions, but they did not consider them cause for abandoning their fight. The only ones who referred to the address publicly were the few Republicans still hopeful of healing the party schism. Ultimately, the recommendations made by the administration were altered and passed by a majority of Democrats and Insurgents after they had been scrutinized by the conservationists and purged of all traces of "Ballingerism."

After Taft intervened in the water power issue in May, 1909, he assumed direct responsibility for Interior Department policy. Although anxious to put Roosevelt's policies on the firm foundation of law, he was equally determined not to give in to the pressures created by his detractors. His real motives for accepting Muir's view of the Hetch Hetchy issue are not clear, but he must surely have known that he would anger Pinchot, Garfield, and many California Republicans. When Ballinger subsequently suspended the federal grant and ordered San Francisco to show cause for its renewal within one year, he was also accused of trying to convince the public that he was a sincere conservationist.[12] The Truckee contract, a second thorn in the Presidential flank, produced similar results. Taft had at first opposed the favor to a private power company, but later he argued that Newell evidently approved of it. Ballinger must have warned him that Newell was speaking for Pinchot, but the President may have been trying to use the case as part of a compromise between the two antagonists. The protests of conservationist William Kent, of California, soon turned the Truckee affair into a hornets' nest, so that Taft was forced into the rueful conclusion that the only persons favoring the contract were Senator Newlands, a Democrat, and Governor Tasker Oddie of Nevada, a progressive

Republican. When Ballinger brought a federal decision to the penulti-
mate stage many months later, the President advised him to delay it
indefinitely. The case remained in limbo for so long that ultimately the
power company withdrew its bid. The Californians remained very
suspicious, however, toward all the administration's actions. By
handling these matters personally, Taft thus offended as many people
as Ballinger himself might have alienated.[13]

The Secretary of the Interior shared the President's interest in
legally delineating the authority of his Department, but he was not
wholly in harmony with the views of his chief. In private, he considered
Taft's suggestions to Congress an extension of the federal landlordism
promoted by Roosevelt, and had no wish to be a mere rubber stamp for
such procedures of the past. After the dismissal of Pinchot momentarily
cleared the air in Interior affairs, Ballinger consulted Acting Forester
Potter about the elimination of lands from national forests, reopened
the issue of the Chugach National Forest in Alaska, and drafted legislation for modified water-leasing policy. Returning to the subject that
he had given particular attention while Commissioner, he also asked
Taft to urge the sale of coal lands in lieu of the existing leasing system.
Requests for decisions on all of these subjects were delayed, however,
while the President's January message was being written, and probably
were not resubmitted for some time because of their obvious conflict
with Taft's statements. Although Ballinger continued to press for their
adoption at Cabinet meetings, he invariably acquiesced in his chief's
cautious delays.[14]

The administration's recommendations for additional resource legislation were immediately dubbed the "Ballinger bills," but, in fact, the
Secretary had slight influence upon their original contents or later
revisions. It was the chairmen of the lands and resources committees
in Congress—Mondell in the House and Carter in the Senate—who
shaped the measures to fulfill Taft's purposes. Indeed, they fell so far
short of the hopes of the critics that Eddy, the Colorado polemicist, accused Ballinger of embracing Pinchotism! The bills did empower the
Secretary to transfer reclamation projects to the states or irrigation dis-
tricts for more efficient operation, but such a transparent reversal of previous policy could not command majority support. Senators Nelson and
Smoot drafted other measures relating to oil, gas, and phosphate reserves. All of the proposals came under the jealous eyes of Pinchot's
supporters among the progressive Republicans; through their inter-
vention, the bills were defeated or were delayed until state control provisions could be struck out of them. Ballinger protested against the

interference of men whom he considered enemies of the administration, but Taft made no public comment about it. It was Pinchot, ironically, who received the thanks of the economic interests whom the President had hoped to win over by his recommendations.[15]

Ballinger was personally interested in the adoption of a bill which would enable claimants who were not satisfied with Interior Department decisions to appeal their cases to the federal courts. Under such a law, Garfield's sweeping interpretation of the Secretary's authority could be effectively challenged and pared down. It was strange that a government official should advocate the diminution of his own powers and those of his successors, but the concept was wholly consistent with Ballinger's original view of reclamation policy. Mondell eagerly agreed to introduce the plan in the House, and Ballinger asked Nelson and Sutherland to insert a recommendation into the report of the investigating committee. Eddy obligingly endorsed the proposal at sessions of the Colorado Conservation Commission. Beyond these efforts, however, the so-called safety-valve bill received no support. Ballinger considered this failure as one of the greatest disappointments of his tenure in office and continued to urge its adoption after he left the Department.[16]

When Congress adjourned in June, 1910, the Interior Department claimed credit for maintaining the policy of conservation while correcting attendant sins of commission and omission. The Secretary's reports noted that new legislation had separated surface title from access to coal deposits, thereby making 90,000,000 acres available to agricultural settlement. Executive proclamations withdrew thousands of acres of coal lands, and the administration surpassed its predecessors in the establishment of oil policy. In September, Taft completed the withdrawals of petroleum lands in southern California begun during the Roosevelt years. Ballinger then investigated the question of applying royalties to the use of these deposits under Indian lands and asked for an opinion from the Attorney General on the matter of oil claims held by the Southern Pacific Railroad. Where Garfield had declined to do so, his successor closed oil reservations to all forms of entry, including mineral entry, but conservationists felt that he dared not do otherwise. Unable to act upon his belief in opening up access to Alaskan resources, the Secretary complained that public agitation had greatly impeded further settlement of the territory. In saying that several claimants in Washington State had been indicted for conspiracy, he was obviously anxious to prove that the Department was not overlooking fraud. He warily refrained, however, from mentioning the Cunningham claims, which were still under scrutiny. Taking characteristic pride in his talent as a renovator, Ballinger publicized the facts that $290,000 in salaries had been saved by the adoption of photocopying methods and that estimates for the expenses of the coming year were actually smaller than the total appropriations for the year before.[17] In sending out press notices containing these boasts the Secretary may have hoped to offset the unfavorable publicity of the preceding months, but the accomplishments described were too technical to have any effect upon public opinion and too few to receive substantial notice.

The subject which was not publicized was Ballinger's attempt to complete the changes in Department personnel which he began during his first months in office. After Newell and Davis testified against him at the congressional investigation, he was determined to remove them from the Reclamation Service. In July, 1910, when he asked the President to approve the dismissal, Taft again decided to avoid stirring up another controversy and the matter remained unresolved. Unable to replace Newell with Seattle city engineer Robert Thomson, Ballinger sought to make Thomson Assistant Secretary of the Interior; but Taft appointed a fellow Ohioan instead. By the end of the year, after completing his second annual report, Ballinger came to the conclusion that he had done as much for the administration as the unusual circumstances of the time permitted; there was little more than he could do in the office.[18]

The critics' campaign against federal conservation could be waged with a paucity of ideas, but it could not succeed without a prominent leader. None of the opponents of the policy was so widely known in the West as Ballinger himself. It would have been both natural and to some extent effective for him to assume leadership of their movement. As one of his friends advised him, a "great mob of common people" was "only waiting for a leader to take up the fight against the theory of this conservation idea." In view of the Secretary's consistent reluctance to take any public stand during the controversy, it is not surprising that he declined such a role, although shortly after the disappointment of the investigation and the frustration of his policy he did become more interested in the critics' efforts. Beginning in June, 1909, Eddy and Beaman bombarded his desk with bulletins of the National Public Domain League, along with letters of praise and advice, but Ballinger's replies were always politely noncommittal. During the months of the investigation, other friends sent reams of testimony concerning abuses in the administration of the public domain. Some of these charges came from disgruntled seekers after privilege and patronage, but many were clearly caused by misunderstanding and pettiness. When one correspondent endorsed state control, Ballinger answered with the statement that he understood the West's view and hoped to assist the administration in bringing about "proper results in the disposition of the public domain." Privately, he even approved of Mondell's attacks on the Interior Department's water power policy. Several of his public pronouncements in 1910 revealed an underlying sympathy with the critics' attitudes. Speaking at a state conservation meeting in St. Paul, he emphasized federal obligations for the disposition of the public lands; a few months later he told audiences in Idaho and Oregon that the government should stay out of the business of transmitting power. Addressing the Commercial Club of Portland, he denounced the sources of disruption. "The demagogue, the fanatic, the sentimentalist, the faddist are crusading under the banner of conservation," he warned, "mainly because it is popular to hold the attentions of the hour." Such extreme theories, he added, engendered an unhealthy distrust of the states and would ultimately bring about government ownership and operation of resources. During the next month he repeated these observations to a cordial gathering of old friends, members of the Arctic Club of Seattle.[19]

Early in the year, Ballinger thought that he perceived a greater understanding of his policy developing among the members of both political parties, and therefore tried to maintain a public appearance of impartiality. In addition, the President had asked him to guard his comments to the press after he had been provoked into a reply to statements made by progressive Republican Miles Poindexter, a congressman from Spokane. The disheartening events of the subsequent months, however, caused him to relax the pose of neutrality. Some of the correspondence he was receiving doubtless facilitated this change. Former Senator Fulton, for example, insisted that the attacks on the Secretary were in reality attacks on the West. Another friend told him that sentiment in that region was solidifying in a remarkable way, favoring practical conservation over the "radical theoretical" type. Eddy intensified his epistolary advice. "Cut out all that 'Dear Gifford' business," he demanded, "& just call him a 'stinker' & put him under the ropes."[20] A second influence upon Ballinger's thoughts was A. N. Brown, who was now his private secretary. A shrewd observer and an able publicist who had served the critics' cause in Washington State, Brown kept his chief informed of the strength of Western support. Although an incurable gossip himself, he sometimes restrained Ballinger from making indiscreet remarks in public.[21]

The critics obviously cultivated the Secretary's support not because of his achievements, but because of the potential advantages involved in the policies he proposed. In the second annual report, for example, he urged the creation of a Bureau of National Parks which would develop areas of truly national character and eliminate the need for state and local parks. Some of his friends immediately anticipated a new crop of patronage plums from this source, while Eddy hoped that the park lands would be supervised by the states and opened to entry and use. At the same time, Ballinger challenged the statutory basis for the creation of the immense Olympic National Monument in his home state. He also announced that the Department would give greater selective authority to local Land Office agents in screening applicants, and he proposed a shorter time limit on appeals. Had these changes been adopted, they doubtlessly would have favored corporations that could afford the costs of legal assistance, and might have encouraged bribery and fraud. Finally, the Secretary must have warmed the hearts of the advocates of state control when he suggested that the states should establish their own conservation programs by withdrawing water sites, protecting forests, and selling or leasing coal lands.[22]

On several public occasions Ballinger lamented over the seemingly widespread public indifference toward true good government and the nation's welfare. "Such indifference," he explained, "gives a free field to the fanatic, the demagogue, and the theorist. Sane and earnest political effort in harmony with our institutions is more essential for our well-being than any other consideration." Yet he himself was unmoved by the "theorists'" efforts. "I am no pessimist," he announced at a later time, "but am old-fashioned enough to believe in the institutions of our fathers and that they will be preserved nothwithstanding new-fangled ideas of government or the flaming fanaticism of the crusader."[23] The attacks of conservationists and progressives encouraged him to seek solace from men who were calmly conservative like himself. This accounted for his dependence upon and loyalty to the President, and it explained his refusal to sully the dignity of office with blatant publicity. After he resigned from the Interior Department, in March, 1911, he was naturally willing to take a bolder stand. When he was a private citizen once again, his first statement seemed to promise an outburst of long-suppressed indignation: "As for Mr. Pinchot and his companions in their plot to injure and defame me, I propose to take ample time in planning a legal campaign for retributive justice." His partisans strongly wished he would do just that, but they could hardly use such delayed and personal tactics in their drive for support. The conservationists, on the other hand, were wholly pleased with the announcement. Gleefully, Pardee observed: "... that man is real mad and is still breathing fire, brimstone and threats of suits for damages and prosecutions for criminal libel and mal practice and treason and lese majeste."[24] But Ballinger had waited too long to speak, and now he failed to seek retribution in the courts or beyond. Within a few months he would repeat the act of self-frustration at the Second Public Lands Convention, in Denver.

ORGANIZATION WITHOUT EFFECT

In 1911, the decision of the Supreme Court in the case of Fred Light provoked the critics into actions which seemed to be the preliminaries to unity. Westerners had not seriously anticipated a successful suit, but they had hoped that the case would point up the administrative difficulties involved in the policy and deter irreponsible agents by limiting their jurisdiction. The Court first revealed its interpretation of federal authority in July, 1910, when it upheld the Reclamation Act and the right of the Secretary of the Interior to acquire water sites within the states. In May of the following year it took up the charges against Light, confirmed the legality of executive procedures and regulations made by the Forest Service, and declared that the policy based upon these measures had the full force of law. The Coloradans who had sponsored the litigation immediately protested the decision and petitioned for a rehearing.[25]

A few days later Governor Shafroth and his advisers dispatched letters to their adherents throughout the West. After considering the responses, they concluded that the issue was critical enough to warrant the regional meeting which had been postponed six months earlier. In June, Shafroth issued a formal call for a second Public Lands Convention which would formulate a plan for the administration of the public domain as "a substitute for that now in force or proposed by the Government" and one which would be more compatible with the interests of the West. Eddy privately contemplated the adoption of a system of state control along the lines of the "Ballinger bills." The organizers of the meeting, who were determined to avoid the fate of the first convention, in 1907, decided to exclude all federal employees and choose only those speakers whose hostility to conservation was unimpeachable. With such a dedicated, united assembly, one delegate hoped, the convention might quickly become "a great power in the country" and eventually replace the National Conservation Association, which had "degenerated into a Cabinet for Gifford Pinchot." That conservationist had, however, no fear of the meeting. When Pardee wrote to express alarm and say that he planned to go to Denver, Pinchot assured him that the convention would be nothing more than the "last fight of the States Rights Bunch." In August, Newell had a conversation with Shafroth, while Killian sounded out opinion in western Colorado. They both confirmed the fact that the preparations were arousing slight interest and advised Pinchot that the meeting would be a one-man show—Eddy's. Whatever the delegates did at Denver could always be discredited by referring to the unrepresentative character of the membership. Until then, Pinchot was happy to let them "stew in their own juice."[26]

When the Second Public Lands Convention opened, politics once again proved to be a major handicap for the critics of conservation, as it had been in 1907 and 1910. The long shadow of an approaching election year even stretched back to disturb the first public announcement of the meeting. When Governor Hay described it to the press as one which would undoubtedly favor the Taft interpretation of federal policy, the progressive Republican *Spokesman-Review* protested. "All the members of the Republican Party of this state," the newspaper warned, "ought to be informed of the true nature of the Denver convention. It is an attack on the Taft Administration and no Republican should take part in it." At the same time the bulletins of Eddy's National Public Domain League asserted that existing resource policy discredited the Republican party. Although his irrepressible partisanship undoubtedly dismayed many of the critics who belonged to that party, Eddy later insisted that political considerations had not been involved in the preliminary arrangements and would not be in evidence during the sessions. Politics also upset the organizers' intentions of keeping the convention free of Pinchot's followers. As Hay had feared, some of the governors elected in 1910 "had swallowed the platform of Pinchot." One of these, California's Governor Hiram Johnson, pointedly selected delegates suggested by Pardee, who was then acting as his adviser on resource policy. When Governor William Mills of New Mexico named delegates, he took the advice of the new Secretary of the Interior, Walter Fisher, who believed that they should be men of sound character and disinterested motives. Spry of Utah again sent members of the state Conservation Commission. Even Hay hoped to appoint some conservationists so that all shades of opinion would be present in Denver, but most of his nominees distrusted the whole affair and declined to serve.[27]

One hundred and thirty-two delegates appeared at the sessions of the convention late in September, 1911, but one hundred and one of

them were Coloradans—an even larger proportion of the total than in
1907. For those who had attended the earlier meeting, the faces and
oratory of the speakers were familiar. Former Senator Teller still had
enough energy to denounce the decisions of the Supreme Court, and
Governor Shafroth again proposed state control as the only proper
alternative to federal tyranny.[28] The words that were most welcome,
however, came from the former Secretary of the Interior. Since his
resignation, Ballinger had been profoundly disappointed by the appointment of Fisher as his successor and by Taft's evident willingness to
endorse that conservationist's policies. In his alarm over what he termed
the "irreverent and dangerous" demand for popular government,
Ballinger's characteristic reticence was momentarily dissolved. When
Eddy invited him to speak at the convention, he consulted his close
friends in Seattle and decided to take the public stand he had shunned
for so long. The news of his plan elicited a personal letter from the
President which expressed surprise that Ballinger would join in such a
disreputable attack on conservation. "You and I have had so many conversations on the subject," Taft reminded him, "that I am quite sure you
will not permit your natural indignation to lead you into a position
that might . . . give color to the attacks which you have in times past met
with an accurate and reasonable view of the public interest." In reply,
Ballinger asserted that he was acting in the belief that the convention
would be able to organize the states on a "conservative and just basis for
the protection of their rights against the vice of ultra-conservation
propaganda in the East." He would participate in order to keep that
movement within "consistent and conservative" bounds, free from any
political complexion whatsoever. Candidly, he told the President that
his attitude toward conservation had not changed; he would continue
to support rational policy and criticize bureaucratic methods such as
those used by the Forest Service. Although he assured Taft that nothing
would tempt him into publicly censuring the administration, he confessed for the first time that he was deeply disappointed by the selection
of Fisher, by the failure of the plan for appeal of land claims, and by
the disallowance of the Cunningham claims. Taft must have read these
admissions with sad regret. In reply, he merely expressed his sorrow to
know that Ballinger would be so indiscreet as to give his enemies comfort and confirm their accusations about his true attitudes.[29] This exchange of letters seemed to support Garfield's belief that the President
had never really understood his Secretary's views on the subject of
conservation. It would be interesting to speculate on what events might
have occurred if Taft had become aware of Ballinger's personal opinions
in May or September of 1909.

Ballinger's address offered the convention "A Portrayal of Bureaucratic Government in America." In it, he warned against the influence of unchecked executive power and those specialists who were responsible neither to party nor to the people. Their actions, he sincerely believed, were antagonistic to the fundamental laws of the nation. Challenging the ideas of all reformers, he pointed out that their theories might very well be the concepts which earlier generations had abandoned as undesirable. He envisioned a nation which was most secure and most fair as, in Tennyson's poem, "A land of just and old renown, / Where Freedom slowly broadens down / From precedent to precedent."[30] Although this revealing speech served to place him in the ranks of the critics for all to see, it was not a clarion call for state control, and it must have particularly disappointed those who expected him to assume the leadership of the anti-conservation campaign. Significantly, even Ballinger's presence failed to increase public attendance at the sessions beyond the average of three hundred spectators. On the final day, however, an address by the President was heard by twelve thousand. Having been warned by W. G. M. Stone, of the Colorado Conservation Commission, and by Fisher, Taft was determined to offset the impression made by Ballinger's speech. Just as Roosevelt had done in the same city a year before, Taft condemned the proposed substitution of state control for federal administration of resources.[31] With that, the whole purpose of the Public Lands Convention appeared to be out of order.

The organizers of the meeting were nevertheless undismayed. They were quite pleased that "the truth" about conservation had been exposed at Denver, and they were soon occupied with further schemes. Eddy thought that all of the convention speeches should be printed and distributed; Shafroth was sanguine enough to begin planning for annual meetings. In April, 1912, he organized a Public Lands Committee to act as an interim secretariat and initiator of future gatherings, and instructed Eddy and Ammons to arrange "some concerted action" to secure state control. After consulting with several Western governors, the advisers decided to begin with a program of education based upon the distribution of speeches made by prominent economic and political leaders. The cost of printing and handling would be borne by assessment of $1,000 from each state. The governors showed little enthusiasm for the plan under that condition and decided on more direct action: several of them traveled to Washington, D.C., to discuss land and resource use with Fisher and Taft. They also agreed to continue the annual conferences in the West. At the next meeting, however, held in Boise in August, 1912, their number was considerably reduced by the demands of electioneering. Shafroth, for example, was running for the Senate and could not attend. Governors West of Oregon and Oddie of Nevada, both progressives who supported federal policy, did come to the meeting, where they blocked the adoption of extreme resolutions. Nothing more could be done about the Public Lands Committee's hopes for another regional convention so long as the state executives were preoccupied with political maneuvers.[32]

The rumblings of the Colorado committee aroused the indefatigable A. N. Brown to draw up his own plan for organized action. "Sending occasional delegations [to Washington, D.C.]," he wrote to Erastus Brainerd, "and passing resolutions in the American Mining Congress get the states nowhere. Concientious organized intelligent effort, supplemented by scientific publicity, is the only way we can beat the bureaucrats and get justice done for the public land states." Believing that the time was "just ripe for it," Brown visualized the formation of a League of Public Land States which would seek to have the public domain "restored" to the West. Each of the states would contribute $1,000 a year to support a "bureau" (*sic!*) in the nation's capital. Using all the publicity techniques of the National Conservation Association, this agency would issue pamphlets and support lobbyists in Congress. Brown hoped that Hay would accept the task of organizing the League, and he recommended Brainerd as the director of the bureau. Once again the financial requirements of such a scheme had little appeal. Moreover, Brainerd was preoccupied with the task of securing an appointment as Commissioner of Indian Affairs.[33]

The failure of the critics' campaign for the alternative policy of state control of resources can be ascribed to their own poor judgment and incompetence. Instead of relying upon leaders with constructive abilities, they depended upon a group of political timeservers and blatant spokesmen for economic interests. Burdened by propaganda, which ignored or distorted the scientific realities of resource use, they convinced few who were not already hostile to federal supervision. By excluding Western conservationists from their conventions, they actually underscored the fact that conservation was supported by many residents of their region. Finally, the impotent view of this minority was to be overwhelmed by the reaction to the Taft administration.

Chapter VII

ON THE PROGRESSIVES' BAND WAGON

Year of Triumphs

THE DISMISSAL of Gifford Pinchot stimulated the critics' campaign, but at the same time it had an effect of far greater consequence. Those citizens who were already dismayed by the course of the Taft administration were now thoroughly shocked. Political leaders on many levels, from the Insurgents in Congress to the minority factions within state party organizations, were armed with a new advantage: the cause of conservation was obviously a part of the progressives' crusade.

There was an ominous sound to the letters and telegrams that poured into the former Chief Forester's office. Stone, of the Colorado Conservation Commission was one of many friends who viewed the removal as an act of martyrdom, complete with Taft's thrusting a spear into Pinchot's side by saying that his usefulness was at an end. "Think of the venom that can be concealed behind two such smiling lips," Stone wrote. "I am not an 'insurgent.' I'm a straight party man but if it were election day today, I fear I should fly to some dark cellar for safety." From California, George Pardee reported that the people were "mad as hatters" about the President's action, adding: "Your legion of friends here are proud of your manly stand. It is unfortunate there are not more like you in the Government." Several other friends, members of the faculty at Stanford University, called a mass meeting to protest the dismissal. Civic organizers in Los Angeles and San Jose sent resolutions to the White House. Charles F. Lummis, editor of *Out West,* hopefully offered Pinchot space in his magazine for any reply to Taft. In Oregon, Joseph Teal found a similar popular response. "Members of fashionable clubs may be against you," he assured his friend, "but the people on the street cars are with you." Such messages came in from every part of the West, including the citadels of criticism, and doubtless confirmed Pinchot's belief that the majority of the people in the country were at last standing with him in his fight. The line between the forces of selfishness and those of justice seemed more clearly drawn than it had ever been before.[1]

During the months that followed there was a striking improvement in local support of conservation throughout the West. Pinchot, now free of official duties, devoted much of his time to sustaining this public awareness by corresponding with new and old adherents and by once again traveling through the states of the region. His disciples also turned out in full force to bolster the publicity campaign and report on the nature of local sentiment. Chief Forester Graves and former Secretary Garfield went to the heart of enemy country to concentrate their energies in Colorado. Graves even called on Elias Ammons—and received Pinchot's "heartiest commiseration" for suffering such an ordeal. By the summer of 1910, the forester could assure his predecessor that "the whole West is absolutely with you." In California, Pardee eagerly sought out another implacable critic, Frank Short, met him in debate before the Los Angeles Chamber of Commerce, and gleefully reported the details of his victory. Short, he wrote Pinchot, had been tired and unprepared for the contest, and his speech had wandered "from Dan to Beersheba, quoting all kinds of scripture and law and things," until half the audience departed. Elsewhere a substantial amount of sympathy for Pinchot was discernible in Ballinger's Washington and in Heyburn's Idaho even before the disastrous fire of August. One Wyoming citizen was sufficiently aroused to write to Senator Warren: "You and your sheep were not elected to feed ... at the expense of the nation.... Mr. Pinchot is right & his way is right & his way is the way for Wyoming." There could hardly have been a more convincing proof of the change taking place in Western attitudes than the letter Governor Hay wrote to his adversary after the debacle at St. Paul. In it, he argued that conservation was too important a program to be undermined by political or personal considerations. Extending an olive branch, he promised to support a sensible and just policy. With characteristic enthusiasm Pinchot interpreted the letter as evidence of the "complete abandonment of the ultra-States Rights policy." It was, more accurately, a prophetic sign that the political repercussions of the controversy were weakening his opponents.[2]

Because of the juxtaposition of these two developments, the conservation issue served to convince many progressives that a realignment of the Republican party would be necessary and inevitable. William Kent, of California, had foreseen this when, at the height of the Ballinger controversy, Taft's actions prompted him to go to Washington, where he had a "very lively time with the large person." When he left the White House, he regretfully concluded that the President was unable to see that conservation and the public interest were at stake. "Just one more flop in the wrong direction," he decided then, "and there will be nothing to it but Teddy." That "flop" obviously occurred when Pinchot was dismissed. Kent was overdramatic in concluding that the affair was a "crisis in the history of the country" which "if settled one way will lead to progress along democratic lines, and if settled the other way will be the harbinger of revolution." Yet, even such a man of deliberation as Chester Rowell, of the Fresno *Republican,* who was then, like Kent, an admirer of Taft, feared that the fires started by the Ballinger controversy might spread farther than anyone could foresee. Other observers who had been hurt by the administration needed no further reason to come to their own conclusions. San Francisco engineer Marsden Manson, disgusted over the suspension of the Hetch Hetchy grant, decided that Pinchot's removal would force the nomination of Roosevelt at the next Republican convention. Governor Curry of New Mexico Territory was more directly affected. Early in 1909, he had planned a trip to the national capital to settle outstanding resource problems and urge the approval of a statehood bill. Through Ballinger, the President denied him permission to make the trip, causing Curry to complain bitterly that the administration had no confidence in him. In March, he sent in his resignation; after a barrage of correspondence and confidential talks, however, he agreed to remain in office. Later, when confronted with the choice between Taft and Ballinger or Roosevelt and Pinchot, Curry predicted that if the President continued to ignore his predecessor's policies he would lose the support of the West. Shortly after Pinchot was removed, Curry decided to support Roosevelt if he were a candidate in 1912.[3]

The Old Guard Republicans at first underestimated the situation when they accused the progressive Republicans of using the "return from Elba" scare as a means of frightening Taft into recommending more extensive conservation legislation. Roosevelt's reaction to the controversy was of a far more significant nature. He had learned of the dismissal while still in Africa and privately confessed that he was appalled by the treatment of this "aggressive, hard hitting leader of all the forces which were slugging for conservation [and] fighting for the general interests as against special privilege." Shortly afterward, he wrote to Pinchot: "It is a very ungracious thing for an ex-President to criticize his successor, and yet I can not as an honest man cease to battle for the principles for which you and I and Jim [Garfield] and [Malcolm] Moody and the rest of our close associates stood." The flying rumors of Roosevelt as a candidate naturally extended to Pinchot himself; one Western editor guessed that the controversy would make him the party's nominee, but there is no evidence that Pinchot was considering that possibility. Instead, he was concentrating his energies toward a more immediate task. Reminded by his brother Amos that "Ballinger is but a symptom of the disease the country is suffering from," and agreeing with Pardee that a new "stir up" was needed,

Pinchot hoped, with the help of his disciples, to make the public see the enormity of the crisis.[4]

In joining their cause to the progessive faction in the states of the West, the conservationists had to tread carefully. In Colorado, for example, the Republican party itself was still weak and the new organization therefore had slight chance of disturbing the Democratic preponderance. Deciding that the safest course would be the defense of resource policy apart from politics, Pinchot, Garfield, and Roosevelt came to the state in August, 1910, addressed civic organizations and stock raisers on "Conservation and Progress," and denounced the heresy of state control. After they left, Judge Ben B. Lindsey, one of the prominent reformers in the state, reported that the talks had made thousands of friends for them. "I have heard men singing your praises who were within six months damning [you]," he wrote to Pinchot, and added: "Conservation and all that it stands for was immeasurably strengthened and helped by your visit."[5]

By way of contrast, a resurgent Democratic organization in Oregon strengthened local support of conservation. The Republicans were weakened by internal dissensions, and a multiplicity of candidates vied for most of the available offices. In addition, the death of editor Scott of the *Oregonian* had removed from the scene a forceful supporter of Taft as well as a constant critic of resource policy. The President's advisers were sufficiently worried about the party's welfare in Oregon to suggest that Ballinger refrain from executing a planned transfer of the Land Office field division headquarters from Portland to Spokane, Washington. Later, the Secretary himself traveled to Portland to defend his interpretation of conservation. Although Republicans scoffed because their opponents—traditionally advocates of states rights—were now supporting federal control of resources, they could not discredit the extensive contributions of prominent Democrats. Joseph Teal, former counsel to lumber corporations, was the moving force behind the state Conservation Commission. His work in securing the coöperation between forest users and federal agents was praised by many Oregonians who despised Pinchot. Former Governor—now Senator—George Chamberlain had become a conscientious convert to the cause of conservation, and was an intimate friend of Pinchot and Roosevelt. Both Teal and Chamberlain were then aiding the gubernatorial campaign of Oswald West, a Democrat and former Railroad and Land Commissioner. Malcolm Moody had first introduced him to Pinchot in 1907 and may now have been instrumental in inducing Roosevelt to endorse West's candidacy publicly. The connection proved beneficial when West won the

office in November. As governor, he immediately asked his legislature
to make up for the past neglect of vital policy by creating the office of
State Forester and by establishing a Board of Forestry. Determined
to bring about a broad acceptance of the board's decisions, he selected
its membership from the ranks of private lumbermen as well as the
Oregon Forestry Association. Finally, by reconstituting the Oregon
Conservation Commission, the legislators repaired the damage done by
his predecessor, Bowerman. West was justifiably proud of Roosevelt's
public tribute to his accomplishments.[6]

The subject of federal resource policy proved to be both a hindrance
and a help for those progressive Republicans who broke with the regular
party organizations when they ran for office in 1910. In Idaho, for
example, they were wholly unable to use the issue because of the
strength of the Old Guard led by Borah and Heyburn. Only Paul
Clagstone, candidate for the governorship, was courageous enough or
ambitious enough to face the odds by supporting conservation. When he
asked for an endorsement from the Roosevelt men, however, Pinchot
concluded that, although Clagstone was an acceptable progressive, he
had no chance of winning. Perhaps because there was no nucleus of
conservationists in the state, such as there was in Colorado, Pinchot
decided not to risk the prestige of the policy by connecting it with a lost
cause. He consequently refrained from giving out any statement about
the candidate, and did not stop in Idaho during his tour of the West
that August.[7]

The case of the progessive Republican effort in California was a
happy contrast. As one Taft newspaper sullenly observed, in terms of
conservation zeal and disloyalty to the party that state was the "worst
offender." In June, 1910, the leaders of the faction urged Pinchot to
participate in their campaign to make Hiram W. Johnson governor.
The local reform organizations throughout the state were eager to have
an intimate of Roosevelt with a national reputation to help their cause,
and they were equally aware of the continuing importance of resource
policy in the economy of their rapidly growing state. During the summer months, Pinchot traveled extensively in California, paying his own
expenses, and renewed friendships with many adherents, including
George Pardee. Another supporter, William Kent, was running as a
progressive Republican candidate for the House of Representatives.
Together, the three conservationists exploited Ballinger, Hetch Hetchy,
and Truckee as potent political issues. On Johnson's behalf, they specifically tied conservation and progressivism together, and he was soon
being described as the only Republican who would "aggressively follow

in California" the policies of Roosevelt, Pinchot, and Garfield. In many instances, Pinchot tellingly equated the fight of the reformers against selfish economic interests in the state with his own struggle against the enemies of conservation. In the public view, he proved to be the next best thing to having Roosevelt himself on the stump. The former President, however, had not yet announced his break with the Old Guard and therefore had to deny that Pinchot spoke for him in California. The Taft supporters gleefully reported that this was evidence of a rift between the two men, and Ballinger brought it to the President's attention in the hope that he would make political capital of it. When the California Republicans also accused Kent of fencing public domain to keep stock from his rangelands, however, Roosevelt issued a public letter of confidence on behalf of the candidate. This endorsement, reproduced by many newspapers, probably served to offset the rumors of the rift with Pinchot. Some Republicans, opposed to Roosevelt, insurgency, and conservation, chose to vote Democratic rather than swallow Johnson, whom they described as a demagogue. The subsequent victory of both Johnson and Kent clearly proved that the conservation issue could be a political blessing under the right conditions.[8]

The triumph of the progressives in California had in turn a direct influence upon the maintenance of resource policy in the state. The incoming Johnson administration established a Committee on Proposed Legislation immediately after the election, and that group included a Conservation Committee under the chairmanship of Pardee, with Kent, Rowell, and former federal attorney Francis J. Heney as members. The new governor was not personally familiar with the complex problems of resource regulation, but he readily accepted the committee's drafts of laws for fire protection and timber cutting, as well as a bill for the creation of a California Conservation Commission. Johnson wisely appointed Pardee as chairman of the latter organization, but Pardee's subsequent tenure was unfortunately marred by disruptive controversies. One of these came after the selection of Louis Glavis, Ballinger's old incubus, as secretary to the commission. Within a year after his appointment Glavis was accused of personally profiting from his office in several cases involving the purchase of timberlands. In order to avoid a scandal that might have injured both the state administration and the progessives' chances in 1912, Johnson and Pardee asked him to resign. The man who had been so recently hailed by half the nation for his exposure of Ballinger's misdemeanors quickly disappeared from the public scene. It is interesting to speculate on the way in which conservation and the progressive revolt might have gone if Glavis's integrity had been similarly muddied two years before.[9]

In interest and significance, the California contest of 1910 was matched by the dramatic nature of the elections in the state of Washington. Although the adherents of Ballinger and Taft were still in control of the party machinery, an increasing number of residents were attracted to the progressive faction, especially in the Spokane area. While the Old Guard was still arguing over the respective merits of Judge Burke and former Senator John L. Wilson as nominees for the Senate seat of Samuel Piles, the progressives rallied around one candidate: Congressman Miles C. Poindexter. For several years Poindexter had been indifferent to the subject of resource policy, but the controversy over Ballinger and the influence of editor Cowles of the *Spokesman-Review* served to arouse his interest. He was especially quick to observe the way in which the issue produced a clear distinction among Republicans. All the "Tories," the "bogus aristocracy," he noted, were against conservation, while the progressives were "heartily in favor of Pinchot, of Roosevelt and . . . their policies and methods." When Poindexter announced his candidacy in December, 1909, he publicly repudiated the "development interpretation of conservation" held by Senators Jones and Piles.[10]

By January, 1910, the President's supporters were fully aware that the resource issue was affecting public opinion in the state. Senator Jones confessed to a friend that he was "a little bit uneasy" about this "strong current of feeling" within the insurgent element. His constituents did not let him forget the connection between the subjects. "Don't go over to the enemy," one of them warned, "or you will go down with Taft—the worst discredited President since Andrew Johnson—Work for the people—not the coal land looters and the giant interests." A lifelong Republican wrote to add that the wave of "Civic Resurgence" which was sweeping the country would not tolerate any such injustice as the whitewashing of Ballinger: "Pinchot may not be an angel but he stands for that which the people *demand.*" Jones first tried to placate these critics with rhetorical twists; he stated, for example, that he agreed with "a great many of the opinions of Mr. Pinchot just as I agree with some of the opinions of Mr. Ballinger." By May, however, he reverted to a public endorsement of Wilson's candidacy and of state control of resources, and delivered several anti-conservation speeches for the candidate.[11]

Many Republicans in the state doubted that Wilson was the best choice for the contest. Some of them remembered the fact that his earlier career in the Senate had been marred by his solicitude for the Northern Pacific Railroad's domination of politics and economic development; others feared that state control of resources, which he advocated, would add "more rottenness" to state government. After the dismissal of Pinchot, several men of the party decided that the strongest of all possible candidates would be the Secretary of the Interior. As the defender of "proper" federal conservation, he could thus give the voters an opportunity to attest publicly to their belief in his interpretation of the policy and their confidence in his personal integrity. Editor Brainerd insisted that this would be the only available solution to the intraparty tension created by the conflicting claims of Burke and Wilson. Ballinger, however, was not interested in the suggestion. "When I get out of my present office," he replied to Brainerd, "I am out of politics and official consideration absolutely [and] the patriotic view will never again permit me to become involved in public life unless under the most extraordinary conditions." Feeling that the present contest was not such a case, he declined the chairmanship of the state Republican convention and decided to take no part in the campaign in Washington.[12]

Taft and his advisers were profoundly worried about the situation in that state, not only because it was Ballinger's home, but also because it had been a party stronghold for many years. Although the President was anxious to see the defeat of Poindexter, whom he described as a "blatant demagogue," he refused to interfere in the dispute of the local organization. Instead he asked Ballinger personally to investigate the problem with a special campaign adviser, Senator W. Murray Crane, of Massachusetts. Because Taft did not want to open himself to the charge of violating his rule of aloofness, he impressed upon both men the absolute need for secrecy. When they met in Minneapolis, in August, Ballinger suggested to Crane that the President should ask both Burke and Wilson whether they would give up their own plans so that the party could unite behind one of them. This request was subsequently made. Burke would not commit himself, but Wilson, whom Ballinger privately favored, agreed to retire from the race. Shortly thereafter he succeeded Brainerd as editor of the *Post-Intelligencer* and continued his attacks on conservation from its pages. Although Burke had once been a supporter of Pinchot's policy, his subsequent friendship for Taft and nearness to party conservatives modified his opinion about conservation. He did not make that subject a principal issue during the campaign, but men like Governor Hay, who spoke for him, repeated the customary criticisms of inordinate federal interference in local economy.[13]

Meanwhile, candidate Poindexter had become identified with the progressive leadership beyond his state. Perhaps through the urging of

Pinchot, he traveled to Roosevelt's home at Oyster Bay, New York, consulted with both men, and returned to Spokane as the seeming champion of their policies. His "adhesion to Pinchotism" was loudly exploited by his opponents during the primary campaign, but he refrained from publicly referring to Ballinger in return. Unlike the situation in Idaho, the cause of conservation was clearly at stake in Washington, Pinchot believed, and he offered to endorse Poindexter if that would help him. The progressive evidently did not need help; he won a majority of the votes cast. His success was promptly described as a "Triumph for Good Government" and a "stinging rebuke" to Ballinger.[14]

Yet the strong showing of the progressive Republicans in Washington was not wholly owing to the issue of conservation. Senator Crane believed that Poindexter won because many Democrats voted in the Republican primary. Moreover, one of the men elected during the campaign that November was a leading opponent of federal resource regulation. Congressman William Humphrey capitalized upon his friendship with Roosevelt by securing a letter of endorsement from him and won easily as a progressive Republican. Humphrey revealed his true sentiments after the election when he replied to a telegram of congratulations from Ballinger. "For the next two years," he announced facetiously, "I am an insurgent of the fiercest kind. I am against rules, against the Speaker, against everything. I may be lonesome, but I will enjoy myself." Roosevelt's endorsement of such a hypocrite, William Allen White told Pinchot after the election, was a "tactical blunder."[15]

BALLINGER OUT—FISHER IN

A few months after the heartening elections of 1910, conservationists again joined with progressives to rejoice over the announcement that Ballinger had resigned as Secretary of the Interior. Rumors of that solution to the controversy had appeared in the press from the time the disagreement with Pinchot was first made public, early in 1909, and had been repeated sporadically ever since. Even after Taft's letter of September 13 destroyed any hope that Ballinger would retire of his own volition, the Pinchot men believed that public pressure would eventually force the resignation. When Senator Crane went to the West in August, 1910, they eagerly speculated that he was being sent to obtain the Secretary's withdrawal; later rumors cast Postmaster General Hitchcock in the role of emissary. Ballinger soon learned of these allegations from his secretary, Donald Carr, and promptly denied that he was planning to resign. Because of the President's request for secrecy about the Crane mission, however, he could not publicly account for the

meeting in Minneapolis. He was evidently unaware of the fact that, at
that same time, certain persons close to Taft were trying to bring about
his resignation. These men, whose identities were not revealed, allegedly
urged the President to get rid of Ballinger because they considered him
a detriment to the chances of the party's candidates in the coming
elections.[16]

Cognizant of these pressures, Paul Norton, private secretary to the
President, decided to make a personal effort to heal the rupture in Republican ranks. He first sought to arrange a reconciliation between
Taft and some of his former friends—Kent and Roosevelt, among others. Just how far these plans were carried is not known, but Norton
evidently was not acting with Taft's knowledge or approval. Ultimately,
the secretary concluded that the greatest single reason for the persist-
ence of factionalism was the Ballinger affair. He therefore concentrated
upon devising a way of removing that stigma from the administration.
During the sessions of the St. Paul congress, in August, Norton approached Governor Hay and asked him to consider the possibility of
urging the Secretary to resign. To support the idea, he argued that
Ballinger's continued presence in the Cabinet would jeopardize the
election of thirty-five candidates for the House of Representatives and
would result in Democratic control of the House. He added, however,
that any action had to be taken by the Republican leaders of Washington State and could not be initiated by the President.[17]

When Hay first heard the rumors of resignation, he wrote to Taft
to reassert the West's claim to the vacancy if it should occur. Although
he recommended no names at that time, a later letter to a friend mentioned a preference for either Senator Jones or Senator Borah. Hay
personally wanted Ballinger to remain in the post, and was therefore
much disturbed when he heard Norton's suggestion. A few weeks later,
after the congressional investigating committee published its report, he
wrote a confidential letter to Jones and told him of Norton's request.
Hay felt he could not urge the resignation, and he doubted that Taft
would accept it unless Ballinger insisted. As he told Jones, the insurgents were after Taft, not Ballinger, whose removal would hardly satisfy them. Nevertheless, he confessed: "[Ballinger is] certainly a load
for President Taft to carry [and] the only grounds that I can see upon
which we could urge his resignation would be that he is hurting a true
friend by longer remaining." In reply, Jones indignantly objected to
the whole scheme: "If the time has come that the [Republican] party
in order to succeed must listen to charges of this kind and must set aside
men who have honestly and faithfully done their duty then it does not

deserve to win at all." But the senator could see the signs: "It looks to me like the country is due for a change and our party had better go down with its flag flying for what it believes to be right than ... compromise our principles because we would then go down to a deserved defeat."[18]

Perhaps Norton disclosed the purpose of his plan to a few close friends of the administration. Rumors were soon being repeated across the country, while a flurry of comment appeared in private correspondence and the public press. Editor Rowell, in California, decided that the selection of a successor to Ballinger would be the principal problem in any rehabilitation of Taft. Privately, he feared that Senator Flint, of his state, would be offered the post because of his part in the congressional absolution of the Secretary. Rowell was even more discomfited when Representative William Englebright asked him for an endorsement for the post—the choice of such a critic of conservation would hardly have solved the President's problems. When rumors of the scheme reached Ballinger himself, he consulted with Vertrees and protested that he had received no intimation from Taft or Crane that the resignation was desired. Significantly, he lamented over the way he was getting the worst of the situation "as usual," simply because the "powers that be" thought it impolitic to give the public the facts about the meeting with Crane. The rumor had appeared about the time that his proposed legislation was rejected and shortly after the minority of the investigating committee announced its censure of him. In view of these events, Ballinger may have decided that to resign then would furnish cause for overwhelming public condemnation. He did not reveal his real thoughts, however, and merely issued a statement in the form of a letter to Crane denying the existence of such a plan. The heart of this message—originally written by Vertrees—strongly implied that Ballinger was especially pained by the idea that his usefulness was impaired. Those who demanded his resignation, he pointed out, based their reasons not on misconduct, but upon this alleged impairment. Yet they were the same persons whose attacks upon his conduct had warped public opinion until his work had been impaired. In reply, Crane hastened to assure him that the President had never mentioned the rumored scheme in his presence, and that no resignation would be requested. Taft assured Hay that there was "not the slightest prospect" of the Secretary's resigning, but he failed to give Ballinger the same assurance. Ballinger's confidence was therefore profoundly shaken. If Norton acted on his own initiative, Taft obviously made no effort to tell Ballinger of the fact. Perhaps he actually allowed his secretary to test the plan and then refused to refer to it after it failed. In the absence of any word from his chief, Ballinger came to his own saddening conclusion.[19]

Until March, 1911, when the resignation was announced, the Secretary of the Interior wore a noncommittal smile before his own staff and whenever he was questioned by reporters. But he had decided early in January that he had fulfilled the tasks for which he remained in office: assisting the President in land and resource policies and legislation, and securing the weight of a congressional exoneration. Still, he was not satisfied with the outcome of these efforts. Generally, he disagreed with Taft's view of federal conservation. Many of his suggestions—judicial review of Department decisions, the Cunningham claims, the Truckee contract, and Hetch Hetchy—had been rebuffed or suspended. Neither Newell nor Davis had been removed from their posts, and suggestions for the appointment of men who would be loyal to him were ignored. Doubting that he could possibly be of use in the future, Ballinger went to the White House and presented a letter which asked the President to let him resign. His characteristic reticence prevented him from expressing his feeling of disappointment, and he probably remembered Taft's earlier impatience with the idea that his usefulness was impaired. The letter therefore referred only to the decline of his law practice and the state of his health. It was certainly true that he had sacrificed a lucrative income to enter the Cabinet, but the only incident in office affecting his physical health seems to have been a shaking-up he received during a wreck on the Baltimore and Ohio Railroad the previous October. It is possible, however, that the unusual pressures of the past two years might have brought on a psychosomatic upset.[20]

President Taft waited a few days before replying that he would never consent to the resignation for any alleged good of the Department or the party, but would do so only in consideration of the Secretary's personal affairs. Actually, he was not yet fully convinced that the resignation was really a desirable thing. When he consulted Charles Taft, his closest confidant, he was advised that it would be better if Ballinger were permitted to leave, thereby relieving the administration of an embarrassment. There were many thousands of people who had held that sentiment for more than a year. Early in March, in the midst of a new wave of rumors, the President finally acquiesced after Ballinger presented a second letter of request.[21]

Taft's letter accepting the resignation fairly burned with righteous indignation. It recapitulated the course of Ballinger's tenure from a point of view that had received scant publicity during the controversy.

The Secretary, it noted, had entered the service under protest and at great personal sacrifice. Although he had earnestly and conscientiously attended to the interests of the government under conditions of great difficulty, he had nevertheless been the object of "one of the most unscrupulous conspiracies for the defamation of character that history can show." He had fought that conspiracy out of a sense of duty to his office and to society in order to show the people that the false impression of him as a man and an administrator was wholly the result of a "malicious and unprincipled plan for the use of the press to misrepresent [and] torture every circumstance, however free from detrimental significance into proof of corrupt motive." Men using "the most pettifogging methods" had "showered" him with suspicion by parading before "an hysterical body of headline readers" matters which were irrelevant to the issues of corruption or inefficiency. Yet those same men, Taft noted bitterly, "like the Pharisees of old," posed as the "only pure members of society" who were activated by the spirit of self-sacrifice for their fellow man. Ballinger's character had thus been blackened, and his honesty and effectiveness obscured. The result, the President lamented, was a "cruel tragedy." As a description of the intentions and methods of the Secretary's detractors, the letter was generally accurate. But it was incomplete in that it failed to take notice of the fact that Ballinger's personal views marred his efficiency as an administrator, and naturally it ignored the way in which Taft's own handling of the controversy had increased public doubts. Neither of these facts was attributable to the influence of the character assassins.[22]

The letter was everything that Ballinger might have desired in his long quest for vindication, but the almost clandestine nature of Taft's decision was strongly resented by some of his colleagues in the Cabinet. During their regular meeting on the same day, the President did not mention the resignation or the acceptance. Because he had asked the Cabinet members for their views of Pinchot's dismissal, in January, 1910, the resignation semed to be an analogous matter. Secretary Knox and Postmaster General Hitchcock were told of the letter of acceptance when they waited on Taft after the meeting adjourned, but the other members did not hear the news until they returned home. Several of them immediately wrote protests to the President, declaring that they would certainly have said something on the subject had they known of it. In reply, Taft explained that he had hastened to decide the matter so that he would not be "exposed to the great difficulty of selection [of a successor] if Ballinger's resignation became known as it was likely to be." He certainly had no wish to undergo the usual flood of suggestions,

pressures, and press comments which would accompany such a controversial Cabinet appointment, but his excuse that he "forgot until it was
too late" to say something at the meeting can only be described as in-
firm. Moreover, it is astonishing in view of the fact that he had already
selected a successor. The President's elusiveness in the matter reveals
that he was really embarrassed by the obvious inconsistency between his
earlier refusal to accept the suggestion of letting Ballinger resign and
his decision to do so based upon the same suggestion.[23]

Ballinger left Washington, D.C., late in March, after receiving expressions of regret and best wishes from many friends in the Department and capital society. Returning to Seattle, he found his personal
finances in a deplorable state and therefore rejoined Alfred Battle and
two new associates in a law partnership. At first he declined to serve
any parties with cases before the Interior Department, but business was
so slight that he later asked Taft for permission to serve the government in special cases there. On several occasions he also wrote to the
President to offer suggestions on patronage matters. Whenever he acted
as speaker at local public functions, Ballinger usually made some reference to the type of man who used calm deliberation in the midst of
popular fanaticism. He remained the object of sporadic attacks, especially during the election campaign of 1912, and, although he grew
callous to such treatment, he never lost his resentment for those who
had ruined his reputation and public career.[24]

Gifford Pinchot was feeling cheerful on the morning of March 7,
1911. The announcement of Ballinger's resignation brought hundreds
of calls to his home and office in Washington, D.C., and a host of reporters to the hotel in New York City where he was staying at the time.
For the press, he remarked that the event was inevitable and would be
received with general satisfaction. Privately, however, he was not particularly anxious to see his adversary resign. Having been "sterilized . . .
pretty effectively," Ballinger was no longer a threat to Pinchot and
could have continued to aid the cause of conservation and progressivism
as a millstone around the neck of Taft. The President's letter to the
Secretary was greeted with jubilation and derision by the Pinchot men.
Pardee declared that he could not understand the inconsistencies involved: "Why should [Ballinger] do it now any more than a year ago?
Hasn't he been VINDICATED, by gosh? And, being VINDICATED, why
should he resign? And why should he get out of the way, anyhow, until
he has accomplished what he was set to do?" Garfield felt that it was a
most unfortunate time for the decision because the popular belief would
be that talk of Ballinger's impeachment had forced the President's

hand: "So ends most disastrously two years of hideous mistakes by Taft."[25]

The newspapers of the West naturally were filled with condolences for Ballinger, but even in Seattle there was a feeling that its favorite son should have resigned long before he did. Some westerners believed that his tenure had served only to complicate the already knotty problems of resource use; others, however, thought that their region had lost an invaluable spokesman for their interests. Democratic and progressive Republican editors agreed that, next to the tariff, he had been the "saddest of all of Mr. Taft's sad handicaps." They were sincerely sorry that he had not stayed in office until election time. Ballinger's supporters felt sure that history would deal justly with his record, but his critics decided that he was not a vindicated man. Rowell's Fresno *Republican* made this perceptive summation: "Taft calls the Ballinger case a tragedy. It is. It is the tragedy of Hamlet. To Ballinger 'the times were out of joint.' To the nation Ballinger was 'out of joint.' His was a mental attitude or bias of mind, a viewpoint that could not and would not fit into the new conditions." Such newspaper comment seemed to show that the resignation came too late to alter opinions about Ballinger or Taft, one way or the other.[26]

The appointment of Walter L. Fisher to be Secretary of the Interior was welcomed by conservationists of East and West as enthusiastically as they had hailed the departure of Ballinger. Fisher was a tall man, of scholarly appearance. He had no national reputation, but had been a leader of civic reform in Chicago for many years, and had earned Pinchot's confidence while serving as an executive officer of the National Conservation Association. Taft thought of him as an "extremist" and somewhat "inclined to Pinchot," but was impressed by the way he had discreetly avoided any public stand during the Ballinger controversy. That fact, coupled with his ability as an administrator and reputation as a reformer, made him politically attractive to the administration in the anxious days before the elections of 1910. It was at that time that he was being mentioned as a possible candidate for mayor of Chicago, as an appointee to the United States Supreme Court, and as the next Secretary of the Interior. When Fisher first learned of these possibilities, he wrote to Pinchot and half-seriously asked: ". . . how would you and [Roosevelt] regard me as a successor to Ballinger?" Of the three posts, Pinchot thought that the court appointment would be the best choice. As for the Cabinet place, he advised his friend that the term would doubtless be limited "in the natural course of events" to six years at the most and possibly to two. Furthermore, after all the discussion of the past years, Pinchot felt that "the Interior Department is likely to go along pretty straight for some time to come." When Fisher was given the post of Secretary, Pinchot announced that the choice was a concession to the "growing determination of the country to be represented by public servants in whose hands the public interests are safe."[27]

Whether pleased by the appointment or not, many observers found it to be further evidence of the President's inconsistencies. Taft was fully aware that Fisher was one of the coterie who had seen the Glavis charges before they were made public, and he knew that the Chicagoan was a close colleague of Pinchot. It may have been secretary Norton who first suggested Fisher, in August, 1910, as the best means of overcoming the stigma of Ballinger before the elections. But Taft probably was more impressed by the character and ability of the man than by any political advantage involved in the selection. A few days before Ballinger left office, Taft and Fisher talked with him in private. The subject of this conversation was not announced, but they might well have agreed upon the necessity of keeping Department business out of the arena of public controversy. When Garfield heard about the meeting, he feared that Fisher might have been induced to accept Taft's opinion of Ballinger's actions, but, on second thought, decided that the new Secretary would have a free hand in the Department. Still, he could not understand why the President had selected a man who was one of the conservationists whom he had branded "foul conspirators." It was, he told Pinchot, "just another one of Taft's incomprehensible actions displaying again his absolute lack of political sagacity as well as dense ignorance regarding conservation questions." Ballinger did not express his own feelings about the choice until several months later. In the course of defending his participation in the Second Public Lands Convention, he admitted to Taft that he found the appointment "hard to bear." The President hastened to assure him that Fisher was not "truckling to Pinchot and his fellow fanatics," but this did not relieve Ballinger's disappointment. Many westerners found it difficult to believe that Taft would deliberately put a Pinchot man in office. The choice, as one editor observed, clearly did not add laurels to Ballinger's brow.[28]

In significant contrast to his behavior with Ballinger, Pinchot was determined to avoid the appearance of having undue influence upon Fisher's policies. He knew that his stewardship of the past was no longer essential, and he was immediately reassured by the new Secretary's initial actions. Two of Pinchot's most dedicated disciples were appointed to the immediate staff. Samuel Adams, of Chicago, became Assistant Secretary in the place of Pierce, who resigned in May, and Philip P. Wells assumed the post of law officer for the Reclamation Service. A few months later, however, Pinchot's resolution wavered a little. He was in one instance an indirect party in the exposure of the so-called "Dick to Dick letter," a futile attempt to document Ballinger's earlier culpability. Of greater importance, he collaborated with his brother Amos on a brief which brought about the cancellation of claims on Controller Bay, Alaska. From the first, Garfield did not hesitate to consult with Fisher on all phases of Department business. He eagerly offered advice on several touchy subjects which the Secretary subsequently disposed of to the satisfaction of the conservationists. Californians who had first feared that Fisher would be "mere putty in Taft's hands" were delighted to learn that he would sustain the Hetch Hetchy grant. He also saw to it that the Truckee contract, with which he had become familiar as counsel for the National Conservation Association, was summarily dropped. The controversial Cunningham claims were reconsidered and finally cancelled in June, 1911; an appeal of the decision was rejected in September of the following year. Those claimants who had already lost their investments during the long period of litigation were almost indifferent to this outcome, but others in the Pacific Northwest bitterly concluded that their demand for the opening of Alaskan resources would never be satisfied so long as Fisher was in office. Generally, the new Secretary hoped to have the government act as arbiter and harmonizer of the conflicting interests of the states. He personally oiled the troubled waters during a trip through the West and, after doing so, concluded that state control of resources was not the real desire of the average westerner.[29] In all of these decisions, Fisher seemed to be the tool of Pinchot; actually, the two friends disagreed upon two important subjects. One of these arose when the Secretary quietly suggested that Graves consider the possibility of transferring the Forest Service back to the Interior Department or else altering its jurisdiction over grazing and water use in the national forests. Secondly, Fisher disliked Newell's inordinate influence in the Department. Like Ballinger, he asked the President to obtain the Director's resignation and was refused; Taft doubtless feared that it would stir up another disastrous public controversy.[30]

Generally, the President also showed an attitude toward Fisher strikingly different from his attitude toward Ballinger. The new Secretary was given a free hand in policy decisions, perhaps because Taft was confident that the best interests would be protected thereby, but equally because he was gratified to have conservationists commend the administration after the long, dark night of criticism. Moreover, as Kent observed, Fisher was politically valuable. If Taft hoped to heal the great breach in the party by thus favoring the Secretary, however, he failed to accomplish anything more than the alienation of his own adherents in the West. "So far as this administration is concerned," A. N. Brown observed with disgust, "the West has been wiped off the map." Old Guard Republicans in Washington State were particularly exasperated by continuing complaints against land use regulations. "Why the h—l [*sic*] doesn't the President wake up and straighten out his Interior Department," Governor Hay demanded. "I understand [it] is honey combed with men who are fighting the President's administration and at the same time bringing this administration into disfavor with the homesteader. I have met a lot of poor politicians," he added with authority, "but I want to take my hat off to President Taft as being the poorest of the bunch." In that particular sentiment, many men of other political persuasions could heartily concur.[31]

The Old Guards found themselves in an unenviable position as election time, 1912, drew near. They could no longer take false comfort in the belief that the "people of prominence" were standing by them. The "Isms" seemed to hold full sway over the masses. Conservation had been one of the issues which provoked the rebellion of the progressives; now the critics of conservation were turning away because of Fisher's policies. Former claimant Miles C. Moore, for example, readily admitted that he was thoroughly embittered by Taft and his Interior Secretaries. Hay believed that the replacement of Fisher with a "good strong western man" would improve the party's chances in the election; if the President had appointed someone "strong enough to have cleaned out the department and laid out a policy that would command the respect and confidence of all our people, I think a large portion of [his] troubles would have ceased." Taft was "in some way . . . hampered and unable to get the action he thinks just," Hay felt, and was also "a little afraid and [catering] too much to the eastern conservationists," who knew "little or nothing about western conditions." One of the governor's correspondents, a Seattle lawyer, confessed that he was so "utterly disgusted" with Taft's land policy that he was going to cross party lines and vote for Woodrow Wilson. Alarmed by these trends, Hay was far more audacious than most of the other Republican candidates in the West. During his campaign for reëlection he readily criticized federal resource policy even though doing so involved an attack on the Republican administration. Feeling as he did, Hay did not ask for or receive an endorsement from the White House. Taft had been warned that any changes in Interior policy might harm the party's chances in the West. Evidently deciding that the subject should be passed over lightly, he merely issued a public letter in defense of Fisher's administration. In election that November, Hay's views on many other subjects proved to be unpopular. His defeat by a Democrat was described as the worst suffered by any candidate on national issues that year. He could not have suffered more, even if Taft had retained Ballinger.[32]

DILEMMA OF THE WESTERN PROGRESSIVES

There were some conservationists in the Republican party who regretted the growth of the progressive faction, but most of them waited expectantly for the "peal from [Roosevelt's] bugle." Pardee thought that Pinchot would do well in "the Fat Man's place," and favored the possibility of a La Follette–Pinchot ticket. The former Chief Forester could have viewed the increasing support of federal conservation as the basis for personal political strength. Indeed, his critics acknowledged that connection when they accused him of using the issue "to gain political notoriety" and office when Roosevelt was reëlected. Since 1910, he had helped bring about a substantial change in public opinion, helped shape much of the resource legislation passed by Congress, and had been prominent in the revolt of the progressives. In July, 1912, he served as one of the midwives at the birth of the new Progressive party, and he loomed large behind the figure of its presidential nominee, Theodore Roosevelt. Pinchot wrote an uncompromising statement for the party's platform, one which not only demanded an extension of conservation policies, but also put them into the context of the prevention of waste in industrial and human resources. Unlike the authors of the planks in the platforms of the other two parties, he paid not the slightest attention to the demand for modifications of use regulations and reserve boundaries. As a result, Western observers were convinced that if Roosevelt returned to the White House the settler's chance of obtaining greater access to the public domain would vanish. "Pinchotic Progressivism" appeared to them to exceed even the Socialists' demand for government ownership. What the critics considered more calamitous was the potential presence of Pinchot, the "Roosevelt evil genius," who was "croaking for revenge." Newspaper editorials in every part of the West repeatedly reminded readers of the terrible consequences of that friendship. The *Coconino Sun* could not believe that Arizona stockmen would support Roosevelt and his "conservationist compadre." After experiencing years of "his special brand of conserving," the idea of Pinchot as Secretary of Agriculture was not appealing to them. In Cheyenne, the *Wyoming Tribune* conjured up a frightening vision of him in that post, wielding "absolute control over the forestry bureau and the tying up of public land." The issue was clear and simple: "Every Wyoming vote for the Bull Moose ticket means a vote for the return to power of Pinchot and Garfield. . . . Do you want them?"[33]

Pinchot's presence in Progressive councils proved to be a substantial problem for the party's organizers in the West. In those states where conservation and progressivism were already strong, as in California, he was a positive asset to the cause. But he was a formidable handicap for the new party in the states which were still hostile to both conservation and progressivism. In Wyoming, for example, Progressive Robert D. Carey confessed that he was very reluctant to "drag Pinchot into the fight" for local support. As he told editor C. Watt Brandon, Roosevelt's appeal in the state was considerably weakened by Pinchot's unpopularity there. When Brandon made further inquiries among prominent citizens to learn how deep that feeling went, he was dismayed to find that, in many instances, the only real objection to Roosevelt's candidacy was his friendship with Pinchot. The Progressives' opponents eagerly exploited the possibility of a Cabinet post—in this case, that of Secretary of the Interior. In near-by Montana, the Great Falls *Leader* also issued a dark warning: "The West knows what Pinchotism is . . . Homesteaders, settlers, stockmen and western businessmen all dodge at the name of Pinchot. But [he] will be the next Secretary of the Interior if . . . Roosevelt is elected." Even the regular Republicans, overwhelmed in the elections that November, took a last crumb of comfort from the thought that Pinchot's candidacy for a Cabinet place was finally eliminated. Roosevelt had, in fact, promised his friend a portfolio—not the one his critics feared, but that of Secretary of State. The apprehension in the West was, however, not unrealistic. As chief counselor to the President, Pinchot would certainly have influenced other Cabinet appointments, as well as the policies made by the Departments of the Interior and of Agriculture.[34]

Apart from personalities, the issue of conservation proved to be a mixed blessing for candidates in the West. Even the Progressives approached the subject warily. In Montana, for example, aware that both the Republican and Democratic state conventions had earlier endorsed state control, they were satisfied with including conservation in the general demand for greater governmental responsibility for the public interest. When the Progressive Republican League held their convention in Billings, they adopted a resolution which made no reference to Roose-

velt or Pinchot, and merely endorsed federal administration of resources until such time as the state government was returned to the
control of the people. The situation was further complicated by the fact
that many political leaders in the West who considered themselves progressives were outstanding critics of federal policy. Senator Borah, of
Idaho, stood with the Insurgents to fight for tariff revision and reci-
procity, but he had no use for the conservationists in the new third
party. Speaking from the floor of the Senate, he warned all Western
candidates for office that they would have to satisfy the people by showing they had "both the purpose and the courage to stand against these
unreasonable and impractical theories which would send that region
with its imprisoned wealth back to the owls and the bats." In New
Mexico, Senator Fall was an admirer of Roosevelt, but he could not
agree with the Progressives' interpretation of resource administration.
Although he disliked Taft's Mexican policy, he decided not to upset
patronage privileges by severing his connection with the administration. Divided loyalties thus forced him to take a passive role in the
campaigns of 1912. His fellow New Mexican, former Governor Hagerman, however, brought the subject of Roosevelt's land policies into the
local political arena, perhaps in order to retaliate against the man who
had removed him from office in 1907. Pinchot asked his friend and
Hagerman's successor, George Curry, to answer these attacks in
speeches throughout the state, but the issue seems to have had no effect
on the handful of votes which the Progressives received there.[35]

The problems encountered by Western candidates who did uphold
conservation in their campaigns were exemplified by contests in Oregon
and Colorado. In Oregon, Jonathan Bourne was running for reëlection
to the Senate. When other Republicans of the Pacific Coast states were
taking a stand against the Taft administration at the height of the
Ballinger controversy, Bourne had retained his friendship with the
President. Not until September, 1910, did he endorse Roosevelt's criticism of his successor. Although he thereafter helped organize the National Progressive Republican League, Bourne was unable to convince
colleagues like Pinchot that he was trustworthy. Once a Populist, then
a Silver Republican, he was ready to change again without disturbing
his personal convictions. In view of the fact that alleged moral irregularities had made him increasingly unpopular during the preceding
year, his decision to board the Progressive wagon may have been made
out of desperation. Thereafter he began to study conservation publicity
for campaign speeches, but he seems never to have changed his private
doubts about federal control. The literature issued on his behalf before

the elections emphasized instead his past efforts in getting lands opened
to settlement and having national forest boundaries altered to suit local
demands. Newspapers critical of conservation, such as the *Oregonian,*
remained unimpressed by all of these gestures. When Bourne refused
to abandon the Republican party label, another opportunist ran against
him as a Progressive. With the support of the traditionally Republican
Oregonian, this opponent made political capital of Bourne's Eastern
interests and high-tariff sympathies. Bourne's disguise as a progressive
Republican failed to convince the voters of his state, but at the same
time Congressman Abraham Lafferty, an advocate of state control, was
reëlected to the House as a Progressive. A similar example of the un-
predictable effectiveness of these two subjects occurred in Washington.
Once again, Representative Humphrey displayed a fine sensitivity to
opportunity, as he had done two years before. Evidently disappointed
by Taft's failure to give him a judgeship, and aware of the unpopularity
of the conservative Republicans, he proclaimed himself a Progressive
and reissued Roosevelt's 1910 endorsement. True Progressives in the
state warned Pinchot that Humphrey privately opposed everything
their party stood for. In March, 1911, the congressman visited Roosevelt at Oyster Bay, but this gesture was not followed by another endorsement. Although the party's national committee refused to support
him, Humphrey nevertheless rode the strong Progressive wave to another victory.[36]

The contest in Colorado was, in comparison, less complex, but it well
illustrated the problems encountered by Progressives in an area where
political and conservation sentiment was traditionally hostile. Authentic Roosevelt Progressives had founded the party's organization in the
state, and many of them were old friends of Pinchot as well. In the
summer of 1912 they selected Edward P. Costigan as their candidate
for governor. Just as Poindexter had done in 1910, Costigan embodied
the connection between the issues of conservation and progressivism in
the West. Years before, he had shared the prevailing irritation over
Forest Service procedures, but his political interests subsequently
brought him into association with local conservationists. Although his
own doubts were transformed into understanding of the federal policy,
he realized as the campaign got under way that his was decidedly a
minority view. Colorado, he observed, was "filled with enemies of the
movement." The substance of a letter shown to him by one of his staff
precisely indicated the embittered opinion that prevailed. The state's
greatest need, the writer insisted, was more settlers on the public domain

and not a "system of espionage that would give Russia a pointer for her secret police." In spite of "Teddy's blowing," the writer added, all that the former President had ever accomplished was the passage of the Pure Food Act—"They have the same goods, only labels are changed"— and he had "about ruined the small stockman of Colorado when he made the public lands Federal Forests." The West had had enough of "Rooseveltism" and "Pinchotism," the letter concluded, "No more for yours truly." The newspapers of Denver, whether Republican or Democrat, echoed such sentiments repeatedly during the campaign months. If the people would support Taft, one claimed, there would be "Neither Roosevelt Nor 'Pinchotism' For Free Colorado." The implacable *Rocky Mountain News* almost surpassed its early record for anti-conservation polemics while advocating the election of Elias Ammons as governor and Shafroth as senator and the reëlection of Congressman Taylor.

Costigan's principal opponent was Democrat Ammons, the confirmed critic of the Forest Service and adviser to the Shafroth campaign for state control. When the two candidates met in public debate, in October, the occasion aroused as much local interest as had the exchange between Ammons and Pinchot three years before. Because of the way in which both antagonists symbolized the opposing views of conservation in the West, the encounter took on an almost epic quality. When it was over, voters of every political persuasion decided that the Democrat had the more impressive arguments. Perhaps the arguments seemed more impressive because they had been heard for so long in the state. Progessives nevertheless continued to believe that Costigan could win the election. Their candidate immediately suggested that the debates be expanded into a full series, but Ammons declined, ostensibly out of respect for Roosevelt, who then lay wounded by a would-be assassin. Whatever the real reason for this refusal, he left the field at a most advantageous juncture. Pinchot offered personal assistance to the Progressives but without effect. In November, Ammons was elected governor by twice as many votes as Costigan received. That victory stunningly demonstrated the fact that, in spite of the encouraging results of 1910, the conservation issue could not bring about political miracles.[87]

That same reality was the source of great disappointment to Theodore Roosevelt. The Progressives had won only California and Washington in the West—states where conservation and reform were already popular. Although the party was a strong second in several parts of the Northwest, it could not match the appeal of the Democrats in the Rocky Mountain states. Roosevelt was particularly upset by the way in which candidates who opposed his policies or straddled the conservation issue came out ahead of those who supported his policies and upheld federal conservation. The results seemed to indicate to him that most of the American people did not appreciate the difference between state and national administration of resources.[38] That observation seemed to be the lament of a proud parent whose favorite child had failed him in time of greatest need.

Chapter VIII

THE DEMOCRATS' OPPORTUNITY

The Beneficiaries of 1912

AFTER Theodore Roosevelt left the White House, in 1909, some of the members of his party feared that the Democrats would make effective political capital of the controversies over federal conservation. During the months that followed, Republican candidates in the Western states found that they could not ignore the Ballinger affair. The election results of 1910 provided additional warning that they could not profit by criticizing resource policy, either. Thereafter, the inconsistent and ineffectual actions of Taft deepened their despair. As the epic contest of 1912 loomed, these Republicans were convinced that their adversaries would successfully attract westerners of both parties with promises of some change in the Pinchot-Roosevelt policy.[1]

Because many prominent Democrats in the West had long been in the vanguard of the critics' campaign against federal conservation, it seemed logical that they would take a bold stand on the issue. By the summer of election year, however, the party was dominated by spokesmen who presented themselves as authentic progressives and promised programs which would avoid the extremes represented by Roosevelt and Taft. Western Democrats seemed willing to support such an appeal because of its obvious usefulness. Some of those who were opponents of conservation recognized the political wisdom of a comprehensive stand. When the party's national convention met in Baltimore, Governor Shafroth of Colorado submitted a draft statement for the public lands plank of the platform, one which he hoped would "appeal to the west without frightening the east." The platform committee evidently did not find his suggestion tactful enough, perhaps because it advocated cession of the public domain to the states. Instead, they adopted a paragraph drafted by Thomas J. Walsh, a candidate for the Senate from Montana. Although this included the well-worn objection to keeping nonforested lands in the national forests, it made no reference to state control. The plank also recognized the need for additional conservation legislation and for the adjustment of the boundaries of federal reserves—both phrases ambiguous enough to attract support from critics and conservationists. Even Senator Fall, of New Mexico, a Republican, grudgingly admitted that the statement would give the Democrats great strength in the West during the campaign.[2]

The party's candidates in the region generally recognized that the

few voters who were actively interested in the subject—either as supporters of federal policy or as advocates of state control—might not
be satisfied by the Republicans or the Progressives. Instead, the idea
of a new trusteeship might seem to be a simple and effective solution.
It was just such a promise that Democratic organs made whenever they
referred to the issue. The *Nevada State Journal,* for example, asserted:

> The cry of the voice of the west has been heard in the wilderness long enough.
> Colonel Roosevelt heard it and placed a bureaucrat with a brand new ax to make
> kindergarten rules on conservation. Mr. Taft heard it and gave to an agent of the
> corporate interests practical sovereignty over a vast empire. The democrats have
> heard it and have brought to light many crying abuses; have passed much bene-
> ficial legislation, and now are entitled to take up as a trust those duties so flagrantly
> neglected and abused by past administrations.

Such an appeal was naturally most effective in those areas where opposition was strongest to both "Pinchotism" and "Ballingerism." In
Colorado, antipathies toward federal control and the party that had
promulgated the policy were exploited by Democratic candidates. Calling themselves "progressives," both Shafroth and Ammons were elected
to high offices after months of slashing attacks on government land and
resource administration, and on the Forest Service particularly. In
other Western states, adherents of the older, conservative traditions of
the party found the progressive reform movement, especially conservation, wholly distasteful. Former Senator William A. Clark, of Montana,
for example, half apologized to Ballinger over the way in which some
Democrats were evidently "hypnotized" by Pinchot, the "pipe
dreamer."[3]

For all concerned, the surest guarantee on the subject of future
Democratic resource policy was the party's presidential nominee,
Woodrow Wilson. His bold and successful administration as governor
of New Jersey had earned him the attention of progressives everywhere.
One of these, Gifford Pinchot, called on him in June, 1911, and was
elated to learn that Wilson favored the retention of federal control. A
year later, however, conservationists were disturbed by the statements
of Wilson, the nominee. In his formal acceptance speech, the candidate
briefly referred to the issue by saying: "Reservation is not the whole of
Conservation. The development of great states must not be stayed indefinitely to await a policy by which our forests and water power can
prudently be made use of." The speaker seemed to intend to show that
he sympathized with the complaints of westerners, but, in view of the
fact that neither of the conditions he mentioned actually existed, the
pronouncement was meaningless rhetoric. In the course of the campaign

of 1912 Wilson was primarily occupied with the outstanding issues of tariffs and trusts, and he rarely mentioned conservation. Whenever he did, his remarks were brief, vague, or merely a point of departure for a discourse on government. In Colorado Springs, for example, he referred to the state fear of federal power and the federal government's equal concern lest the public domain be ruined by the spoilers. Both dangers, he pointed out, clearly argued for greater mutual trust and disinterestedness, and for full coöperation between state and federal agencies.[4]

Wilson's running mate, Thomas Marshall, of Indiana, provoked more definite assumptions about the direction which a future Democratic administration would take. A party regular who was conservative enough to satisfy some of the Republican Old Guard, Marshall knew nothing about conservation, but well knew what his audiences wanted to hear. Speaking in Washington State, for example, he made an outright appeal for state control of lands and water power. Throughout the region, Democratic candidates could take their cue from Marshall's provincialisms or Wilson's ambiguities. Conservationists might be worried by the conflicting statements, but many other voters in the West were sufficiently impressed by Wilson's reform zeal to believe that he would, as President, correct abuses in public land administration and expand federal resource policy. Generally, Western Democrats could encompass many shades of opinion on the issue because they were not haunted by the specters of Pinchot or Ballinger. Such a negative appeal doubtless contributed to the victory of the party in the eight states which it won in the West.[5]

ANOTHER WESTERNER IN THE INTERIOR DEPARTMENT

Western interest in the post of Secretary of the Interior, already sharpened by the controversial tenures of Hitchcock, Garfield, Ballinger, and Fisher, was now transformed into new hope by the Democratic triumph. In anticipation, the *Oregonian* spoke for those who were "tired of impractical theories and bureaucratic methods," and demanded the appointment of a man from the West who would carry out the "sane" land and resource planks of the Democratic platform. In making such a choice, the newspaper observed, Wilson would have the opportunity of drawing a definite line between "real" conservation and the "theoretical" variety. During the months after the election, westerners endorsed more than the usual number of favorite sons for the post, but few of them had substantial support throughout the region or beyond. In Colorado, state party leaders recommended Alva

Adams, a former governor with a clouded record who had just been defeated in the primaries as a candidate for the Senate. Shafroth, who won the seat, and Ammons, the new governor, supported him not only because he shared their views, but also to console him for being rejected by the voters. The suggestion alarmed Dodge, of the Colorado Springs *Gazette*. Adams, he told his friend Pinchot, would be "worse than Ballinger" and would set federal conservation back ten years if appointed. The recommendation of the Colorado Democrats was further marred by the fact that they had not favored Wilson's nomination at Baltimore. In the same class as Adams were Governors James H. Hawley of Idaho and John E. Osbourne of Wyoming. Editors and businessmen of Idaho praised Hawley as a man who would right past wrongs and give the West a chance to develop. Osbourne, a Bryan Democrat who had helped swing his state's delegation to Wilson, would allegedly remove the grip of a "fantastic, bureaucratic, imperialistic land administration" that had suppressed the region for a decade.[6]

Western conservationists also had their favorites for the Interior post. Senator Newlands sought the appointment of a "sane" reformer, a "progressive without wheels in his head," and thought that Clay Tallman of Nevada would be an excellent choice. As a member and presiding officer of the state senate from 1909 to 1911, Tallman had directly assisted in the adoption of a primary elections law, a pure food act, and a mine inspection bill. He ran for the national House of Representatives in 1912, but lost the contest by seventy votes in a four-way race. Three Oregonians were mentioned for the appointment, all of them leaders of state and federal conservation. One, Senator Chamberlain, was needed by the new administration in his legislative capacity; another, Governor West, could not be chosen, according to the *Oregonian*, because his strong views were not in accord with those of influential Democrats from the West. Seemingly, only Joseph N. Teal could depend upon the support of conservationists and Democrats within his state and beyond. Although Teal was not a politician, his experience and success in serving private and public resource interests and his role as organizer of the state Conservation Commission had won widespread respect. A similar reputation was held by Franklin K. Lane, of California, the favorite choice of the San Francisco *Call*. Before serving as a member of the Interstate Commerce Commission under both Roosevelt and Taft, he had been city attorney of San Francisco, and he was as well acquainted with problems of resource use as his onetime political opponent, George Pardee. The *Call* asserted that Lane was competent enough to hold any Cabinet post, but agreed with several other Western newspapers that he would most likely be offered the Interior portfolio.[7]

Thomas J. Walsh, who had shared his party's triumph by winning election to the Senate, was deeply concerned about the appointment. A moderate critic of federal conservation since the Public Lands Convention of 1907, he now hoped to persuade leading Western Democrats to combine their influence so that the selection would not be left to mere chance. His letters to Newlands and others set forth in precise terms just what kind of a man he thought the new Secretary should be. The Department needed a "live western man" who would understand the laws he administered because of his familiarity with the conditions which had prompted their creation. Such a man must also be "imbued with the democratic spirit and attached to the principle of local self government." Because of the controversies of the past, however, the candidate had to be one against whom there could be made "no just imputation ... such as drove Ballinger from the Taft household." Walsh clearly emphasized the political importance of the appointment by warning that the West expected the Democrats to inaugurate a new land use policy and remove the tinge of scandal from the Reclamation Service specifically. The future of the party, he implied, depended upon the liberal legislation passed by the new Congress and upon the actions of the Interior Department. The senator-elect soon decided that the man who would satisfy all of these considerations was Governor Edwin Norris of Montana. One of the first Western chief executives to take a personal interest in correcting existing land use laws, Norris had secured the passage of measures regulating timber and water resources in Montana, and he soon became one of the leading advocates of state control of conservation policy. As a prominent Democratic governor, he had met Wilson and supported him even before the Baltimore convention, but had not taken an active part in the campaign. Because he was publicly noncommittal on the subject of a Cabinet position, Norris evidently relied upon Walsh's efforts to advance his candidacy.[8]

Eastern conservationists were equally interested in the selection of a new Interior Secretary. Although Pinchot's influence with the incoming administration was slight, he was naturally concerned about the future policies of the Department. The rumor that Wilson was attentive to the demand for a westerner caused him to look over the list of names being mentioned by the press. Out of all of them, only Teal, of Oregon, satisfied him as trustworthy and qualified. Teal, however, told him that he was personally not interested in the post and that he doubted whether his health was equal to the burdens of present tasks, not to mention the enormous duties of government office. Pinchot nevertheless refused to alter his conclusion. In an effort to weaken the appeal of the other leading contender, Norris, he compiled a lengthy argument and presented it to Wilson through Louis Brandeis and Walter Hines Page, two old friends who were now advisers to the President-elect. The indictment claimed that the Montanan's accomplishments in securing resource legislation were fully offset by his prominence in the movement for state control. According to Pinchot, Norris's true attitude was represented by the resolution opposing federal conservation which he had sponsored at the St. Paul congress. Other allegations, connecting the governor with the Anaconda copper trust, were repeated by Pinchot's supporters and printed in Eastern newspapers. The object of these attacks remained silent in public. Privately, he wrote several letters that did not increase the likelihood of his appointment. One of them asked Governor Hay to recommend him to Wilson. In another, he wrote to the President-elect to deny the charge that he was a tool of the corporate interests that dominated his state. Those who were vilifying him, Norris asserted, were actually trying to destroy the candidacy of all westerners. If the administration would be embarrassed by his presence, he would not accept the Cabinet post. Shortly thereafter, Newlands and Kent, of California, assured Pinchot that the danger of Norris' selection was rapidly disappearing. Indeed, the Montanan's letter to Wilson might by itself have given sufficient reason for removing his name from further consideration. Pinchot then wrote to Teal and confided: "It looks to me as if a certain question [is] going to be put up to you and when it is, there must be but one answer." Just to make sure that the choice would be to his liking, however, he suggested to Brandeis that Congressman Kent was the only other desirable westerner for the post.[9]

The ultimate selection of the Secretary of the Interior was determined neither by the West's demands nor by the efforts of Pinchot. Although Wilson had assured Walsh that he was impressed by the arguments in favor of a Western appointee, his private opinions were unknown even to his party advisers. In reality, he was not at all convinced of the desirability of a westerner as Secretary of the Interior, particularly one from a Mountain state. In that respect he felt just as Roosevelt had, believing that a man from such a background would be subject to many local pressures. In addition, he was acutely conscious of the political danger involved. As Pinchot had reminded Brandeis, the new administration must not be made a target for "the same troubles which Ballinger brought on Taft," troubles which could harm both the party and the country. Wilson allegedly shared Kent's opinion that if Taft had selected Fisher first, instead of Ballinger, he would have been reëlected in 1912. William Jennings Bryan, the Secretary of State designate and virtual leader of a large segment of the Democratic party, similarly questioned the desirability of a westerner, particularly one from the Pacific Coast states, the home of Ballinger and of Mitchell of the timberland frauds. Disturbed by certain unidentified rumors about Teal, he decided that Norris at least was competent, but he made no written recommendation. Wilson eventually expressed his personal choice by asking a close friend, Newton D. Baker, of Ohio, to take the Interior Department. When Baker declined the offer, the President-elect's personal interest was discharged and he left the matter to Edward M. House, of Texas, his chief adviser on Cabinet appointments.[10]

Colonel House was not primarily interested in satisfying the claims of any particular region for a specific post. His purpose in selecting candidates was to bring about the best possible geographic distribution for maximum political strength. Some indication of his view of the West's demands was the fact that he originally considered Walter Hines Page, of North Carolina, for either the Interior or the Agriculture office. Later, while traveling across the country to consult party leaders on appointments and legislative plans, he corresponded with Franklin K. Lane, of California, a personal friend. When he was asked to recommend a good man for the Interior Department, Lane replied that the election contribution of the Pacific Coast states substantiated their claim to that place, and went on to praise the qualifications of Teal and James D. Phelan, the former mayor of San Francisco. Lane did not consider himself a candidate, however, because, like Ballinger before him, he felt that his personal finances could not bear the expense of Cabinet life. He preferred to remain with the Interstate Commerce Commission, where he could deal with the problems he had handled so successfully during the preceding years. A man of a genial and orderly nature, Lane was decidedly repelled by the prospect of controversy and chaos associated with the Interior Department. Moreover, he had never met Wilson, and had even doubted whether he would carry the West during the election. The Californian answered the hopes of his friends with the confession that he was "not at all enamoured of the honor of a Cabinet place," but was willing to let the matter "rest on the knees of the gods." Colonel House was aware of Lane's reluctance, but he concluded that his friend's ability, prominence, and place of residence would readily combine to satisfy political, popular, and geographic considerations. After Baker's declination, he therefore recommended the appointment of Lane. In the middle of February, 1913, Wilson overrode Lane's reticence in much the same way as Taft had Ballin-

ger's—by appealing to his desire to serve the administration. Like
Ballinger, Lane found that his initial feeling of doubt and depression
turned to hopeful determination after he received the President's
cordial greeting on the day before the inauguration.[11]

Had the Wilson men acted with the sole purpose of satisfying the
West, the response to Lane's appointment would have been a tribute to
their wisdom. Among the flood of letters of praise sent to the President
and his Secretary of the Interior was one from Teal, who thought no
better choice could have been made; there was also a note of congratulations from Roosevelt. Editorial comments in the Western press included
the prediction that Lane would become "one of the touchstones of the
Wilson administration" and a Secretary whose actions would avoid the
"tight" policies of Garfield and Fisher. Critics of federal conservation
were similarly confident. The *Post-Intelligencer,* for example, certified
that Lane was not inoculated with the "Pinchot microbe." That particular organism himself called on the new Secretary soon after the
inauguration and was pleased with what he saw; privately, however, he
still regretted that Teal did not get the post. Seemingly, only Norris's
supporters were dejected by the decision, especially since they did not
learn that the governor was out of the running until the last moment.
Generally, westerners hailed the appointment of Lane as a sign that the
Wilson administration recognized their long-time demand. In their
elated mood, they reasoned from external evidence. The actual circumstances of the choice indicated that the traditions of Cabinet-making
had not been altered by the Ballinger affair or by the long campaign
for modification of federal resource policy. Those controversies, certainly, had made the Democrats more wary and helped bring about the
selection of a candidate who was not opposed by conservationists or their
critics. Beyond these considerations, however, the decision was again
made by the President-elect and his immediate advisers, men who were
concerned more with political acceptability than with specific views
about resource policy.[12]

Franklin Lane's success during his first year in office to a great extent
accounted for the continuation of a vigorous conservation policy without the political complications of the past. Handsome, warmhearted,
and imaginative, he seemed to be a welcome contrast to the austerity
and reticence of his two immediate predecessors. The new Secretary
immediately took up the continuing problem of reorganization, begun
by Garfield and Ballinger. Particularly impressed by the latter's unfortunate experiences with his staff, Lane was anxious to choose co-
workers whose abilities would be obvious to men of every political

persuasion. He asked Teal to serve as his Assistant Secretary, but the Oregonian declined the offer in order to serve the cause of conservation in the West. (Pinchot, still in a "sour grapes" mood, thought the post too small for Teal's talents.) Andrew A. Jones, of New Mexico, a Progressive and friend of former Governor Curry, then accepted the place. Clay Tallman, of Nevada, became Commissioner of Public Lands. The establishment of greater intradepartmental coöperation was a second paramount purpose in the Secretary's plans. Reviving the idea of Roosevelt's Public Land Commission, he formed a "Land Cabinet" consisting of the Assistant Secretary, the Land Commissioner, and the Director of the Geological Survey. Later, the same idea was applied to reclamation policy, but Lane saw to it that Director Newell did not dominate the group. A year afterward, that old foe of Ballinger resigned from the Department, but no cry of alarm was raised by the Pinchot men. Lane's initial actions were characteristically tactful and pleasing to both westerners and conservationists. Shortly after assuming office he secured legislation for a Bureau of National Parks, for example. His sense of timing in that case was in significant contrast to Ballinger's initial procedures.[13]

After setting the Department in order, the new Secretary embarked on an inspection trip through the West during the summer of 1913. Aware of local dissatisfaction with reclamation projects, he sent a close friend from his staff over the route he was to take, two weeks ahead of his own departure. This agent, who did not reveal his connection with the Department, was able to observe actual conditions and learn the opinions of many residents. Lane thereby avoided the blandishments and distortions of the vested interests who customarily monopolized the attention of federal officials. In several other ways, he devoted much of his own time and that of his staff to the task of overcoming the remainder of Western opposition to the Department's policies. When Governor Ammons of Colorado called another conference of Western governors at Salt Lake City, the Secretary promptly dispatched the chiefs of the field divisions in the region to take part in the discussions. The presence of these men strengthened the efforts of Governor West of Oregon in his stand against an endorsement of state control. When Ammons also opened the Third Public Lands Convention, at Denver, Lane was in the midst of his summer tour. After obtaining President Wilson's personal approval, the Secretary went to the meeting himself and helped turn it into an expression of confidence in the administration's land-use policies. The following year, he wisely undercut this source of controversy by sponsoring the Denver meeting.

Although some sputterings were heard there, few remarks were directed against the agents of the Interior Department.[14]

During his first year in office, Lane thus made innovations in Department procedures, matured plans for legislation, and secured the cooperation of men of all views on conservation. In doing these things he was not subjected to close Presidential supervision, as Ballinger had been. The full measure of his compromise between the planners of federal programs and the users of resources was not apparent until 1915, at which time he was criticized by Pinchot and other conservationists. Until then, however, he was able to gain their confidence by continually favoring their interpretation of federal interests in crucial issues, such as the confirmation of the Hetch Hetchy grant in December, 1913. The crusaders occasionally tried to cast suspicion upon members of his staff, but Lane answered these criticisms himself and in one instance remarked pointedly that a difference in viewpoint did not mean that a man was dishonest. Taft had asserted that same idea—in vain—four years before.[15]

Like his chief, Lane was willing to retain federal authority wherever there seemed to be danger of monopoly by unregulated private enterprise. He therefore continued Garfield's broad interpretation of the Department's jurisdiction. But he was especially anxious to allay the West's doubts and opposition toward federal actions. His first annual report noted that the basic source of discontent was the inadequate administrative machinery which had been used in the past:

We have called a halt on methods of spoilation which existed, ... but we have failed to substitute methods, sane, healthful, and progressive, by which the normal enterprise of an ambitious people can make full use of their own resources. We abruptly closed opportunities to the monopolist, but did not open them to the developer.

In order to overcome this impediment, the Secretary meant to encourage greater state participation in federal plans and proceedings. The report noted several examples of cordial relations between state agencies and federal reclamation projects in the Pacific Northwest and suggested the leasing of other resources in the region. Any state in the West, Lane argued, would "well appreciate the efforts of the Nation when it makes sacrifice itself, and nothing could more induce the success of the Nation's effort than to have some local check and interest." With federal policy affirmed by his own administration, greater state participation was not only encouraged, but was deemed positively desirable.[16]

For the first time since Ballinger became Secretary, the political and economic spokesmen of the West—no matter what their views on conservation—were satisfied with the administration of the Interior Department. With the help of his many friends in both parties, Lane quickly secured the respect of some of the principal critics of past policy: Democrat Ammons and the Colorado delegation in Congress, and Republican Senators Borah and Fall. He consulted these men on specific problems, explained his aims in personal correspondence and official publicity, and thus practiced from the first the effective public relations which Ballinger never fully utilized. The satisfactory course of his tenure was attested to by every faction; even Senator Jones, of Washington, the Republican Old Guard's reliable critic of conservation, was pleased with the contrast to Fisher. Perhaps the most convincing evidence of Lane's initial success was the description of him by lobbyist A. N. Brown: "Any man who can get both the Ballinger and the Pinchot forces to approve [of] him is a smooth individual."[17]

THE STORM SUBSIDES

By the end of 1913 conservation policy was no longer a political issue in the West. After reaching a peak of intensity during the Ballinger-Pinchot controversy, the subject had been exhausted by years of publicity and campaigns. Criticism still flashed sporadically, sparked by private persons and commercial organizations. An Idaho legislator urged the adoption of a memorial which would condemn the Forest Service as incompetent, inefficient, and dishonest. A Home Industry League in California issued a similar denunciation. Edward H. Thomas, J. L. Wilson's successor as editor of the Seattle *Post-Intelligencer*, arraigned federal resource policy in the columns of his newspaper and in *Pearson's Magazine*. Playing upon existing public antipathy toward monopolies, Thomas reversed the cry of the crusaders and described conservation as the real source of entrenched wealth and stifler of healthy competition. The article aroused Pinchot to write a personal reply in the same magazine. In it, he claimed that the editor had misrepresented Western opinion. The fact that the people of the West had elected such men as Poindexter, with conservation as the specific issue, was proof that they recognized the policy as beneficial. This exchange of views might have received national notice three years before; by now the arguments were too familiar to provoke further response.[18]

The accession of Elias Ammons as governor of Colorado accounted for the continuation of criticism from that state. In his inaugural address of January, 1913, he repeated Shafroth's performance of four years before: preservation without development was deplored, the dangers of monopoly or resource exhaustion were denied, and the desirability of state control was proclaimed. In company with his predecessor, now senator-elect, Ammons appeared before the Denver Chamber of Commerce the next day and repeated these clichés. Then with the omnipresent assistance of J. Arthur Eddy and D. C. Beaman he launched another publicity campaign. The Democratic state legislature responded favorably, but some members of the executive branch were unwilling to support the attack on conservation. Stone, of the Conservation Commission, by now an experienced warrior in the battle for resources, wrote to urge the governor that federal control was the only effective way to guard natural wealth. Ammons returned a strongly worded reply which argued that, from his own experiences as a stockman, he knew the Forest Service failed to protect the state's forests and mining industries. Denouncing Stone's commission as a tool of federal agencies, he threatened to organize another group to combat its influence in the state. The conservationists of Colorado took the governor's blusterings seriously. In order to answer his attacks, Clarence Dodge and Edward Costigan quickly initiated an educational campaign, distributed broadsides defending the work of the Forest Service, and obtained reprints of articles written by Pinchot and Overton Price for distribution to newspapers throughout the state. Many private citizens and some state legislators were convinced by these articles that Ammons' charges were false. The governor himself abandoned his campaign before the end of the year, evidently satisfied by having gained the attention of Secretary Lane and the promise of greater state participation in federal policy.[19]

It was inevitable that conservation would continue to be discussed in the chambers and committee rooms of the new Democratic Congress. During the election campaign of 1912 the behavior of several candidates had convinced Pinchot that an all-out fight would be made against the policy when the session began. He therefore turned down an invitation from Stewart Edward White to go to Africa and remained in the capital to lead the battle against what he called the "States Right Abomination." Although he was assured by Teal that Wilson was on the "right side" of the question, Pinchot feared that the President might not be able to stand up against the pressures of men in his party who were hostile to federal resource regulation. To that Sixty-Third Congress came Senators Shafroth and Thomas, of Colorado, the former wielding substantial influence upon the legislation considered that year. There were, however, several key Democrats in the Senate who had even greater influence, among them Newlands and Chamberlain. Moreover, the President had already consulted two Progressives, Poindexter and

Kent, about desirable resource legislation. On the other hand, the old phalanx of Republican critics had been reduced to a few impotent orators. Heyburn and Carter were dead; Smoot no longer exercised the power he had enjoyed under Republican majorities. Fall occasionally interjected well-worn phrases into the debates, but most of his attention during these months was concentrated upon the plight of American investors in revolutionary Mexico.[20]

In spite of the presence of several critics of conservation in the new Congress, the only organized attack on the policy was planned by an outsider: lobbyist A. N. Brown. With the facility of a veteran he composed "anti-Pinchot stuff" which he "fed" to such members as Representative Humphrey, of Washington, who, Brown observed smugly, "spouted it" from the floor of the House. He found another opportunity in the growing discontent among Democrats from the South over the boundaries of the newly created Appalachian National Forest. Some of them agreed with Brown that the power of the Forest Service was an impediment to the purchase of private tracts within the reserve. Senator Lee Overman, of North Carolina, had offered a resolution the previous July calling for an investigation of Forest Service activities, but it had not come to a vote. A similar motion by Humphrey was denounced in the new Congress by his fellow Washingtonian, Representative J. W. Bryan, who acidly noted the incompatibility of his colleague's anti-conservation views and alleged progressivism. Apart from Mondell and Taylor, the proposed investigation was ignored by the Democrats from the West.

Brown's intrigues were no match for the influence of Gifford Pinchot. Working through his many devoted supporters in the Congress and the executive branch, Pinchot saw to it that any bill deemed destructive to existing resource policy was blocked. After the Colorado delegation called on the President to obtain his official favor for the cession of national forests to the states, Wilson listened to Chief Forester Graves' defense of federal trusteeship and decided to continue the Pinchot tradition. Pinchot's influence was naturally far less than it had been during the Roosevelt years, but his intimate knowledge of Western problems and his opinions still commanded the attention of congressional committees and presidential advisers. His personal efforts alone were effective enough to elicit a complaint from former Senator Clark, of Montana, who wrote to Borah at the end of the year to say that there was no use in making further attempts to change federal policy "with that fellow Pinchot in control."[21]

The West's willingness to accept adjustment and compromise on the issue of conservation was also marked by a decline of interest in the alternative of state control. After a decade of obvious material results, no locality was ready to give up reclamation projects, watershed protection, fire control, or equitable regulation of land use in order to return to the chaos that existed before Roosevelt and Pinchot. The arguments which undermined the appeal of state control were succinctly summarized in a special report of the Oregon Conservation Commission in 1913. It pointed out that to continue the irresponsibility and waste of state administration was not only undesirable, but financially impossible. The enormous costs of maintaining the forests alone would amount to a large part of the state's total expenditures. Moreover, state-owned forests would not be subject to taxation, whereas revenue received from federal use fees and repaid to the states exceeded the amount which could be brought in by existing taxes. The Commission agreed that the details of policy were the proper concern of the state, but it asked whether "this purely administrative question, or irritating rules or acts of too zealous subordinates," should furnish an excuse for "abandoning the public forests and turning over the heritage of all to enrich the few."[22] State control of resources may have been an administrative possibility, but it was economically impractical.

Specific resource problems continued to arise in the Western states, but they did not provoke widespread controversy, nor did they produce conventions and leagues comparable to those of the preceding period. The demand for state control was also made during the subsequent years. In two instances, that alternative was favored by Secretaries of the Interior from the West. Albert B. Fall's intentions were largely frustrated during his short term in office and were fully discredited by the Teapot Dome scandal after his resignation. Later, Secretary Ray Lyman Wilbur, from California, shared the Hoover administration's faith in greater state responsibility. He recommended the creation of a commission to study the possibility of transferring the remaining public domain to the states, but this scheme crumbled under the impact of the national economic crisis. Thereafter the public-land states were hopelessly divided on the issue of state administration of resources. A vigorous federal policy, such as that envisioned by the Roosevelt men, was upheld and expanded as an essential part of the New Deal.[23]

The struggles of these years of crusades and controversies were decisive. The cause of the conservationists was adopted by the nation because of the political abilities of a handful of men in the West and the East, men whose influence was enhanced by the events of the Progressive era. Their opponents, weakened by faulty ideas and ineffectual actions, were ultimately discredited. Those who were not silenced by the Ballinger affair were impressed by the economic realities of federal administration. Finally, many citizens who had been confused and angered by the alarms and excursions of a decade welcomed the promise of a new regime. The workings of politics thus removed the traditional obstacles of provincialism and partisanship. The desirability of federal conservation was no longer an issue.

NOTES

NOTES

CHAPTER I: TRIALS AND ERRORS

[1] *Congressional Record*, 54th Cong., 2nd sess., to 55th Cong., 1st sess. (Feb. 28 to June 8, 1897).

[2] *Ibid.*, 55th Cong., 1st sess. (May 5, 1897), 912–914. W. S. Stewart to W. W. Dixon, March 1, 1897, William S. Stewart Papers, Nevada State Historical Society.

[3] Portland *Oregonian*, April 4, 1897. Great Falls, Mont., *Leader*, March 7, 1897. *Argonaut* (San Francisco) 15 (May 17, 1897) 3. Salt Lake City, *Deseret Weekly*, April 10, 1897. J. Muir to R. U. Johnson, March 6, 1897, Robert Underwood Johnson Papers, Bancroft Library. Muir to T. P. Lukens, April 25, 1898, Theodore P. Lukens Papers, Henry E. Huntington Library.

[4] *Congressional Record*, 55th Cong., 1st Sess. (May 10, 1897), 986–987.

[5] A study of the influence of personal politics upon Interior Department policy in an earlier period is in Elmo R. Richardson and Alan W. Farley, *John Palmer Usher: Lincoln's Secretary of the Interior* (Lawrence, Kansas: University of Kansas Press, 1960).

[6] Finley Peter Dunne, *Mr. Dooley: In the Hearts of His Countrymen* (Boston, 1899), p. 147.

[7] J. Muir to R. U. Johnson, June 18, 1897, Johnson Papers.

[8] Among westerners considered for the Secretaryship of the Interior in an earlier period were Edward D. Baker, of Oregon, and Cornelius Cole, of California, during and after the Civil War: R. J. Stevens to C. Cole, Oct. 3, 1871, and Cole to O. Cole, April 30, 1875, Cornelius Cole Papers, University of California at Los Angeles, Library. John W. Noble, Benjamin Harrison's Secretary of the Interior, became interested in forest reservation after a holiday in the Rocky Mountains: Noble to R. U. Johnson, May 14, 1908, Johnson Papers.

[9] *Congressional Record*, 53rd Cong., 1st sess. (Oct. 12, 1893), 2431–2432, and 54th Cong., 1st sess. (Dec. 16, 1894), 755. E. A. Bowers to R. U. Johnson, Feb. 29, 1896, and C. D. Walcott to Johnson, Oct. 6, 1908, Johnson Papers. Lawrence Rakestraw, "A History of Forest Conservation in the Pacific Northwest, 1891–1913" (unpublished doctoral dissertation, University of Washington, 1955), pp. 82–83, 88, 169–170.

[10] Gifford Pinchot, *Breaking New Ground* (New York, 1947), pp. 162–165. A specific example is W. S. Stewart to B. Hermann, March 28, 1902, Stewart Papers.

[11] W. S. Duniway to President Chapman, Dec. 19, 1896, William P. Lord Papers, Oregon State Archives. J. Minto, draft of article, *c.* 1898, and draft of report to State Board of Horticulture, *c.* 1898, John Minto Papers, Oregon State Library. *Oregonian*, March 29, 1899. A full discussion of the Minto-Muir controversy is in Lawrence Rakestraw, "Sheep Grazing in the Cascade Range: John Minto *vs.* John Muir," *Pacific Historical Review*, Vol. 27, No. 4 (Nov., 1958), pp. 371–382.

[12] Laramie, Wyo., *Boomerang*, Jan. 4, 1899. *Congressional Record*, 55th Cong., 3d sess. (Feb. 13, 1899), 1781. Evanston, Wyo., *Wyoming Press*, March 17, 1900.

[13] T. Ryan to M. A. Otero, March 2; B. Hermann to Otero, July 10; and W. W. Miller to Otero, June 20, 1899, Miguel A. Otero Papers, New Mexico Historical Society.

[14] *Message of Frank Steunenberg, Governor of the State of Idaho, to the Fourth State Legislature* (Boise, 1899), p. 13. F. W. Hunt to H. Heitfeld, Jan. 31 and Feb. 7, 1901, Frank W. Hunt Papers, Idaho Historical Society.

[15] Paul W. Morrison, "The Establishment of the Forest Service within Roosevelt National Forest" (unpublished Master's thesis, University of Colorado, 1945), pp. 68, 70, 76, 78–81. *Official Proceedings . . . Twelfth Trans Mississippi Commercial Congress* (Cripple Creek, 1901), pp. 87, 148–149.

[16] Murray Morgan, *The Last Wilderness* (New York, 1955), p. 169. T. B. Catron

to P. Perea, Nov. 23, 1899, Thomas B. Catron Papers, University of New Mexico Library.

[17] E. S. Gosney, "The American Woolgrowers Association, 1898–1909," typescript, pp. 1–3, 56, copy in Arizona Pioneers Historical Society. Bert Haskett, "History of the Sheep Industry of Arizona," *Arizona Historical Review*, 7 (July, 1936), 37–38. Information furnished to me by L. F. Kneipp, ranger in the Arizona forest reserves at this time.

[18] Haskett, *op. cit.*, p. 38. *Session Laws of the Eleventh Legislative Assembly of ... Arizona* (Phoenix, 1899), p. 38. Gosney, *op. cit.*, pp. 5–7, 9–13, 20–22. Gosney to G. F. Kitt, Oct. 7, 1931, E. S. Gosney Papers, Arizona Pioneers Historical Society. A. F. Potter to G. Pinchot, July 5, 1939, Gifford Pinchot Papers, Library of Congress.

[19] J. J. Wagoner, "History of the Cattle Industry in Southern Arizona, 1540–1940," *Social Science Bulletin Number 20*, University of Arizona (April, 1952), p. 55. Mary E. Lauver, "A History of the Use and Management of the Forested Lands of Arizona, 1862–1936" (unpublished Master's thesis, University of Arizona, 1938). Phoenix *Arizona Gazette*, Jan. 23, 1901. Flagstaff, Ariz., *Coconino Sun*, Jan. 19 and Feb. 16, 1901. *Hearing ... San Francisco Mountain Forest Reserve ... 1901* (Washington, 1906), pp. 20–46. Gosney, *op. cit.*, p. 23. A. F. Potter to W. C. Barnes, Dec. 31, 1934, excerpt, Box 339, Pinchot Papers.

[20] *Biennial Report of the Forest Commission of the State of Colorado ... 1889 and 1890* (Denver, 1891), p. 17. W. J. Morrill, "Forestry," in J. D. Baker and L. R. Hafen (eds.), *History of Colorado* (Denver, 1927) II, 768. A full administrative history of California forests is given in C. Raymond Clar, *California Government and Forestry ...* (Sacramento, 1959). The work of the American Forestry Association in the West is described in Andrew D. Rodgers, *Bernard Eduard Fernow* (Princeton, N.J.: Princeton University Press, 1951).

[21] *Message of Governor Robert B. Smith to the Fifth Legislative Assembly of the State of Montana ...* (Helena, 1897), pp. 25–26. *Message of Governor J. H. McGraw to the Legislature of 1897* (Olympia, 1897), p. 7. *Third Biennial Report of the Board of State Land Commissioners ...* (Olympia, 1898), p. 68.

[22] H. M. Wells to B. E. Fernow, Oct. 17, 1896, Heber M. Wells Papers, Utah State Archives. *Deseret Weekly*, Jan. 16, 1897.

[23] Lewis R. Rist, "Historical Sketch of the White River National Forest," p. 155, typescript, C. W. A. project file, Colorado State Historical Society. *Memorial to the Senate and House of Representatives*, Seattle, Nov. 14, 1893, copy in Johnson Papers. Rakestraw, *op. cit.*, pp. 29–30, 39, 42. Information furnished to me by L. F. Kneipp. Albuquerque, N. M., *Citizen*, Sept. 19, 1895. See also George W. James, *Reclaiming the Arid West* (New York, 1917).

[24] C. D. Robinson to R. U. Johnson, Aug. 10, Sept. 19 and Oct. 14 and 27, 1890; J. M. Robinson to Johnson, Sept. 17, 1891; G. N. Mackenzie to J. W. Noble, Nov. 1, 1890, copy; J. M. Hutchings to Johnson, Sept. 14 and Oct. 4, 1890; H. Smith to Johnson, March 23, 1893; J. P. Irish to J. Muir, Sept. 1, 1890; Noble to Johnson, Feb. 27 and March 27, 1891, Johnson Papers. Irish to J. Wilson, March 24, 1910, John P. Irish Papers, Stanford University Library.

[25] San Francisco *Chronicle*, Dec. 1, 1891. "The Yosemite Valley," and "Parks and Reservations," *California Illustrated Magazine*, July, 1892, p. 329, and Nov., 1893, pp. 802–808. E. R. Scidmore to R. U. Johnson, Nov. 11, 1890, and J. W. Noble to Johnson, Sept. 27, 1892 and enclosures, copies, Johnson Papers.

[26] J. Muir to R. U. Johnson, Dec. 6, 1894, and C. D. Robinson to Johnson, June 20, 1893, Johnson Papers.

[27] J. Muir to R. U. Johnson, Jan. 23 and Feb. 3, 1893; Oct. 29 and Dec. 13, 1894; April 11, Sept. 12, and Dec. 13, 1895; and April 24, 1896, Johnson Papers. Muir to T. P. Lukens, Dec. 25, 1896, and Jan. 30 and Feb. 14, 1897, Lukens Papers.

[28] C. D. Robinson to R. U. Johnson, July 3, 1893; J. Muir to Johnson, March 14

and 29, 1893, July 9 and Aug. 3, 1898, and Jan. 23, 1899; C. N. Bliss to Johnson, May 11, 1898; C. H. Castle to Bliss, May 10, 1898, copy; G. N. Mackenzie to Bliss, May 16, 1898, copy; and to Johnson, May 12, and June 6 and 21, 1898, Johnson Papers.

²⁹ J. Muir to T. P. Lukens, July 4, 1899; G. H. Maxwell to Lukens, Nov. 11, 1899; A. Kinney to Lukens, Sept. 1, 1900, Lukens Papers. Los Angeles *Times*, April 20, 1900. G. Pinchot to Kinney, July 3, 1899, Abbott Kinney Papers, University of California at Los Angeles, Library. W. Kerckhoff to T. P. Gerson, July 21, 1899, and T. R. Bard to Kerckhoff, March 28, 1900, T. Perceval Gerson Papers, University of California at Los Angeles, Library. Forest and Water Association to B. Hermann, Feb. 6, 1900, copy, and Lukens to Kinney, Nov. 29, 1901, Lukens Papers.

³⁰ *The Forester* (Washington, D.C.) Feb., 1899, p. 39. San Francisco *Chronicle*, Aug. 5, 1899. *Should the Forests be Preserved?* (San Francisco, 1903). Pinchot, *op. cit.*, p. 170.

CHAPTER II: ROOSEVELT, PINCHOT, AND THEIR DISCIPLES

¹ T. Roosevelt to C. S. Rice, Dec. 25, 1892, and to J. Hay, Aug. 9, 1903, Theodore Roosevelt Papers, Library of Congress. Theodore Roosevelt, *An Autobiography* (New York, 1921). Andrew D. Rodgers, *Bernard Eduard Fernow* (Princeton, 1951), p. 105.

² Theodore Roosevelt, *Works* (New York, 1926) XV, 21, 53–54. Roosevelt to C. LaFarge, Feb. 9 and 16; to G. B. Grinnell, March 14; and to G. McAneny, June 5, 1900, Roosevelt Papers.

³ T. Roosevelt to H. Smith, April 7, 1894, to G. B. Grinnell, Aug. 24, 1897, and to National Irrigation Congress, Nov. 16, 1900, Roosevelt Papers.

⁴ Roosevelt, *Works*, XV, 102, 109, 114. Roosevelt, *An Autobiography*, pp. 384–388. A useful discussion of federal action in the field of resource use during the Roosevelt administration is E. Louise Peffer, *The Closing of the Public Domain* (Stanford, Calif.: Stanford University Press, 1951).

⁵ T. Roosevelt to W. A. Richards, May 21, 1903, to S. Low, Feb. 24, 1905, to C. W. Fulton, May 13, 1905, and to F. J. Heney, Feb. 8, 1906, Roosevelt Papers. Natason, comp., "The Diary of a Land Fraud" typescript, copy in Oregon State Library.

⁶ T. Roosevelt to J. Wilson, July 2, and to C. F. Lummis, Aug. 20, 1902, Roosevelt Papers. W. E. Smythe, "A Reply to Secretary Shaw ..." and "Which is the Party of Irrigation ...," both bound in "Speeches, Etc. of Mr. Newlands," Nevada State Historical Society. Roosevelt, *An Autobiography*, pp. 384–387. The significant contribution of Senator Newlands is discussed in Samuel P. Hays, *Conservation and the Gospel of Efficiency* (Cambridge, Mass., 1959).

⁷ T. Roosevelt to J. Muir, July 3, 1903, to R. S. Baldwin, Oct. 13, 1903; to E. A. Hitchcock, May 7, 1902, and May 19, 1903; to W. A. Richards, May 21, 1903, and April 24, 1904; to R. U. Johnson, Jan. 17, 1905; to J. C. Needham, Jan. 4, 1905; and to G. C. Perkins, June 5, 1906, Roosevelt Papers. *Second Biennial Message of Governor Henry T. Gage to the Legislature of the State of California* (Sacramento, 1903), pp. 15–20. Needham to G. Pinchot, Jan. 13, 1905, James C. Needham Papers, Stanford University Library. J. A. Wilson to G. C. Pardee, May 13, 1903, and Pardee to Muir, July 11, 15, 1904, George C. Pardee Papers, Bancroft Library. Muir to Johnson, Sept. 12 and 21, 1902; Sept. 30, Oct. 26, and Dec. 27, 1904; Jan. 30, 1905; and July 5, 1906, Robert Underwood Johnson Papers, Bancroft Library.

⁸ Lander, Wyo., *Clipper*, Nov. 7, 1902. A. A. Anderson, *Experiences and Impressions* (New York, 1933), pp. 91–93, 96–110. W. A. Richards, "Notes on Interviews between Roosevelt [and] Richards ...," March 7, 1903," typescript, copy, and F. Dennett to Richards, Nov. 13, 1906, Alice Richards McCreery Collection, Wyoming Historical Society. G. Pinchot, Diary, 1907, entry for Nov. 9, Gifford Pinchot Papers, Library of Congress.

⁹ *Preliminary Report of the Public Lands Commission, March 7, 1904* (Washing-

ton, 1904). Fenimore Chatterton, "Autobiography" pp. 68–75, typescript, copy in Wyoming Historical Society. F. E. Warren to G. Pinchot, Dec. 23 and 28, 1903, and Jan. 1, 1904, Francis E. Warren Papers, University of Wyoming Library. Pinchot: minutes of meeting of Public Lands Commission, Jan. 23, 1904; Diary, 1904, entries for Jan. 9, 10, and 23; Chatterton to Pinchot, Aug. 20, and Pinchot to Chatterton, Aug. 23, 1904, Pinchot Papers. Cheyenne, *Wyoming Tribune*, Jan. 23, 1904.

[10] [Ethan A. Hitchcock], *Report of the Secretary of the Interior* (Washington, 1906), pp. 4–5. J. R. Garfield, Diary, 1907, entry for April 13, James R. Garfield Papers, Library of Congress. Livingston, Mont., *Enterprise*, July 3, 1909. G. Pinchot to W. Loeb Jr., Jan. 17, 1906; T. Roosevelt to Hitchcock, Oct. 6, 1907, Roosevelt Papers. Richards, *op. cit.* After examining the Hitchcock Papers in 1940 for biographical material, historian Elting Morison concluded that there was no evidence to prove that Western Senators brought about the Secretary's resignation: E. A. Hitchcock folder, Pres. Appt. file, Secretary of the Interior, Interior Records, National Archives. Morison did not, however, see the Richards memoranda used herein.

[11] [James R. Garfield], *Report of the Secretary of the Interior* (Washington, 1907), pp. 3–8, 12 ff, 73.

[12] M. Nelson McGeary's recent biography, *Gifford Pinchot: Forester-Politician* (Princeton, N.J.: Princeton University Press, 1960), fails to examine the significance of Pinchot's annual inspection trips throughout the West, and makes only passing reference to a few of his many disciples in that region.

[13] The most perceptive account of Pinchot's ideas, contributions, and disputations with other conservationists is in Samuel P. Hays, *Conservation and the Gospel of Efficiency* (Cambridge, Mass., 1959).

[14] G. Pinchot to T. E. Burke, April 3, 8, and 18, 1902, Thomas E. Burke Papers, University of Washington Library. Gifford Pinchot, *Breaking New Ground* (New York, 1947), pp. 125–126, 198. The role of Senator Smoot in the formulation of federal resource legislation can be traced in the Pinchot Papers, the Heber M. Wells Papers, and the John C. Cutler Papers, both in Utah State Archives. Unfortunately, Smoot's own correspondence was destroyed, according to Mrs. Smoot. Pinchot, Diary, 1904, entry for Feb. 12, Pinchot Papers. C. W. Brandon to H. A. Wallace, *c.* 1937; clipping from Rock Springs, Wyo. *Rocket*, Jan. 23, 1908 in C. Watt Brandon Papers, University of Wyoming Library. Cheyenne, Wyo., *Tribune-Leader*, July 31, 1935. Information furnished to me by William H. Mondell.

[15] Pinchot, *op. cit.*, pp. 177–182. Elers Koch, [Reminiscences] in Jessie Thompson (ed.), *Early Days in the Forest Service* (Washington, 1955), I, 92–95. E. T. Allen to Pinchot, Sept. 26, 1905, Pinchot Papers. *Tenth Report of the Board of Agriculture, Labor, and Industry of the State of Montana . . . 1906* (Helena, 1906), p. 46. Harold D. Langille, "Mostly Division 'R' Days . . . ," *Oregon Historical Quarterly*, 57 (Dec., 1956), 301–313. W. C. Barnes, [Letters Received], Arizona State University Library. Barnes, Diaries, 1907–1908, Will C. Barnes Papers, Arizona Pioneers Historical Society. L. F. Kneipp to F. Winn, Dec. 2, 1942, Frederic Winn Papers, Arizona Pioneers Historical Society. E. S. Gosney, "The Arizona Woolgrowers Association, 1898–1909," typescript, pp. 20, 22, copy in Arizona Pioneers Historical Society. Information furnished to me by H. B. Embach, former secretary of the Arizona Woolgrowers Association, Phoenix, and by Thornton T. Munger, then with the Forest Service in Oregon.

[16] *Message of Bryant B. Brooks, Governor of Wyoming, to the Eighth State Legislature, 1905* (Sheridan, 1905), p. 9. Brooks, "Menace of Federal Control," typescript, copy in Bryant B. Brooks Papers, University of Wyoming Library. Clippings from the Rock Springs, Wyo., *Miner*, Oct. 14, 1905, and the Brighton County, Wyo., *News*, Jan. 25 and 31, 1906, in the Brandon Papers. Pinedale, Wyo., *Roundup*, Jan. 10, 1906.

[17] Cheyenne, Wyo., *Leader*, June 7, 1907.

¹⁸ William M. Raines and Will C. Barnes, *Cattle, Cowboys, and Rangers* (New York, 1930), p. 307. R. A. Rodgers, "How and Why I Went Into the Forest Service," typescript, copy, and F. Winn, "History of Coronado National Forest," typescript, copy in Winn Papers. Barnes to A. F. Potter, Dec. 1, 1908, Barnes Papers. Roscoe G. Willson, " 'Teddy's Pets' Fought Hostility in Early Days of the Forest Service," *Arizona Republican Magazine* (Phoenix), March 4, 1956, pp. 18–19.

¹⁹ Elers Koch and Albert E. Cole, [Reminiscences] in Thompson (ed.), *op. cit.* I, 92–95, 97.

²⁰ *Message of Governor Joseph K. Toole to the Tenth Legislative Assembly of the State of Montana, 1907* (Helena, 1907), p. 22.

²¹ *Message of George E. Chamberlain, Governor of Oregon to the Twenty-Third Legislative Assembly, Regular Session* (Salem, 1905), pp. 42–44. E. Herness to J. Minto, April 26, 1907, John Minto Papers, Oregon Historical Society.

²² *Report of the State Fire Warden for the Year 1905* ... (Olympia, 1906), pp. 7–18. Seattle *Post-Intelligencer*, July 12, 1906. Lawrence Rakestraw, "A History of Forest Conservation in the Pacific Northwest, 1891–1913" (unpublished doctoral dissertation, University of Washington, 1955), pp. 210, 287, 289, 300.

²³ A. E. Mead to T. Roosevelt, Feb. 13 copy; G. Pinchot to Roosevelt, March 2 copy; Roosevelt to Mead, March 3, 1907, copy; Mead to Senate of the State of Washington, March 12, 1907, Albert E. Mead Papers, Washington State Archives.

²⁴ Thompson (ed.), *op. cit.*, I, 20–28. F. A. Fenn to G. Pinchot, March 12, 1907, Pinchot Papers. Coeur d'Alene, Idaho, *Press*, Dec. 29, 1906.

²⁵ Claudius O. Johnson, *Borah of Idaho* (New York, 1936), p. 90. P. H. Miller to W. E. Borah, May 28, 1907, William E. Borah Papers, Library of Congress.

²⁶ Anecdote furnished to me by L. F. Kneipp, then supervisor of the Montana-Idaho national forests.

²⁷ D. Vickers to W. B. Heyburn, March 12, 1897; E. Wilson to Heyburn, March 21, 1903; L. Prince to Heyburn, March 26, 1903; J. Sharp to Heyburn, May 12, 1903; D. W. Standrod to Heyburn, May 30, 1903; Heyburn to C. J. Shoemaker, Sept. 13, 1904, Weldon B. Heyburn Papers, University of Idaho Library. Coeur d'Alene, Ida., *Mining Record*, Sept. 1, 1904.

²⁸ W. B. Heyburn–T. Roosevelt correspondence printed in *Forest Reserves in Idaho* (Washington, 1905). G. Pinchot, Diary, 1904, entries for March 31 and June 6, Pinchot Papers. W. B. Heyburn to W. H. Balting, Nov. 29, 1905, Heyburn Papers. Roosevelt to Heyburn, June 13, 1905, Roosevelt Papers.

²⁹ G. Pinchot, Diary, 1905, entry for April 25, Pinchot Papers. F. T. DuBois to T. Roosevelt, May 5, 1905, printed in *Forest Reserves in Idaho*, p. 40.

³⁰ Information furnished to me by L. F. Kneipp. G. Pinchot to J. W. Pinchot, Sept. 8, and to T. Roosevelt, Sept. 22, 1905; Roosevelt to Pinchot, Sept. 15, 1906, Pinchot Papers. *Inaugural Message of Frank R. Gooding, Governor of Idaho, to the Eighth Session of the Legislature* (Boise, 1905), p. 13. Gooding to C. J. Munson, April 23, 1907; W. D. Humiston to Munson, March 17, 1906; H. E. O'Donnell to Munson, June 17, 1905, C. J. Munson Scrapbooks, Idaho Historical Society. Gooding to Laclede Lumber Company, Jan. 17, 1905; to D. T. Ham, Jan. 12, 1905; Pinchot to Gooding, Nov. 22, 1905, and Feb. 7, and May 5, 1906; Gooding to Pinchot, May 8, 1906, Frank R. Gooding Papers, Idaho Historical Society. Pocatello, Idaho, *Tribune*, Jan. 20, 1909; Gooding, speech printed in *Fifth Biennial Report of the Commission of Immigration, Labor, and Statistics, 1907–1908* (Boise, 1909), pp. 121–122. J. B. Waldo to Pinchot, May 26, 1906; C. W. Woodruff to Pinchot, June 20, 1907, Pinchot Papers.

³¹ *Congressional Record*, 59th Cong., 2nd sess. (Feb. 14, 18, 19, 21 and 23, 1907), 2957–2959, 3194–3202, 3283–3295, 3514–3517, 3532–3542, 3611–3618, 3720–3721. T. Roosevelt, memorandum, March 2, 1907, Roosevelt Papers.

³² Denver *Record-Stockman*, Nov. 29 and Dec. 21, 1905; Jan. 11 and 30, 1906; Feb. 21 and 23, 1907. *Procedings of the First Annual Convention of the American*

Livestock Association ... 1906 (Denver, 1906), pp. 20 ff. *Rocky Mountain News,* Feb. 2, 1906. Denver *Republican,* Feb. 3, 1906. W. G. M. Stone to H. A. Buchtel, March 5, 1907, Henry A. Buchtel Papers, Colorado State Archives.

[33] H. A. Buchtel, statement, resolutions of the Colorado legislature, *c.* May, 1907, Buchtel Papers.

[34] H. A. Buchtel to F. C. Goudy, June 11; to D. C. Beaman, May 28; J. A. Eddy to Buchtel, May 29 and June 4, 1907, Buchtel Papers.

[35] J. R. Garfield, Diary, 1907, entry for June 6, Garfield Papers. T. Roosevelt to J. Wilson, June 7, 1907, Denver Land Convention file, Interior Records, N.A. G. Pinchot to W. H. Corbin, April 25, 1907, Pinchot Papers.

[36] *Record-Stockman,* June 13, 1907. *Rocky Mountain News,* June 17, 19–21, 1907. M. Woodruff to R. A. Ballinger, Aug. 12, 1910, Richard A. Ballinger Papers, University of Washington Library. P. P. Wells to R. U. Johnson, July 5, 1907, Johnson Papers. I. Hale to T. Roosevelt, June 21, 1907, Denver Land Convention file, Interior Records, N.A. Denver *Republican,* May 31, 1907. Cheyenne *Wyoming Tribune,* June 24, 1907. Santa Fe *New Mexican,* June 21, 1907.

[37] P. P. Wells to R. U. Johnson, July 5, 1907, Johnson Papers. Fred C. Johnson (ed.), *Proceedings of the Public Lands Convention ...* (Denver, 1907). Las Vegas, N. M., *Optic,* June 19, 1907. Albuquerque, N. M., *Journal,* June 23, 1907. J. H. Kibbey to H. A. Buchtel, June 11, 1907, Buchtel Papers. J. C. Cutler to Buchtel, and to J. Y. Smythe, May 23, 1907, Cutler Papers. Oswald West, "Reminiscences and Anecdotes ...," *Oregon Historical Quarterly,* 51 (June, 1950), 109–110.

[38] G. Pinchot, remarks, copy, Pinchot Papers. J. R. Garfield, notes for speech, Denver Land Convention file, Interior Records, N.A. R. A. Ballinger, speech, copy, Ballinger Papers. P. P. Wells to R. U. Johnson, July 5, 1907, Johnson Papers.

[39] A. E. Mead to H. A. Buchtel, April 22, 1907, Buchtel Papers. Resolutions printed in *Proceedings of the Public Lands Convention ...,* pp. 9–11. Sacramento, Calif., *Union,* June 22, 1907.

[40] *Record-Stockman,* June 27, 1907. *Post-Intelligencer,* June 20–22, 1907. *Salt Lake Tribune,* June 23, 1907. *Oregonian,* June 20–22, 1907. Colorado Springs *Gazette,* June 22, 1907. *Arizona Gazette,* June 18, 1907.

[41] G. Pinchot to L. Murray, June 29, 1907, Pinchot Papers. *Rocky Mountain News,* Oct. 10, 1907. R. A. Ballinger to M. D. McInery, July 1, 1907, Ballinger Papers. J. R. Garfield to F. E. Warren, July 14, and T. H. Carter to T. Roosevelt, June 25, 1907, Denver Land Convention file, Interior Records, N.A.

[42] Walter A. Voss, "Colorado and Forest Conservation" (unpublished Master's thesis, University of Colorado, 1931), p. 76.

[43] Virginia City, Mont., *Madisonian,* April 4, 1907. Voss, *op. cit.,* p. 76. *Rocky Mountain News,* June 22, 1907. Leonard D. Shoemaker, "History of Holy Cross National Forest," typescript, pp. 57–60, copy in Colorado State Historical Society.

[44] R. Smoot to H. M. Wells, Nov. 11, 1903; Wells to Smoot, Dec. 5, 1903; to J. Graham, Feb. 17, 1904; Smoot to Wells, March 25, 1904; G. Pinchot to Wells, Jan. 23, 1904, Wells Papers. J. C. Cutler to T. Roosevelt, Nov. 19, 1907; to the New York *World,* Nov. 19, 1907; to D. Eccles and G. Austin, July 23, 1908; to Pinchot, Sept. 2 and 11, 1908; to J. R. Garfield, April 8, 1908; to Roosevelt, June 6 and 12, 1908, Cutler Papers. *Mining and Scientific Press* (Los Angeles), Jan. 30, 1909, p. 180.

[45] A. J. Beveridge to G. Pinchot, Oct. 22, 1905, Pinchot Papers. H. J. Hagerman to T. Roosevelt, Feb. 4, and W. H. Spockman to Hagerman, Feb. 26, 1907, Herbert J. Hagerman Papers, New Mexico Historical Society. W. C. Barnes to Hagerman, Feb. 15, 1907, Barnes Papers. *Optic,* March 21, 1907. R. E. Twitchell, *The Leading Facts of New Mexican History* (Cedar Rapids, 1912), II, 549–561. Roosevelt to Hagerman, May 1, 1907, Roosevelt Papers. Hagerman to Roosevelt, May 15, 1907, printed in Twitchell, *op. cit.,* pp. 558–559. H. A. Jastro to Pinchot, April 25, 1907, and Pinchot to Jastro, April 26, 1907, Pinchot Papers. Copies of all correspondence and of Hagerman's self-defense are in his *Matters Relating to the Administration*

and Removal of Herbert J. Hagerman (N.p., 1908), pamphlet in Bronson Cutting Papers, Library of Congress.

[46] Twitchell, *op. cit.*, II, 562–563. T. Roosevelt to P. B. Stewart, April 16, and to O. McHarg, July 31, 1907, Roosevelt Papers.

[47] *New Mexican*, Aug. 22 and Oct. 26, 1907. G. Curry to O. McHarg and to C. J. Bonaparte, Aug. 17, 1907; D. D. Bronson to Curry, Nov. 29, 1907; J. W. Owen to Curry, Jan. 22, 1908; Curry to G. Pinchot, Jan. 13, 1908, George Curry Papers, New Mexico Historical Society.

[48] J. W. Owen to G. Curry, Jan. 22, Curry to Owen, Jan. 30; to M. Sanchez, Feb. 11; to W. H. Andrews, Feb. 11; G. Pinchot to Curry, Feb. 19, 1908, Curry Papers. W. C. Barnes to H. A. Jastro, Feb. 3, and Jastro to Barnes, Feb. 13, 1908, Barnes Papers. Curry to H. W. Kelly, Aug. 6; C. Hightower to Curry, Aug. 31; E. H. Clapp to Curry, Sept. 15 and 20; Curry to S. Luna, *et al.*, July 18; to J. R. Garfield, Aug. 22, 1908; and to Pinchot, Dec. 22, 1909, Curry Papers. *New Mexican*, Jan. 20, 1910. For a fuller account of Curry's conversion see Elmo R. Richardson, "George Curry and the Politics of Forest Conservation in New Mexico," *New Mexico Historical Review*, 33 (Oct., 1958), 277–284.

[49] G. Pardee to A. Kinney, June 16 and 25, 1903; Kinney to Pardee, June 22, 1903; T. Ryan to Pardee, Oct. 6, 1903; Pardee to A. Brodie, Feb. 3, 1904; to F. W. Richardson, June 27, 1905; to F. H. Newell, March 14, 1906; to G. Pinchot, Feb. 26, 1906; Pinchot to Pardee, Feb. 16, 1905, and May 7, 1906; Pardee-Pinchot correspondence concerning appointment of E. T. Allen, June 6–Aug. 11, 1905, Pardee Papers. *First Biennial Message of Governor George C. Pardee . . .* (Sacramento, 1905), and *Second Biennial Message . . .* (Sacramento, 1907). J. McAlpine to R. A. Ballinger, Aug. 18, 1909, Ballinger Papers. Los Angeles *Times*, Feb. 21, 1905. San Francisco *Chronicle*, June 5, 11, 20, and 30, 1905. Pinchot, *op. cit.*, p. 406. The details of the forestry work of the Pardee administration are in C. Raymond Clar, *California Government and Forestry . . .* (Sacramento, 1959), pp. 185–265.

[50] J. Muir to R. U. Johnson, March 23, 1905; G. Pinchot to M. Manson, May 28 and Nov. 15, copies, Johnson Papers. T. Roosevelt to Muir, Sept. 16, 1907, Roosevelt Papers. W. F. Badé to J. R. Garfield, Jan. 30, 1909, copy; W. E. Colby to Johnson, Aug. 17, 1908, Johnson Papers. Pinchot to A. Chamberlain, Aug. 11, 1909, Pinchot Papers. A more detailed account of the Hetch Hetchy controversy is in Elmo R. Richardson, "The Struggle for the Valley . . .," *California Historical Society Quarterly*, Vol. 38, No. 3 (Sept., 1959), pp. 249–258.

[51] F. Gooding's remark printed in *Fifth Biennial Report of the Commission of Immigration, Labor, and Statistics, 1907–1908* (Boise, 1909), pp. 121–122. T. Roosevelt to G. Pardee, June 8, 1908, Pardee Papers. On the Governors Conference, see Hays, *op. cit.*, pp. 139–140.

[52] G. Curry's address printed in *Proceedings of the Legislative Council of the Territory of New Mexico . . .* (Santa Fe, 1909), pp. 8–42. *New Mexican*, March 19, 1909.

[53] J. F. Merrill to J. C. Cutler, Oct. 6, 1908, Cutler Papers. W. Spry's message is printed in *Journal of the Eighth Session of the Legislature . . .* (Salt Lake City, 1909), pp. 48–49. Spry, proclamation, July 20, 1909, copy; Merrill to Spry, Dec. 13, 1910, and Spry to G. Pinchot, Dec. 16, 1909, William Spry Papers, Utah State Archives. Spry later served as Commissioner of the Land Office from 1921 to 1929. *Preliminary Report of the Utah Conservation Commission . . .* (Salt Lake City, 1909), pp. 117–118, and *First Biennial Report . . .* (Salt Lake City, 1913), pp. 13, 186.

[54] *Message of Lieutenant and Acting Governor Denver S. Dickerson to the Legislature of 1909* (Carson City, 1909), pp. 164, 221.

[55] H. A. Buchtel to G. Pinchot, Dec. 1, 1908, Buchtel Papers.

[56] O. West, *op. cit.*, p. 109. *Message of George E. Chamberlain, Governor of Oregon, to the . . . Legislative Assembly . . .* (Salem, 1909), pp. 19–20. *Second Annual Report of the Oregon Conservation Commission . . .* (Salem, 1909). *Journal of*

the Senate . . . (Salem, 1909), p. 282. Joint memorial no. 11, Feb. 23, 1909, certified sealed copy, Jonathan Bourne, Jr., Papers, University of Oregon Library. W. H. Manss to C. S. Ucker, Aug. 11, 1909, Ballinger Papers. G. Pinchot to J. Teal, July 23, 1909, Pinchot Papers.

[57] *Message of Governor Edwin L. Norris to the* . . . *Legislative Assembly* . . . (Helena, 1909), p. 23. William B. Greeley, "The Administration of the National Forests," copy of speech, Feb., 1909, in Forest Service Regional Office, Missoula, Montana.

[58] C. H. Bailey to A. E. Mead, Aug. 27, and W. Elwood to Mead, Aug. 31, 1908, Mead Papers. Mead's message is printed in *Journal of the Senate* . . . (Olympia, 1909), p. 17. Mead to E. Brainerd, Feb. 25, 1908, Erastus Brainerd Papers, University of Washington Library.

CHAPTER III: BALLINGER'S BEGINNINGS

[1] G. Pinchot, Diary, 1906, entries for Oct. 20, 22, 24, 26, and 27; Pinchot to R. T. Platt, Jan. 8, 1907, Gifford Pinchot Papers, Library of Congress. T. Roosevelt to Pinchot, Jan. 11, 1907, Theodore Roosevelt Papers, Library of Congress. J. R. Garfield, Diary, 1907, entry for Jan. 11, James R. Garfield Papers, Library of Congress.

[2] "Biographical Memorandum of Richard Achilles Ballinger," typescript (perhaps autobiographical), copy, and Ballinger to W. C. Bowen, Feb. 15, 1911, Richard A. Ballinger Papers, University of Washington Library. *Investigation of the Department of the Interior* . . . (Washington, 1911), VII, 3549–3550.

[3] Copies of some of the records of Ballinger, Ronald, Battle, and Tennant, 1898–1908; A. J. Tennant to R. A. Ballinger, Dec. 17, 1909; Ballinger to E. Smith, Jan. 31, 1910, Ballinger Papers. *Investigation* . . . , III, 3–5, and VII, 3552–3554.

[4] Notes, perhaps for a speech, undated, Ballinger Papers. A description of the contemporary political scene is Keith A. Murray, "Republican Party Politics in Washington During the Progressive Era" (unpublished doctoral dissertation, University of Washington, 1946).

[5] R. A. Ballinger to J. R. Garfield, Jan. 16 and 17, 1907, copies, Pres. Appt. file, Interior Records, National Archives. T. Roosevelt to Ballinger, Jan. 16, 1907, Roosevelt Papers. Seattle *Post-Intelligencer*, Jan. 19, 1907. *Investigation* . . . , VII, 3555.

[6] J. R. Garfield, Diary, 1907, entries for Feb. 18 and 19, Garfield Papers. R. A. Ballinger to A. J. Tennant, Feb. 21, 1907, Ballinger Papers.

[7] J. R. Garfield, Diary, 1907, entry for May 16, Garfield Papers. Unidentified clipping, R. A. Ballinger folder in Pres. Appt. file, Interior Records, N.A. Ballinger to Garfield, March 5, 1908, Ballinger Papers. Minutes, "Meeting of Bureau Chiefs, Nov. 16, 1907," Adm. Gen. file, Interior Records, N.A.

[8] Typescript account of controversy, I, 596, Pinchot Papers. G. Pinchot, *Breaking New Ground* (New York, 1947), p. 402.

[9] *Investigation* . . . , IV, 1330, and VII, 3613.

[10] F. Dennett to R. A. Ballinger, July 24, and Ballinger to J. R. Garfield, Aug. 5, 1907, Ballinger Papers. *Investigation* . . . , IV, 1147–1149, and VII, 3744.

[11] *Investigation* . . . , III, 173, IV, 950, 1334, 1146, and VII, 3501, 3578, 3581. R. A. Ballinger to J. R. Garfield, July 26; E. F. Baldwin to Ballinger, Dec. 27; Ballinger to Baldwin, Dec. 28; and E. E. Garrett to Ballinger, Oct. 7, 1907, Ballinger Papers. W. E. Borah to E. Eagleson, Nov. 7, 1907, and Jan. 24, 1908, William E. Borah Papers, Library of Congress.

[12] *Investigation* . . . , VII, 3555. J. H. McGraw to R. A. Ballinger, Feb. 27, and S. H. Hedges to Ballinger, Oct. 9, 1907, Ballinger Papers. J. R. Garfield, Diary, 1907, entry for Nov. 2, Garfield Papers.

[13] C. N. Hanford to R. A. Ballinger, April 6 and Dec. 26, 1907; Ballinger to Hanford, Dec. 26, 1907, and Jan. 2, 1908; memorandum, M. Bien to F. Dennett,

May 4, 1907, copy, Ballinger Papers. *Investigation* . . . , V, 1606.

[14] J. R. Garfield, Diary, 1908, entries for Feb. 16 and March 2, Garfield Papers. R. A. Ballinger to T. Roosevelt, Jan. 4, 1908, Ballinger Papers. Roosevelt to Ballinger, Jan. 6, 1908, Roosevelt Papers. L. R. Glavis to Ballinger, Jan. 31, and Ballinger to Glavis, Feb. 5, 1908, Ballinger Papers. *Investigation* . . . , VII, 3591, 3593.

[15] R. A. Ballinger to A. W. Lafferty, April 30, 1908, R. S. Ryan to Ballinger, Dec. 14, 1907, and March 10, 1908; Ballinger to F. W. Mondell, March 30, 1908, Ballinger Papers. *Investigation* . . . , II, 162–168.

[16] R. A. Ballinger to J. R. Garfield, April 8, 1908, copy; Garfield to Ballinger, April 16, 1908; A. Battle to C. Gross, Jan. 15, 1908, copy; Battle and A. J. Tennant to Ballinger, Nov. 10, 1909; J. T. Ronald to L. Abbott, Oct. 25, 1909, copy, Ballinger to H. White, Nov. 17, and to M. P. Kinkaid, Oct. 9 and Nov. 10, 1908, Ballinger Papers. *Investigation* . . . , II, 625, IV, 1508, and V, 1517.

[17] *Investigation* . . . , II, 623, 655–658, V, 1619–1620, and VII, 3553–3554.

[18] S. A. D. Puter and H. Stevens, *Looters of the Public Domain* (Portland, 1908), pp. 478–480. O. Lawler to R. A. Ballinger, June 29, 1908, and memorandum attached; Ballinger to F. Pierce, June 30, and to Lawler, June 30, 1908, Ballinger Papers. *Investigation* . . . , V, 1613.

[19] J. M. Carey to H. Plunkett, Nov. 7, 1907, copy; J. N. Teal to G. Pinchot, Jan. 2, 1908; Pinchot to J. W. Pinchot, Oct. 11, 1907; to W. H. Taft, Sept. 12, 1908; to W. C. Barnes, Oct. 30, 1908; to W. L. Fisher, Feb. 23, 1909, Pinchot Papers. *Investigation* . . . , IV, 1160.

[20] H. A. Moody to G. Pinchot, Feb. 15, 1909, Pinchot Papers. J. R. Garfield, Diary, 1909, entry for Dec. 22, and Diary, 1910, entries for Jan. 4, 20, 22, 25, Garfield Papers. Cf. Harold L. Ickes, *Autobiography of a Curmudgeon* (New York: Reynal and Hitchcock, 1943), p. 152.

[21] G. G. Hill to R. A. Ballinger, Jan. 4, 1909, Ballinger Papers. W. G. Miller to G. Pinchot, May 26, 1940, Pinchot Papers.

[22] W. H. Taft to P. C. Knox, Dec. 23, 1908, William H. Taft Papers, Library of Congress.

[23] C. Rowell to M. Lissner, Nov. 28; Lissner to W. H. Taft, Nov. 30; Lissner to Rowell, Dec. 4, 1908, Meyer Lissner Papers, Stanford University Library. Rowell to J. C. Needham and T. R. Bard, Jan. 12, 1908, copies, Alice Rose Collection, Stanford University Library.

[24] R. A. Ballinger to F. Hitchcock, Nov. 6, 1908; to T. H. Cavanaugh, Jan. 25, 1908; to M. C. Moore, Feb. 15, 1908; J. H. Burke to Ballinger, Feb. 6, 1909; F. Pierce to Ballinger, Jan. 8, 1909; Ballinger to W. H. Lorton, Dec. 26, and to G. G. Hill, Dec. 29, 1908, Ballinger Papers. *Investigation* . . . , VII, 3801, 3847, 3854.

[25] W. H. Taft to P. C. Knox, Dec. 22, 1908, and to H. Taft, Feb. 1, 1910, Taft Papers.

[26] W. H. Taft to R. A. Ballinger, Nov. 8, 1908; O. McHarg to C. W. Nagel, Aug. 31, 1909, copy; Ballinger to Taft, June 24, 1908, Ballinger Papers.

[27] J. C. Needham to C. Rowell, Jan. 30, and T. R. Bard to Rowell, April 1, 1909, Chester H. Rowell Papers, Bancroft Library. Rowell, statement, March 24, 1911, copy, Rose Collection. E. T. Parsons to W. H. Taft, Jan. 19, and Taft to C. R. Edwards, Dec. 28, 1909, Taft Papers. John Hays Hammond, *Autobiography* (New York, 1935), II, 542–543. F. Hitchcock to R. A. Ballinger, Jan. 12, 1909, Ballinger Papers.

[28] J. R. Garfield, Diary, 1909, entry for Feb. 1, Garfield Papers. R. A. Ballinger to H. A. Garfield, March 12, and F. Hitchcock to Ballinger, Feb. 2, 1909, Ballinger Papers. Hammond, *op. cit.*, p. 543.

[29] D. A. McKenzie, statement, June, 1909; G. Pinchot, typescript account of controversy, I, 616; J. L. Mathews to Pinchot, Jan. 8, 1910, Pinchot Papers. *Investigation* . . . , IV, 994.

[30] *Post-Intelligencer,* March 5, 1909. S. L. Lemmon to W. H. Taft, Jan. 30, 1909, Taft Papers. R. Smoot to R. A. Ballinger, Feb. 1; D. M. Carr to Ballinger, Feb. 22, E. B. Pieper to Ballinger, Feb. 26; J. E. Chilberg to Ballinger, May 4, 1909, Ballinger Papers.

[31] C. R. Pierce to G. Pinchot, May 28, 1940, Pinchot Papers.

[32] G. W. Rauch to W. L. Jones, March 3, 1909, Wesley L. Jones Papers, University of Washington Library. F. Cushman to R. A. Ballinger, Dec. 20, 1908, copy; H. White to E. B. McFarland, Jan. 5, 1909, encl. in McFarland to Ballinger, April 8, 1910; J. P. Lavin to Ballinger, Feb. 14, 1909, Ballinger Papers.

[33] T. Roosevelt to G. Pinchot, Feb. 24, 1909, copy, Garfield Papers.

[34] A. N. Brown to E. Brainerd, April 30, 1911, Erastus Brainerd Papers, University of Washington Library.

[35] E. L. Baldwin to W. H. Taft, Jan. 13, 1909, Taft Papers.

[36] J. R. Garfield, Diary, 1909, entries for March 6 and 8, Garfield Papers. R. A. Ballinger, statement, *c.* March, 1909, Ballinger Papers.

[37] R. A. Ballinger to E. F. Baldwin, May 10, 1909, Ballinger Papers.

[38] *Investigation . . . ,* VII, 3686.

[39] *Ibid.,* pp. 3643 ff.

[40] *Ibid.,* pp. 3728–3729. When F. Pierce had first been appointed in 1907, the Butte, Mont., *Miner* remarked that the selection was the next best thing to having a westerner as Secretary of the Interior: clipping in F. Pierce folder, Pres. Appt. file, Interior Records, N.A.

[41] *Investigation . . . ,* I, 81, and VII, 3505–3506.

[42] *Ibid.,* VII, 3613–3614. F. Newell to G. Pinchot, Oct. 8, 1909, Pinchot Papers.

[43] *Investigation . . . ,* V, 1717, 1729–1730, and VIII, 4462–4468. *Post-Intelligencer,* Feb. 28, 1909; Boise *Idaho Statesman,* June 8, 1909. Seattle *Times,* July 14, 1909.

[44] J. R. Garfield, Diary, 1909, entries for March 29, April 2 and 15, May 2, 8, and 18, Garfield Papers. F. Newell to G. Pinchot, April 17 and May 12, Pinchot Papers.

[45] G. Pinchot to W. L. Fisher, April 28; to F. Newell, May 22; J. B. Lippincott to Pinchot, April 3; W. B. Hoggett to Pinchot, May 24, 1909, Pinchot Papers.

[46] *Investigation . . . ,* VII, 3613, 4141.

Chapter IV: Pinchot's Gambit

[1] Portland *Oregon Journal,* March 31, 1909. *Oregonian,* March 7, 1909. Denver *Republican,* March 13, 1909. Seattle *Post-Intelligencer,* May 16 and July 14, 1909. Big Pine, Calif., *Owens Valley Herald,* May 14, 1909. Independence, Calif., *Inyo Independent,* May 14, 1909. Boise *Idaho Statesman,* June 3, 1909. Los Angeles *Times,* July 21, 1909.

[2] R. A. Ballinger to M. C. Moore, Jan. 13, 1908, Richard A. Ballinger Papers, University of Washington Library.

[3] *Investigation of the Department of the Interior . . .* (Washington, 1911), III, 226.

[4] *Ibid.,* III, 209.

[5] M. C. Moore–R. A. Ballinger correspondence, May, 1909, copies attached to Ballinger to W. H. Taft, Sept. 4, 1909, Ballinger Papers.

[6] R. A. Ballinger to O. Lawler, Aug. 10, and G. W. Wickersham to Ballinger, Sept. 3, 1909, Ballinger Papers. *Investigation . . . ,* I, 51, and III, 224, 313–314, 380.

[7] O. Lawler to R. A. Ballinger, Aug. 12, 1909, Ballinger Papers. Memorandum to P. P. Wells, Oct. 21, 1909, and reply to Ballinger, attached to O. Price to A. Pinchot, March 22, 1910; G. Pinchot to W. H. Taft, Aug. 12, 1909, Gifford Pinchot Papers, Library of Congress. *Investigation . . . ,* II, 89, III, 314, and VII, 3613, 3756.

[8] J. R. Garfield to G. Pinchot, Aug. 17, 1909; Garfield, Diary, 1909, entries for Aug. 5 and 6, James R. Garfield Papers, Library of Congress. Pinchot to C. L. Pack, Aug. 19, 1909, Pinchot Papers.

[9] R. A. Ballinger to W. E. Clark, Aug. 7, and to W. H. Taft, Sept. 4, 1909, Ballinger Papers.

¹⁰ W. H. Taft to R. A. Ballinger, Aug. 22 and Sept. 13, 1909; O. Lawler to Ballinger, July 31, 1909, Ballinger Papers. *Investigation* ..., VIII, 4496–4527.

¹¹ W. H. Taft to G. Pinchot, Sept. 13, 1909, Pinchot Papers. *Investigation* ..., III, 313.

¹² G. Pinchot to M. Pinchot, Aug. 5, 1909, Pinchot Papers. J. R. Garfield, Diary, entries for Sept. 21 and 30, Garfield Papers.

¹³ W. A. Beard to G. Pinchot, July 23, 1909, Pinchot Papers. *Official Proceedings of the Seventeenth National Irrigation Congress* ... (Spokane, 1909), esp. pp. 96, 222, 229, 291. Spokane, Wash., *Spokesman-Review*, Aug. 10–15, 1909. A. A. Barstow to D. A. McKenzie, Jan. 13, 1910, copy, Ballinger Papers. *Investigation* ..., VI, 3326–3328.

¹⁴ C. H. Rowell to M. Manson, Aug. 17, 1909, Chester H. Rowell Papers, Bancroft Library. Flagstaff, Ariz., *Coconino Sun*, Aug. 20 and 27, 1909. Phoenix *Arizona Republican*, Aug. 13, 1909. Portland *Oregonian*, Sept. 1, 1909. *California Weekly* (San Francisco), I (Aug. 13, 1909) 594–595, (Sept. 17, 1909) 681.

¹⁵ C. H. Rowell to M. Manson, July 31; to J. C. Needham, July 20; Needham to Rowell, Aug. 26, 1909, Rowell Papers.

¹⁶ C. H. Rowell to W. H. Taft, Aug. 27, 1909, Rowell Papers.

¹⁷ W. S. U'Ren to J. Bourne, Aug. 27, 1909, Jonathan Bourne, Jr., Papers, University of Oregon Library.

¹⁸ F. Dennett to R. A. Ballinger, Oct. 11, 1909, Ballinger Papers.

¹⁹ O. Lawler to R. A. Ballinger, July 21 and Aug. 13; Ballinger to O. McHarg, Aug. 25; to C. S. Ucker, Aug. 26; to E. Brainerd, Aug. 25; to J. McAlpine, Aug. 31; to W. C. Cowles, Dec. 9, 1909, Ballinger Papers.

²⁰ T. H. Carter to R. A. Ballinger, July 21, 1909, Ballinger Papers. D. Carr to E. P. Hopson, Sept. 30, 1909, Western Trip, 1909, file, Interior Records, National Archives. *Investigation* ..., V, 1730, 1732. J. Muir to R. U. Johnson, Oct. 27 and Nov. 16, 1909, Robert U. Johnson Papers, Bancroft Library. Ballinger, speech, Aug. 11, 1909, copy, Ballinger Papers.

²¹ [Letters received], bound files, Aug.–Dec., 1909, Ballinger Papers. W. H. Taft to R. Ogden, April 21, 1909, William H. Taft Papers, Library of Congress. H. Ryckman to G. Pinchot, Jan. 28, 1910, Pinchot Papers.

²² F. K. Lane to R. A. Ballinger, Nov. 20, 1909, Ballinger Papers.

²³ Estimate based upon examination of the volume and content of letters received in the Ballinger and Pinchot Papers, and in the Interior Records, N.A.

²⁴ A list of the principal articles in *Hampton's, La Follette's,* and *Collier's Weekly,* Aug.–Dec., 1909, is in the Ballinger Papers. The series in *Collier's* began in Nov., 1909, and ended in May, 1910. R. A. Ballinger, undated statement to San Francisco *Examiner*, Ballinger Papers.

²⁵ E. F. Baldwin to R. A. Ballinger, Nov. 12, 1909, with notation in Ballinger's handwriting at bottom, Ballinger Papers.

²⁶ J. Ronald to L. Abbott, Oct. 25, 1909, copy; to R. A. Ballinger, Nov. 12, 1909; J. H. McGraw to H. Waterson, Jan. 3, 1910, copy, Ballinger Papers. T. Burke to H. L. Stimson, Sept. 7, 1909, copy, Pinchot Papers. J. J. Donavan to editor of *Collier's Weekly*, Nov. 12, 1909, copy, Brainerd Papers.

²⁷ R. A. Ballinger to C. H. Patterson, Nov. 1 and Dec. 29, and W. B. Heyburn to Ballinger, Nov. 10, 1909; folders of allegations against the Forest Service, arranged by state, Ballinger Papers. Ballinger, statement, Nov. 20, 1909, copy, Pinchot Papers. *Investigation* ..., V, 1781.

²⁸ R. A. Ballinger to E. Brainerd, Nov. 22; to J. F. Miller, Nov. 19; E. L. Baldwin to Ballinger, Nov. 9 and 15; Ballinger to Baldwin, Nov. 18, 1909, Ballinger Papers.

²⁹ R. A. Ballinger to H. W. Mabie, Oct. 4; to L. Abbott, Nov. 17; to E. L. Baldwin, Nov. 12, 1909, Ballinger Papers.

³⁰ *Investigation* ..., V, 1909.

[31] R. A. Ballinger, Cabinet memoranda, Aug.–Dec., 1909; Ballinger to E. L. Baldwin, Nov. 10, 1909, Ballinger Papers.

[32] W. H. Taft to H. P. Taft, Oct. 18, 1909, Taft Papers.

[33] G. Pinchot, memorandum of conversation with Taft, Sept. 24, 1909, Pinchot Papers.

[34] G. Pinchot to G. Pardee, Nov. 21, and S. E. White to Pinchot, Oct. 18, 1909.

[35] *Investigation* . . . , IV, 1290.

[36] G. Pinchot to W. H. Taft, Nov. 26, 1909, Pinchot Papers.

[37] R. A. Ballinger to E. Brainerd, Dec. 28, Erastus Brainerd Papers, University of Washington Library. Ballinger to W. L. Jones, Dec. 2, 1909, Ballinger Papers. G. W. Norris to A. Lief, May 4, 1934, copy, Pinchot Papers.

[38] J. R. Garfield, Diary, 1909, entries for Nov. 11 and 14; Garfield to G. Pinchot, Dec. 1, 1909, Garfield Papers. [Richard A. Ballinger], *Report of the Secretary of the Interior* (Washington, 1909), pp. 6, 19, 21.

[39] G. Pinchot to T. Roosevelt, Dec. 31, 1909, Pinchot Papers.

[40] G. Pinchot to W. H. Taft, Dec. 4, 1909, Pinchot Papers. *Investigation* . . . , IV, 1292–1293, 1397–1399, 1453.

[41] W. H. Taft, statement, quoted in G. Pinchot, memorandum of conversation, Sept. 24, 1909, Pinchot Papers.

[42] W. H. Taft to H. Taft, Oct. 3, 1909, Taft Papers.

[43] J. Wilson to G. Pinchot, and W. H. Taft to Pinchot, Jan. 7, 1910, Pinchot Papers.

[44] E. Brainerd to R. A. Ballinger, Feb. 5, 1910, Ballinger Papers.

[45] *Salt Lake Tribune*, March–May, 1910. *Idaho Statesman*, May 11, 1910. Joel F. Paschal, *Mr. Justice Sutherland: A Man Against the State* (Princeton, 1951), pp. 61–62.

[46] *Investigation* . . . , VII, 3658.

[47] M. D. McInery to R. A. Ballinger, Sept. 8, 1910, Ballinger Papers.

[48] O. McHarg to R. A. Ballinger, Feb. 1, 1910, Ballinger Papers.

[49] R. A. Ballinger to J. H. Lewis, Feb. 12, 1910, Ballinger Papers. Out of the total legal fee, Ballinger paid $10,000 to Vertrees and $5,000 to his assistant, Carl Rasch, an attorney for the Interior Department. Pierce paid the remainder because the case for the defense involved his actions as well as the Secretary's: F. Pierce to Ballinger, July 6, 1910, with enclosure, Ballinger Papers.

[50] *Investigation* . . . , III, 449, and IV, 1319, 1320, 1403. A. N. Brown to E. Brainerd, March 31, 1910, Brainerd Papers.

[51] *Investigation* . . . , III, 421, 435, 604, and IV, 1311, 1437, 1445, 1455.

[52] *Ibid.*, IV, 1443, 1491, 2000–2001.

[53] *Ibid.*, VII, 3747, 4140. H. P. Taft to W. H. Taft, March 9, 1910, Taft Papers.

[54] *Investigation* . . . , VI, 3190–3191, and VII, 3789, 3801, 3863, 3870, 3895, 3904, 3931, 3994, 4115.

[55] *Ibid.*, II, 290, and VII, 4136–4137.

[56] *Ibid.*, VII, 4395–4425, and VIII, 4452–4461. G. Pinchot to T. Roosevelt, May 18, 1910, Pinchot Papers.

[57] *Investigation* . . . , IV, 1143–1144.

[58] *Ibid.*, I, 1–89.

[59] *Ibid.*, 100–147.

[60] R. A. Ballinger to C. Rasch, July 1, and to W. M. Crane, Sept. 10, 1910, Ballinger Papers. Reno, Nev., *Gazette*, Sept. 21, 1910.

[61] R. A. Ballinger to A. Battle, April 9 and 11, and Battle to Ballinger, April 13, 1910, Ballinger Papers.

CHAPTER V: THE CRITICS' CAMPAIGN

[1] Denver *Post*, Oct. 15, 1908. Denver *Record-Stockman*, Nov. 19, 1908. G. Pinchot to W. G. M. Stone, Aug. 28, and J. Vivian to Pinchot, Nov. 20, 1908, Gifford Pinchot Papers, Library of Congress.

² M. Smith to S. Adams, Aug. 2, and W. H. Rosecrans to Adams, Aug. 5, 1911, Denver Land Convention file, Interior Records, National Archives. J. A. Eddy to R. A. Ballinger, Aug. 23, 1910, Richard A. Ballinger Papers, University of Washington Library. Eddy to J. R. Garfield, Dec. 18, 1908, National Public Domain League file, G.L.O., Interior Records, N.A. Eddy to W. H. Taft, Jan. 29, 1909, William H. Taft Papers, Library of Congress.

³ Denver *Post*, Jan. 4, 1909. J. A. Shafroth, inaugural message, in *Journal of the General Assembly* . . . (Denver, 1909), esp. p. 81. J. A. Eddy to Shafroth, Jan. 15, and J. B. Killian to Shafroth, Feb. 2, 1909, John A. Shafroth Papers, Colorado State Archives.

⁴ Concurrent resolution of the Colorado legislature, Feb., 1909, copy; D. C. Beaman to J. A. Shafroth, Feb. 23 and 24; F. C. Goudy to Shafroth, Feb. 2; J. A. Eddy to Shafroth, Feb. 7 and 20, 1909, Shafroth Papers.

⁵ Lake City, Colo., *Phonograph*, and Glenwood, Colo., *Avalanche*, as quoted in Denver *Democrat*, Feb. 6, 1909. Denver *Rocky Mountain News*, March 1, 1909.

⁶ Meeker, Colo., *Herald*, as quoted in Denver *Democrat*, June 12, 1909. Leonard C. Shoemaker, "History of the Holy Cross National Forest," p. 60, typescript, copy in Colorado State Historical Society. Theodore Shoemaker, [Reminisences], typescript, copy in the possession of Mr. Shoemaker, who was supervisor of Pike National Forest at this time. J. A. Eddy to J. A. Shafroth, June 21, and R. W. Shaw to W. G. M. Stone, July 22, copy, Shafroth Papers.

⁷ Denver *Republican*, March 2, 13–18, 1909. *Rocky Mountain News*, March 17–18, 1909. Grand Junction, Colo., *News*, March 26, 1909. John H. Keep, "Early History of Uncompahgre National Forest," pp. 241–243, typescript, copy in Colorado State Historical Society. *Record-Stockman*, April 22, 1909.

⁸ J. A. Eddy to S. C. Smith, Oct. 18, 1909, copy, Ballinger Papers. Eddy to T. H. Carter, Aug. 22, 1909, Thomas H. Carter Papers, Library of Congress. There are copies of most of the League's bulletins in the Shafroth Papers and in the National Public Domain League file, G.L.O., Interior Records, N.A. F. C. Goudy to J. A. Shafroth, June 16, 1909; Shafroth, statement, June 14, 1909; Shafroth to D. C. Beaman, Aug. 16, 1909, Shafroth Papers. *Official Proceedings of the Trans Mississippi Commercial Congress* . . . (Denver, 1909), pp. 74, 77, 94, 194.

⁹ *Official Proceedings of the Colorado Conservation Commission* . . . (Denver, 1910), pp. 11, 25, 30–32, 82–88. D. C. Beaman to K. L. Fahnstock, and to W. G. M. Stone, *c.* April, 1910, and to J. A. Eddy, Jan. 17, 1910, copies; Eddy to J. A. Shafroth, Oct. 9, 1909, and Jan. 15, 1910; F. C. Goudy to Shafroth, Dec. 20, 1910, Shafroth Papers. J. Arthur Eddy, "The Public Domain . . . ," typescript, copy, National Public Domain League file, G.L.O., Interior Records, N.A. Denver *Republican*, Oct. 2 and 4, 1910; W. G. M. Stone to T. R. Shipp, May 4, and to G. Pinchot, June 29, 1910, Pinchot Papers.

¹⁰ E. T. Allen to G. Pinchot, June 8, 1909, Pinchot Papers. Press notice, Nov. 1, 1910, Interior Records, N.A. Seattle *Post-Intelligencer*, Aug. 26–29, 1909.

¹¹ L. K. Armstrong to M. E. Hay, June 3, 1910, enclosure, constitution and bylaws of the Western Conservation League of Spokane, Marion E. Hay Papers, Washington State Archives. "Western Conservation Bulletin," enclosure with T. R. Shipp to G. Pinchot, July 10, 1911, Pinchot Papers. Armstrong to R. A. Ballinger, July 26, 1909, Western Trip, 1909, file, Interior Records, N.A. Hay to Armstrong, Jan. 6, and J. J. Browne to Armstrong, Jan. 28, 1910, copy, Hay Papers.

¹² L. K. Armstrong to M. E. Hay, March 3, 1910, Hay Papers. *Post-Intelligencer*, Jan. 9, 1910. E. H. Libby to R. A. Ballinger, Feb. 19, 1910, Western Trip, 1909, file, Interior Records, N.A. F. G. Flower to G. Pinchot, Feb. 11; L. Pease to Pinchot, Sept. 13; H. M. Montgomery to Pinchot, Jan. 7; G. W. Chamberlain to Pinchot, July 5; E. T. Allen to Pinchot, July 20, 1910, Pinchot Papers. M. D. McInery to Ballinger, May 21, 1910, Ballinger Papers.

¹³ R. A. Ballinger to A. J. Beveridge, April 10, 1909; G. U. Young to Ballinger, Dec. 21, 1909, and Jan. 4, 1910, Ballinger Papers.

[14] G. O. Freeman to T. H. Carter, Jan. 15, 1910, Carter Papers.

[15] C. Cobb to G. Pinchot, *c.* Aug., 1909; H. B. Walker to Pinchot, Aug. 19; Pinchot to Walker, Aug. 25; J. A. Sargent to Pinchot, Aug. 3 and 4, 1910, Pinchot Papers. Boise, *Idaho Statesman*, July 18 and 25, 1910.

[16] *Post-Intelligencer*, Jan. 8 and 9, 1910. *Idaho Statesman*, Jan. 14, 1910. Portland *Oregonian*, Jan. 9, 1910. Tucson *Arizona Star*, Jan. 9, 1910. Albuquerque, N.M., *Journal*, Jan. 9, 1910. Los Angeles *Times*, Jan. 9, 1910. *Salt Lake Tribune*, Jan. 8, 1910. Big Pine, Calif., *Owens Valley Herald*, Jan. 14, 1910. *Rocky Mountain News*, Jan. 8 and 9, 1910. Boise *Capital News*, Jan. 13, 1910.

[17] Laramie, Wyo., *Boomerang*, Jan. 17, 1910. Denver *Republican*, Jan. 9 and 10, 1910. Reno, Nev., *Gazette*, Jan. 7 and 10, 1910.

[18] *Salt Lake Tribune*, Jan. 8 and 12, 1910. W. Spry to R. Smoot, Jan. 12, 1910, William Spry Papers, Utah State Archives. Butte, Mont., *Miner*, Jan. 9, 10, and 12, 1910.

[19] Phoenix, *Arizona Gazette*, Jan. 8, 1910. W. C. Barnes to W. F. Potter, Jan. 12, 1910, Will C. Barnes Papers, Arizona Pioneers Historical Society, Tuscon.

[20] Las Vegas, N.M., *Optic*, Jan. 10, 1910. *Salt Lake Tribune*, Jan. 11, 1910. *Post-Intelligencer*, Jan. 18, 1910.

[21] Gifford Pinchot, *Breaking New Ground* (New York, 1947), p. 459. O. Price to W. C. Barnes, Jan. 29; P. P. Wells to Barnes, Feb. 6; Pinchot to Barnes, March 17; Barnes to H. A. Jastro, June 28, 1910, Barnes Papers. H. A. Smith to Pinchot, Jan. 29; H. S. Graves to Pinchot, Aug. 26, 1910; A. F. Potter to Pinchot, July 14, 1941; Potter, "The Treaty of 1910," typescript, copy, Box 339, Pinchot Papers.

[22] Flagstaff, Ariz., *Coconino Sun*, Jan. 14, 1910. Butte *Miner*, Jan. 19, 1910. W. C. Barnes to H. A. Jastro, June 28, 1910, Barnes Papers.

[23] P. Gibson to G. Pinchot, Jan. 4, 1910, Pinchot Papers. E. L. Norris, address printed in *Twelfth Report of the Department of Agriculture, Commerce, and Industry of the State of Montana, for the Years 1909–1910* (Helena, 1910) I, 18–29. *Governor's Message Relating to Conservation* . . . (Helena, 1911).

[24] Olympia, Wash., *State Capital Record*, Aug. 12, 1911. J. J. Underwood, *The Crime of Conservation* ([Seattle?], 1911), and "A Possible Peril to Our Republic . . . ," *Leslie's Illustrated Weekly Newspaper*, April 24, 1913, pp. 446–447, copies of both items in Pinchot Papers. George L. Knapp, "The Other Side of Conservation," *North American Review*, 191 (April, 1910), 465–481.

[25] Frank H. Short, *An Open Letter to Mr. Gifford Pinchot* . . . (n.p., n.d.), copy in Jonathan Bourne, Jr., Papers, University of Oregon Library. Los Angeles *Times*, Feb. 23 and 25, 1910.

[26] Frederick S. Titsworth, "Notes on the Legal Aspects of the Conservation Problem," *Proceedings of the Colorado Scientific Society*, 9 (March, 1910), 315–334, copy in Pinchot Papers.

[27] Bellingham, Wash., *Herald*, Sept. 11, 1910. J. J. Donavan to M. E. Hay, July 16, 1910, Marion E. Hay Papers, Eastern Washington State Historical Society. Clipping, undated, San Francisco *Recorder*, enclosure in R. L. Dunn to R. A. Ballinger, May 3, 1910, Ballinger Papers.

[28] H. J. Hagerman, article, copy, enclosure in H. Hurd to R. A. Ballinger, March 9; A. O. Repetto to Ballinger, July 8 and 20, 1910, Ballinger Papers. G. W. Edwards, *Conservation and Our Republic* (n.p., 1911), copy in Bourne Papers.

[29] *Attitude of the Seattle Chamber of Commerce on Conservation* . . . (Seattle, 1910), copy in Bourne Papers. Francis W. Harris and Andrew P. Johnson, *The Neglected West* (Seattle, 1911), copy in Ballinger Papers.

[30] *Owens Valley Herald*, Sept. 23, 1910. Oregon City *Enterprise*, Jan. 21, 1910. Clipping, *c.* Jan., 1910, and John Minto, "The Forester: What Is to Be His Relation to the State and to the Nation," MS of article, *c.* 1910, John Minto Papers, Oregon Historical Society.

[31] "Forest Fires of Coeur d'Alene" and "I" files, James H. Brady Papers, Idaho

Historical Society. *Idaho Statesman,* Aug. 24 and 25, 1910. Los Angeles *Times,* Aug. 26, 1910. Missoula, Mont., *Missoulan,* Aug. 27, 1910.

³² M. E. Hay to G. A. Haynes, Aug. 10, 1910, and Hay to "My Dear Governor," undated, Hay Papers, Eastern Washington. A draft of this second letter, dated July 30, 1910, with revisions evidently made by Brainerd of the *Post-Intelligencer* is in the Erastus Brainerd Papers, University of Washington Library.

³³ J. H. Brady to J. A. Shafroth, teleg., Aug. 11, 1910, copy, Spry Papers. B. B. Brooks to M. E. Hay, Aug. 8; W. M. Arthur to Hay, Aug. 12, 1910, Hay Papers, Eastern Washington. W. Spry to Hay, Aug. 4, to St. Paul, Minn., *Dispatch,* Aug. 11, 1910, Spry Papers. Hay to J. A. Shafroth, Aug. 8, Shafroth to the governors of the western states, Aug. 15, 1910, Shafroth Papers. *Salt Lake Tribune,* Aug. 7, 1910. *Post-Intelligencer,* Aug. 19, 1910. E. T. Allen to G. Pinchot, Aug. 4; T. R. Shipp to Pinchot, Aug. 14, Pinchot to Shipp, Aug. 15; R. Smoot to Pinchot, Sept. 21, 1910, Pinchot Papers. J. A. Eddy to R. A. Ballinger, Aug. 23, and Ballinger to Eddy, Sept. 1, 1910, Ballinger Papers. Draft of resolutions of this Salt Lake City governors conference; "An Observer" to Hay, *c.* Aug., 1910, Hay Papers, Eastern Washington.

³⁴ R. A. Ballinger to M. E. Hay and to D. Carr, and Carr to Ballinger, Aug. 21, 1910, Ballinger Papers.

³⁵ G. Pinchot to A. O. Eberhart, July 9; C. L. Pack to Pinchot, July 22; Pinchot to Pack, July 29; T. R. Shipp to Pinchot, July–August; E. T. Allen to Pinchot, Aug. 4, 1910, Pinchot Papers. *Investigation of the Department of the Interior . . .* (Washington, 1911), V, 1803, 1819. H. R. Logan to T. H. Carter, July 16, 1910, Carter Papers. J. A. Eddy to R. A. Ballinger, Aug. 20; L. Hill to Ballinger, July 6; Ballinger to Hill, July 18, 1910, Ballinger Papers. Hill to M. E. Hay, Aug. 8, 1910, Hay Papers, Eastern Washington.

³⁶ M. E. Hay to T. R. Shipp, Aug. 30; to L. K. Armstrong, April 30; T. E. Roling to Hay, *c.* Aug. 30, 1910, Hay Papers. E. L. Norris to Hay, Aug. 4, 1910, Hay Papers, Eastern Washington. J. Bowerman to R. A. Ballinger, Jan. 18, 1911, Ballinger Papers. A. N. Brown to E. Brainerd, Sept. 9, 1910, Brainerd Papers.

³⁷ E. T. Merritt to W. Spry, Sept. 1, 1910, and enclosure, Spry Papers.

³⁸ G. Pardee to G. Pinchot, Aug. 21, 1910, Pinchot Papers. Denver *Republican,* Aug. 30, 1910. Los Angeles *Times,* Sept. 5–7, 1910.

³⁹ M. E. Hay to J. A. Shafroth, Sept. 21, 1910, Shafroth Papers. *Idaho Statesman,* Jan. 5, 1911. Los Angeles *Times,* Sept. 9–13, 1910. *Oregonian,* Oct. 11, 1910. E. L. Norris to M. E. Hay, Sept. 24; R. E. Sloan to Hay, Sept. 28; W. Spry to Hay, Oct. 17; J. Gillett to Hay, Oct. 4, 1910, Hay Papers, Eastern Washington.

⁴⁰ M. E. Hay to F. O. Hudnut, Oct. 14, 1910, Hay Papers, Eastern Washington. S. Norman to G. Pinchot, June 16, 1910, Pinchot Papers. Los Angeles *Times,* Aug. 27, Sept. 1 and 27–30, 1910. W. E. Pedrich to J. A. Shafroth, Sept. 14 and Oct. 4, 1910, Shafroth Papers.

CHAPTER VI: THE LIMITS OF REACTION

¹ M. E. Hay to E. C. McDonald, Sept. 19, and to G. Pinchot, Oct. 12, 1910, Marion E. Hay Papers, Eastern Washington State Historical Society.

² E. Grandjean to G. Pinchot, Dec. 26, 1912, Gifford Pinchot Papers, Library of Congress. M. E. Hay to M. S. Lewis, Nov. 16; to G. A. Haynes, Aug. 10; to R. A. Ballinger, Sept. 26; to F. O. Hudnut, Oct. 14; to G. Pinchot, Oct. 12, 1910, Hay Papers, Eastern Washington.

³ M. E. Hay to F. O. Hudnut, Oct. 14; to W. T. Heacock, Oct. 15, and to E. C. McDonald, Sept. 13, 1910; Hay, *The State's Interest in Conservation* (Olympia, 1910), copy in Hay Papers, Eastern Washington. *Second Message of Governor M. E. Hay to the Legislature of 1911* (Olympia, 1911), pp. 21–22.

⁴ Cartoon in Boise *Idaho Statesman,* Jan. 21, 1911.

⁵ Message of Jay Bowerman, *Acting Governor of Oregon, to the . . . Legislative Assembly . . .* (Salem, 1911), pp. 18–19. *Journal of the Senate . . .* (Salem, 1911),

pp. 31, 257, 310, 549. Portland *Oregonian,* Jan. 22–23 and March 7, 1911. J. Teal to G. Pinchot, Feb. 9, 1911, Pinchot Papers.

[6] *Journal of the Senate*... (Denver, 1911), pp. 425, 643. *Governor's Message Relating to Conservation*... (Helena, 1911), pp. 3–6.

[7] J. A. Shafroth to E. T. Taylor, April 15, 1912, John A. Shafroth Papers, Colorado State Archives. H. J. Riebling to G. Pinchot, Jan. 20, 1910, Pinchot Papers. T. H. Carter to S. Gordon, Feb. 7, 1910, Thomas H. Carter Papers, Library of Congress. *Congressional Record,* 61st Cong., 2nd sess. (May 24–June 11, 1910), pp. 6518–6521, 6532, 7077–7086, 7538–7561. A. N. Brown to E. Brainerd, Jan. 14, 1911, Erastus Brainerd Papers, University of Washington Library. Pinchot, Diary, 1911, entry for March 3, and T. W. Gray to T. W. Tomlinson, March 7, 1911, copy, Pinchot Papers. W. B. Heyburn to P. Norton, Feb. 14, 1911, William H. Taft Papers, Library of Congress.

[8] *Congressional Record,* 61st Cong., 1st sess. (Aug. 11, 1911), p. 3838. A. W. Lafferty to G. Pinchot, June 19, and Pinchot to Lafferty, Aug. 29, 1911, Pinchot Papers.

[9] *Congressional Record,* 62nd Cong., 2nd sess. (May 13–16, 1912), pp. 6391–6393, 6488–6495, 6549–6560, and especially 6561.

[10] J. H. Brady to R. A. Ballinger, July 6, 1910, Richard A. Ballinger Papers, University of Washington Library. Brady to M. E. Hay, Sept. 3, 1910, Hay Papers, Eastern Washington.

[11] G. L. Knapp to T. Burke, April 15, 1910, Thomas E. Burke Papers, University of Washington Library.

[12] W. H. Taft to R. A. Ballinger, Oct. 9, 1909, Ballinger Papers. Los Angeles *Times,* Feb. 28, 1910.

[13] W. H. Taft to W. L. Fisher, Sept. 25, 1909, copy, Pinchot Papers. W. Kent to Taft, June 22, and Sept. 10, 1909; Taft to Kent, Sept. 1, 1909; R. A. Ballinger to Taft, Jan. 9 and Feb. 2, 1911; T. Oddie to Taft, Feb. 9, 1911; Taft to Oddie, March 2, 1911, Taft Papers. See also Samuel P. Hays, *Conservation and the Gospel of Efficiency* (Cambridge, Mass., 1959), pp. 154–165.

[14] R. A. Ballinger to J. A. Eddy, July 15, copy attached to Ballinger to W. H. Taft, July 24, 1911, Taft Papers. *Investigation of the Department of the Interior*... (Washington, 1911), VII, 3748–3749, 4146. Ballinger to D. Carr, Aug. 10, 1910; Ballinger, "The Public Domain and National Obligations Regarding its Disposition," MS of speech, March 16, 1910; Ballinger to C. L. Mosher, Feb. 26, and to C. W. Shaffer, Feb. 11, 1910; Cabinet memoranda, Dec. 31, 1909, and Jan. 25 and 28, 1910, Ballinger Papers.

[15] J. A. Eddy to R. A. Ballinger, Jan. 29, 1910, Interior Records, National Archives. F. Mondell to Ballinger, Nov. 22, 1909; A. C. Campbell, memorandum, enclosed in Ballinger to T. H. Carter, Feb., 1910; Cabinet memoranda, Feb. 8 and 11, and April 1, 1910, Ballinger Papers. P. P. Wells to G. Pinchot, April 12, 1910, Pinchot Papers. J. R. Garfield, Diary, 1910, entry for Feb. 16, James R. Garfield Papers, Library of Congress.

[16] F. Mondell to R. A. Ballinger, Jan. 11 and June 11; Ballinger to G. Sutherland, Sept. 26; Sutherland to Ballinger, Oct. 4; Ballinger to W. H. Taft, Oct. 22; J. A. Eddy to Ballinger, Nov. 16, 1910, Ballinger Papers. [Richard A. Ballinger], *Report of the Secretary of the Interior* (Washington, 1910), pp. 21–22. Ballinger to Taft, July 25, 1911, Taft Papers.

[17] Interior Department press notices, June 22, 1910, Interior Records, N.A. R. A. Ballinger, Cabinet memoranda, April 19, Oct. 2, and Nov. 25, 1910, Ballinger Papers. Hays, *op. cit.,* pp. 89–90. P. P. Wells to G. Pinchot, Aug. 1, 1910, Pinchot Papers.

[18] Interior Department press notice, Nov. 5, 1910, Interior Records, N.A. R. A. Ballinger to D. Carr, July 8, and to F. Curtis, June 4, 1910; confidential memorandum, perhaps prepared by Lawler, sent to W. W. Robertson, July 27, 1910; index to

testimony of Newell and Davis, typescript; W. H. Taft to Ballinger, May 13, 1910; Cabinet memorandum, Dec. 16, 1910, Ballinger Papers.

[19] G. U. Young to R. A. Ballinger, Jan. 4, 1910, Ballinger Papers. J. A. Eddy to Ballinger, June 28, July 15, Sept. 6, 1909, and April 23, 1910; to W. H. Taft, April 25, 1910; to R. Smoot, April 23, 1910, National Public Domain League file, G.L.O., Interior Records, N.A. Ballinger to D. C. Beaman, Nov. 16, 1909, Denver Land Convention file, Interior Records, N.A. T. M. Patterson to Ballinger, Jan. 6, and Ballinger to Patterson, Jan. 10, 1910, General Forestry, National Forest, and Forest Service files, arranged by state; E. M. Holbrook to Ballinger, June 21; A. R. Titlow to Ballinger, Feb. 14; M. D. McInery to Ballinger, Aug. 30; C. W. Shaffer to Ballinger, Feb. 4; Ballinger to Shaffer, Feb. 11, 1910; and to E. L. Baldwin, Dec. 30, 1909; drafts and copies of speeches, March 16, July 23, 24, and 27, Aug. 11 and 12, and Sept. 7, 1910, Ballinger Papers.

[20] R. A. Ballinger to J. J. Vertrees, June 29; W. J. Mills to Ballinger, July 7; M. D. McInery to Ballinger, June 29; C. W. Fulton to Ballinger, Aug. 29; C. H. Hartson to Ballinger, Aug. 5; J. A. Eddy to Ballinger, Nov. 20 and 25, 1910, Ballinger Papers. Ballinger to W. H. Taft, July 13, 1910, Taft Papers. A. N. Brown to E. Brainerd, Oct. 21, 1910, Brainerd Papers.

[21] Interior Department press notices, Nov. 1, Dec. 15 and 23, Interior Records, N.A. A. N. Brown to E. Brainerd, Dec. 11, 1910, Brainerd Papers.

[22] R. A. Ballinger to W. E. Humphrey, Dec. 19, and to M. E. Hay, Oct. 4, 1910; J. A. Eddy to Ballinger, Jan. 20, 1911, Ballinger Papers.

[23] Interior Department press notice, Nov. 24, 1910, Interior Records, N.A. R. A. Ballinger, speech to the Arctic Club, July 27, 1910, and speech at Williams College, Jan. 26, 1911, copies; Ballinger to R. Beach, Feb. 25, 1911, Ballinger Papers.

[24] Colusa, Calif., *Sun*, March 22, 1911. *Salt Lake Herald*, March 9, 1911. G. Pardee to G. Pinchot, March 30, 1911, Pinchot Papers.

[25] *Idaho Statesman*, Jan. 9, 1911. Denver *Rocky Mountain News*, May 17, 1911. Denver *Record-Stockman*, May 18, 1911.

[26] J. A. Eddy to J. A. Martin, Aug. 7, 1911, copy, Denver Land Convention file, Interior Records, N.A. R. Atkinson to J. H. Hawley, Aug. 5, 1911, James H. Hawley Papers, Idaho Historical Society. Eddy to J. A. Shafroth, May 19, undated copy, June 17, Sept. 2 and 12, 1911, Shafroth Papers. G. Pardee to G. Pinchot, July 22 and 28; F. Newell to Pinchot, Aug. 8; D. W. Aupperle to Pinchot, Sept. 12; Pinchot to Mrs. J. W. Pinchot, May 30; to Pardee, July 21 and 28, 1911, Pinchot Papers.

[27] M. E. Hay to Spokane, Wash., *Chronicle*, Sept. 4, and to Spokane *Spokesman-Review*, Sept. 5; to J. R. McKee, March 31, 1911, Marion E. Hay Papers, Washington State Archives. Public Lands Convention Bulletin No. 2, and supplement, enclosed in E. Mills to G. Pinchot, Aug. 16, 1911; G. Pardee to Pinchot, Aug. 2, 1911, Pinchot Papers. W. J. Mills to W. L. Fisher, July 19 and Fisher to Mills, July 25, 1911, Denver Land Convention file, Interior Records, N.A. W. Spry to J. A. Eddy, Aug. 16 and Sept. 26, 1911, William Spry Papers, Utah State Archives.

[28] *Rocky Mountain News*, Sept. 26 and Oct. 3, 1911.

[29] Clipping, enclosed in A. Johnson to R. A. Ballinger, July 12, 1911, Ballinger Papers. Ballinger to J. A. Eddy, July 15, copy; to W. H. Taft, July 24 and 28; Taft to Ballinger, July 21 and 31, and Aug. 3, 1911, Taft Papers.

[30] R. A. Ballinger, speech at Second Public Lands Convention, copy, Folder 1061, Taft Papers.

[31] J. A. Shafroth to J. Charlton, Oct. 9, 1911, Shafroth Papers. W. G. M. Stone to W. L. Fisher, Sept. 18, 1911, Denver Land Convention file, Interior Records, N. A. Fisher to W. H. Taft, teleg., Sept. 30, 1911, Walter L. Fisher Papers, Library of Congress. *Rocky Mountain News*, Oct. 3, 1911.

[32] J. A. Shafroth to J. A. Eddy, Dec. 14, 1911; J. W. Mussen to Shafroth, April 2 and May 4, 1910; E. L. Norris to Shafroth, Jan. 9, March 20, April 19, and July 29,

1912; Shafroth to Norris, July 25, and to Mussen, April 30, 1912; L. W. Strickland to Shafroth, May 6, 1912; A. Chappell to Shafroth, July 25, 1912, Shafroth Papers. J. H. Brady to J. D. Works, Nov. 22, 1911, John D. Works Papers, Bancroft Library. Norris to W. H. Taft, Nov. 16, 1911, Taft Papers. J. H. Hawley to Norris, Nov. 6 and 8, 1911, and March 18, 1912, Hawley Papers. Conference of Western Governors file, G.L.O., Interior Records, N.A.

[33] A. N. Brown to E. Brainerd, Sept. 7; W. L. Jones to Brainerd, Sept. 16; M. E. Hay to Brainerd, Sept. 30, 1912, Brainerd Papers.

CHAPTER VII: ON THE PROGRESSIVES' BANDWAGON

[1] W. G. M. Stone to G. Pinchot, Jan. 27, 1910, Gifford Pinchot Papers, Library of Congress. G. H. Marx to F. Hichborn, Jan. 11, 1910, Franklin Hichborn Papers, University of California at Los Angeles, Library. Los Angeles *Herald*, Jan. 9, 1910. W. C. Barnes to Pinchot, Jan. 12, 1910, Will C. Barnes Papers, Arizona Pioneers Historical Society. C. L. Edholm to Pinchot, Jan. 8; J. Teal to Pinchot, Jan. 8; G. Pardee to Pinchot, Jan. 8; M. Alexander *et al.* to Pinchot, Jan. 8; M. Bond to Pinchot, Jan. 10; Pinchot to G. Stanton, Feb. 16; to F. Crawford, March 14; to A. C. Ringland, March 8, 1910, Pinchot Papers.

[2] W. G. M. Stone to G. Pinchot, March 17 and May 6; S. Riley to Pinchot, Jan.; W. T. Cox to Pinchot, Sept. 11; C. Rutherford to Pinchot, April 28; J. H. Beatty to Pinchot, Sept. 3; P. Gibson to Pinchot, Sept. 13, 1910, Pinchot Papers. North Yakima, Wash., *Yakima Herald*, Feb. 2, 1910. A. S. Hosmer to F. E. Warren, Jan. 10, 1910, Francis E. Warren Papers, University of Wyoming Library. J. R. Garfield, Diary, 1910, entry for April 18, James R. Garfield Papers, Library of Congress. Pinchot to A. C. Ringland, March 8; to D. D. Olds, Feb. 17; to E. T. Allen, Aug. 22; to W. Mills, June 27; to M. E. Hay, Nov. 10; to G. M. Cornwall, Nov. 29; A. M. Drew to Pinchot, Feb. 21 and March 15; Allen to Pinchot, July 20; G. Pardee to Pinchot, June 23; H. S. Graves to Pinchot, May 7 and Aug. 16; Pinchot to Graves, July 29, 1910, Pinchot Papers.

[3] W. Kent to W. Washburn, Sept., 1909, and to G. Pinchot, Jan., 1910, quoted in Elizabeth Kent, *William Kent, Independent* (privately printed, 1950), pp. 191–192. Kent to C. H. Rowell, Feb. 3, and Rowell to Kent, Jan. 12, 1910, Chester H. Rowell Papers, Bancroft Library. M. Manson to Pinchot, Jan. 9, 1910, Marsden Manson Papers, Bancroft Library. G. Curry to A. C. Voorhees, Dec. 27, 1909; to C. Lyon, Jan. 11 and to A. B. Fall, Feb. 21, 1910, George Curry Papers, New Mexico Historical Society.

[4] Unsigned letter to J. A. Eddy, Jan. 11, 1910, copy, John A. Shafroth Papers, Colorado State Archives. Tucson, Ariz., *Citizen*, Jan. 8, 1910. T. Roosevelt to G. Pinchot, March 1, 1910, copy; Pinchot to E. T. Allen, Aug. 16, 1910, Pinchot Papers. Phoenix *Arizona Republican*, Jan. 8 and 9, 1910. A. Pinchot to Pinchot, May 8, and G. Pardee to Pinchot, March 21, 1910, Pinchot Papers.

[5] B. B. Lindsey to F. W. Scripps, April 7, copy; C. P. Dodge to G. Pinchot, July 20; J. E. Painter to Pinchot, Aug. 21 and Nov. 18; Lindsey to Pinchot, Sept. 3, 1910, Pinchot Papers.

[6] R. A. Ballinger to P. Norton, Aug. 11, and L. L. Sharpe to F. Dennett, Aug. 23, 1910, copy, Richard A. Ballinger Papers, University of Washington Library. Portland *Oregonian*, Jan. 10, Nov. 2 and 14, 1910. E. T. Allen to G. Pinchot, Aug. 4, 1910; H. Moody to Pinchot, April 19, 1907; J. Teal to Pinchot, Nov. 10, 1910, Pinchot Papers. Information furnished to me by former Governor Oswald West. *Message of Oswald West, Governor of Oregon to the . . . Legislative Assembly . . .* (Salem, 1911), pp. 19–21. *Fourth Annual Report of the Oregon Conservation Commission* (Salem, 1912), p. 15.

[7] A. L. Filson to R. A. Ballinger, July 6, 1910, Ballinger Papers. P. Clagstone to G. Pinchot, July 8, and to G. Pardee, July 6; Pardee to Pinchot, July 24; Pinchot to Clagstone, July 28, and to Pardee, Aug. 17, 1910, Pinchot Papers.

⁸ M. Manson to A. Giannini, June 18, 1910, Manson Papers. H. W. Johnson to E. A. Dickson, June 12, 1910, Edward A. Dickson Papers, University of California at Los Angeles, Library. M. Stimson to G. Pinchot, Sept. 24; W. Kent to Pinchot, June 25; Pinchot to Kent, June 30; M. U'Ren to Pinchot, Aug. 30; Pinchot to U'Ren, Aug. 25, 1910, Pinchot Papers. F. Hichborn to F. J. Heney, July 6, and J. J. McCarthy to Hichborn, June 14, 1910, Hichborn Papers. Los Angeles *Express,* July 19 and 21, Aug. 11, 1910. Los Angeles *Herald,* Aug. 7, Sept. 15 and 17, 1910. Los Angeles *Times,* July 22, Aug. 2 and 5, 1910. R. A. Ballinger to W. H. Taft, Aug. 19, 1910, Ballinger Papers. T. Roosevelt to W. Kent, Aug. 5, 1910, Theodore Roosevelt Papers, Library of Congress. F. C. Sharp to M. E. Hay, Sept. 8, 1910, Marion E. Hay Papers, Eastern Washington.

⁹ The formulation of state conservation policy by the Hiram Johnson administration may be traced in the papers of Pardee, Rowell, and Lissner. The foregoing discussion is based upon these specific items: Committee on Proposed Legislation list, Edward A. Dickson Papers. M. Lissner to H. W. Johnson, Nov. 25; E. E. Keech to Lissner, Nov. 23; Lissner to Keech, Nov. 29; W. Kent to Lissner, Dec. 1, 1910, Meyer Lissner Papers, Stanford University Library. Lissner to Johnson, Jan. 23 and 24, 1911, and G. Pardee to F. Hichborn, Feb. 5, 1912, Hichborn Papers. *Inaugural Address of Governor Hiram W. Johnson . . .* (Sacramento, 1911), p. 12. *First Biennial Message of Governor Hiram W. Johnson . . .* (Sacramento, 1913), pp. 12–13. On the work of the California Conservation Commission, see C. Raymond Clar, *California Government and Forestry . . .* (Sacramento, 1959), pp. 329–349, and on the Glavis affair see *ibid.,* pp. 331–334.

¹⁰ J. J. Browne to L. K. Armstrong, Jan. 28, 1910, copy, Marion E. Hay Papers, Washington State Archives. F. G. Flower to G. Pinchot, Feb. 11, 1910, Pinchot Papers. M. E. Hay to W. Heacock, Oct. 15, 1910, Hay Papers. "Manifesto of Eastern Washington League of Republican Editors," Nov., 1909, typescript, copy in Wesley L. Jones Papers, University of Washington Library. M. C. Poindexter to John L. Wilson Senatorial Club, Dec. 31, 1909, and to W. L. Jones and S. Piles, Feb. 8, 1910, Miles C. Poindexter Papers (film copy), University of Washington Library.

¹¹ F. H. Turner to W. L. Jones, Jan. 7; H. L. McLean to Jones, March 9; W. D. Sargent to Jones, April 13; W. D. Jones to Jones, March 9; H. W. Wentworth to Jones, April 19, 1910; Jones, draft of speech to state Republican convention, *c.* April, 1910; Jones Papers.

¹² A. O. Repetto to R. A. Ballinger, July 20, 1910, Ballinger Papers. Ballinger to W. H. Taft, July 15, 1910, William H. Taft Papers, Library of Congress. Seattle *Times,* Aug. 23, 1910. F. C. Jones to Jones, Feb. 7, 1910, Jones Papers. J. Stringer to Ballinger, Jan. 24, and E. Brainerd to Ballinger, Feb. 5, 1910, Ballinger Papers. J. J. Donavan, statement, Aug. 6, 1910, copy; Ballinger to Brainerd, Feb. 10, 1910, Erastus Brainerd Papers, University of Washington Library. Ballinger to W. H. Taft, July 15, 1910, Taft Papers.

¹³ W. H. Taft to J. L. Wilson, May 16, 1910, Taft Papers. M. E. Hay to Taft, Aug. 22, 1910, Hay Papers, Eastern Washington. P. Norton to R. A. Ballinger, July 29 and Aug. 11, 1910, Ballinger Papers.

¹⁴ A. N. Brown to E. Brainerd, Aug. 15, and J. J. Donavan to Brainerd, Sept. 11, 1910, Brainerd Papers. M. C. Poindexter to G. Pinchot, July 24; A. G. Fleming to Pinchot, Sept. 9; Pinchot to Poindexter, Aug. 16 and Sept. 10 and 14, 1910, Pinchot Papers. Poindexter to F. O. Martin, Sept. 26, and K. T. Webber to Poindexter, Sept. 14, 1910, Poindexter Papers.

¹⁵ R. A. Ballinger to W. M. Crane, Sept. 21; Crane to Ballinger, Sept. 19; Ballinger to W. E. Humphrey, teleg., Nov. 10; Humphrey to Ballinger, Nov. 11, 1910, Ballinger Papers. W. A. White to G. Pinchot, Dec. 5, 1910, Pinchot Papers.

¹⁶ G. Pinchot to A. W. Maltby, April 27; G. Pardee to Pinchot, June 23; Pinchot to G. P. Ahern, Oct. 15; F. A. Turner to Pinchot, Jan. 12; F. W. Culbertson to

Pinchot, Jan. 15, 1910, Pinchot Papers. J. G. Lawrence to W. L. Jones, May 5, 1910, Jones Papers.

[17] D. Carr to R. A. Ballinger, Aug. 15; Ballinger to Carr, Aug. 15; Carr to Ballinger, Aug. 16 and 23; G. G. Hill to Ballinger, Aug. 9, 1910, Ballinger Papers. T. R. Shipp to G. Pinchot, March 25, and W. Kent to Pinchot, June 25, 1910, Pinchot Papers. A. N. Brown to E. Brainerd, Aug. 15, 1910, Brainerd Papers. M. E. Hay to W. L. Jones, Sept. 12, 1910, Hay Papers, Eastern Washington.

[19] C. H. Rowell to L. K. Bell, Aug. 24, and to W. Englebright, Nov. 18 and 21, 1910, Rowell Papers. R. A. Ballinger to J. J. Vertrees, Aug. 26; Vertrees to Ballinger, Aug. 13; Ballinger to W. M. Crane, Sept. 10; Crane to Ballinger, Sept. 19, 1910, Ballinger Papers. W. H. Taft to M. E. Hay, Aug. 29, 1910, Hay Papers, Eastern Washington.

[20] A. N. Brown to E. Brainerd, May 26, 1910, Brainerd Papers. R. A. Ballinger to D. H. Kelsey, Oct. 17, 1910, and to W. H. Taft, Jan. 19, 1911, copy, Ballinger Papers.

[21] C. P. Taft to W. H. Taft, Jan. 26, 1911, Taft Papers. G. Pinchot to G. Pardee, Feb. 6, 1911, Pinchot Papers. R. A. Ballinger to Taft, March 6, 1911, Taft Papers.

[22] W. H. Taft to R. A. Ballinger, March 7, 1911.

[23] J. M. Dickerson to R. A. Ballinger, March 7, 1911, Ballinger Papers. W. H. Taft to F. MacVeagh, March 7, 1911, Taft Papers.

[24] R. A. Ballinger to W. L. Fisher, April 10, 1911, Walter L. Fisher Papers, Library of Congress. W. H. Taft to R. A. Ballinger, April 17, June 5, and Sept. 4, 1911; Ballinger to C. D. Hilles, March 15, 1912, and Aug. 28, 1911; Taft to M. Bradley, May 25 and Aug. 19, 1911; Ballinger to Taft, May 31, 1911, Taft Papers. Seattle *Post-Intelligencer*, Nov. 11, 1912.

[25] P. S. Stahnlicker to G. Pinchot, memorandum, March, 1911; Pinchot to T. Roosevelt, Jan. 21, 1911; Pinchot, Diary, 1911, entry for March 7; Pinchot, statement at New York City, March 7, 1911, copy; G. Pardee to Pinchot, Feb. 15, 1911, Pinchot Papers. J. R. Garfield to Pinchot, March 7, 1911; Garfield, Diary, 1911, entry for March 7, Garfield Papers.

[26] Laramie, Wyo., *Republican*, March 9, 1911. Flagstaff, Ariz., *Coconino Sun*, March 10, 1911. Great Falls, Mont., *Leader*, March 8, 1911. Boise *Idaho Statesman*, March 13, 1911. L. J. Morrison to W. L. Jones, Feb. 26, 1911, Jones Papers. J. M. Carey to Pinchot, March 10, 1911, Pinchot Papers. Phoenix *Arizona Democrat*, Dec. 14, 1910. *Arizona Republican*, March 8, 1911. Helena, Mont., *Independent*, March 8, 1911. San Francisco *Call*, March 8, 1911. Fresno, Calif., *Republican*, March 8, 1911.

[27] W. H. Taft to C. P. Taft, Dec. 24, 1909, Taft Papers. W. L. Fisher to Pinchot, Oct. 10 and 20, 1910; Pinchot to C. R. Crane, Sept. 12, 1908; Pinchot, statement at New York City, March 7, 1911, copy, Pinchot Papers.

[28] W. Kent to G. Pinchot, March 13, and J. R. Garfield to Pinchot, April 5, 1911, Pinchot Papers. R. A. Ballinger to W. H. Taft, July 28, and Taft to Ballinger, July 29 and Aug. 3, 1911, Taft Papers. Missoula, Mont., *Missoulan*, March 9, 1911. Helena *Independent*, March 8, 1911. *Idaho Statesman*, March 8 and 9, 1911. J. F. Reihl to W. H. Taft, March 9, 1911, Taft Papers. Denver *Rocky Mountain News*, March 8, 1911.

[29] Philadelphia *Public Ledger*, April 23, 1911. G. Pinchot to M. Manson, Aug. 21, and to G. Pardee, Nov. 24, 1911, Pinchot Papers. Asst. Secy. folders, Pres. Appt. file, Interior Records, N.A. J. R. Garfield to W. L. Fisher, March 11 and 25, and April 25, 1911, Fisher Papers. Pinchot, Diary, 1911, entry for July 28, Pinchot Papers. Samuel P. Hays, *Conservation and the Gospel of Efficiency* (Cambridge, Mass., 1959), pp. 77, 79–80. Washington, D.C., *Herald*, April 25, 1911. A. N. Brown to E. Brainerd, April 30 and May 14, 1911, Brainerd Papers. R. A. Ballinger to W. H. Taft, July 28, 1911, Taft Papers. [Walter L. Fisher], *Report of the Secretary of the Interior* (Washington, 1911), pp. 17–20. Fisher to W. Kent, Dec. 16, 1909, Fisher Papers.

³⁰ Hays, *op. cit.*, p. 247. G. Pinchot, Diary, 1911, entry for Nov. 24, Pinchot Papers. H. S. Graves to W. L. Fisher, Oct. 21, 1911, Transfer of the Forest Service file, G.L.O., Interior Records, N.A.

³¹ G. Pinchot, Diary, 1911, entry for May 25, Pinchot Papers. A. N. Brown to E. Brainerd, May 14, 1911, Brainerd Papers. M. E. Hay to W. L. Jones, July 20, 1912, Jones Papers.

³² R. A. Ballinger to W. H. Taft, April 24, 1911, Taft Papers. M. C. Moore to M. E. Hay, Oct. 2, 1911, and Hay to M. Leehey, Sept. 28, 1912, Hay Papers, Eastern Washington. Hay to W. L. Jones, July 10, 1912, and Jones to L. L. Stewart, July 15, 1912, Jones Papers. Ballinger to C. D. Hilles, May 20, 1912; T. A. Marlow to Hilles, Dec. 31, 1911; L. Hill to Hilles, Sept. 13, 1912, Taft Papers. *Oregonian,* Nov. 2, 1912. *Post-Intelligencer,* Oct. 29, 1912. J. J. Callahan to Hay, Jan. 8, 1913, Hay Papers, Eastern Washington.

³³ G. Pardee to G. Pinchot, Dec. 7, 1910, and March 5, 1911, Pinchot Papers. C. W. Thuringer to M. E. Hay, Aug. 12, 1910, Hay Papers, Eastern Washington. S. Gordon to Pinchot, April 25, 1911; Pinchot to T. Roosevelt, Dec. 10, 1910; to J. M. Dixon, Feb. 12, 1911; to Roosevelt, July 13, 1912; C. E. Wantland to Pinchot, March 12, 1912, Pinchot Papers. W. L. Jones to L. L. Stewart, July 15, 1912, Jones Papers. Los Angeles *Times,* Aug. 17 and 21, 1912. *Idaho Statesman,* May 25 and June 4, 1912. *Coconino Sun,* Oct. 4, 1912. Cheyenne *Wyoming Tribune,* Oct. 8, 1912.

³⁴ H. W. Johnson to G. Pinchot, June 3, 1912, and F. Cuttle to Pinchot, March 14 and April 2, 1912, Pinchot Papers. R. D. Carey to C. W. Brandon, March 5, 1912, and Brandon to A. Sims, June, 1912, C. Watt Brandon Papers, University of Wyoming Library. Great Falls *Leader,* Oct. 11, 1912. Los Angeles *Times,* Nov. 6, 1912. T. Roosevelt to G. Pinchot, Nov. 11, 1912, copy, Pinchot Papers, and July 11, 1916, Roosevelt Papers.

³⁵ *Resolutions Adopted by the Progressive Republican League of Montana . . . 1912* (n.p., 1912?), copy in William A. Clark Library. *Congressional Record,* 62nd Cong., 2nd sess. (Aug. 7, 1912), p. 10338. A. B. Fall to H. B. Holt, July 22, 1912, Albert B. Fall Papers, Henry E. Huntington Library, information furnished to me by David H. Stratton, Fall's biographer.

³⁶ G. Pinchot, Diary, 1911, entry for Jan. 21; R. T. Platt to Pinchot, Feb. 15, 1911, Pinchot Papers. F. S. Barnwell to J. Bourne, Sept. 14, 1910; Bourne to M. Ballam, Feb. 15, and to J. A. Schoonover, Nov. 28, 1911; I. Arneson to W. W. Prescott, March 21, 1911, copy; clippings in Conservation folder; Bourne to W. L. Fisher, Oct. 22, 1912; and A. J. Hinckley to Bourne Club of Seattle, Jonathan Bourne, Jr., Papers, University of Oregon Library. C. S. Chapman to Pinchot, May 24, and Pinchot to Chapman, May 29, 1912, Pinchot Papers. R. A. Ballinger to W. H. Taft, Jan. 13 and March 5, 1912, Taft Papers. W. Humphrey to M. E. Hay, March 7, 1911, Hay Papers, Eastern Washington. H. McLean to Pinchot, Dec. 23, 1911; Pinchot to McLean, Dec. 28, 1911; T. Roosevelt to Pinchot, Jan. 3, 1912, Pinchot Papers.

³⁷ E. P. Costigan to G. Pinchot, Oct. 2, 1908; H. H. Eddy to Costigan, Nov. 2, 1912; A. A. Foote to J. S. Temple, Feb. 10, 1912; Costigan to F. Johnson, Oct. 17, 1912; F. Cline to Costigan, Oct. 31, 1912, Edward P. Costigan Papers, University of Colorado Library. J. Causey to W. L. Fisher, Feb. 5, 1913, Fisher Papers. Denver *Republican,* Feb. 26, 1912. *Rocky Mountain News,* Sept. 1 and 4, and Oct. 31, 1912.

³⁸ T. Roosevelt to G. Pinchot, Nov. 13, 1912, Roosevelt Papers.

CHAPTER VIII: THE DEMOCRATS' OPPORTUNITY

¹ D. C. Beaman to R. A. Ballinger, Dec. 9, 1910, Richard A. Ballinger Papers, University of Washington Library. Denver *Republican,* Nov. 20 and 22, 1910. C. A. Coffin to P. Norton, Jan. 6, 1911, William H. Taft Papers, Library of Congress.

² E. T. Taylor to J. A. Shafroth, June 4 and Shafroth to Taylor, and to A. J. Van Tilbourg, June 19, 1912, John A. Shafroth Papers, Colorado State Archives.

H. A. Slattery to G. Pinchot, July 5, 1912, Gifford Pinchot Papers, Library of Congress. T. J. Walsh to T. D. Long, July 12, 1912, Thomas J. Walsh Papers, Library of Congress. Kirk H. Porter and Donald Bruce (comps.), *National Party Platforms*... (Urbana, 1956), pp. 172–173. A. B. Fall to H. B. Holt, July 22, 1912, Albert B. Fall Papers, Henry E. Huntington Library, information furnished to me by David H. Stratton, Fall's biographer.

³ Reno *Nevada State Journal*, Oct. 23, 1912. J. M. Carey to H. Plunkett, Dec. 30, 1911, copy, and to G. Pinchot, Jan. 18 and Feb. 8, 1912, Pinchot Papers. F. E. Warren to C. D. Hilles and to W. H. Taft, Nov. 9, 1912, Taft Papers. Denver *Rocky Mountain News*, Nov. 4, 1912. T. Shoemaker, [Reminiscences], typescript in Mr. Shoemaker's possession. W. A. Clark to R. A. Ballinger, Dec. 9, 1910, Ballinger Papers. Information furnished to me by F. Lee Kirby, formerly with the Forest Service in the Southwest.

⁴ W. Wilson to G. Pinchot, July 4, 1911; Pinchot, Diary, 1911, entry for July 21, 1911, Pinchot Papers. R. S. Baker and W. E. Dodd (eds.), *The Public Papers of Woodrow Wilson* (New York, 1924–1927), II, 307, 355, 371, 470. Helena, Mont., *Independent*, Oct. 4, 1912. *Rocky Mountain News*, Oct. 8, 1912. Portland *Oregonian*, Nov. 6, 1912.

⁵ Spokane, Wash., *Spokesman-Review*, Oct. 29, 1912. G. Pinchot to J. Teal, Oct. 14, 1912, Pinchot Papers. A. C. Voorhees to T. B. Catron, July 23, 1912, Thomas B. Catron Papers, University of New Mexico Library.

⁶ *Oregonian*, Nov. 30, 1912. *Rocky Mountain News*, Jan. 13 and 15, 1913. H. L. Myers to T. J. Walsh, Nov. 22, 1912, Walsh Papers. C. P. Dodge to G. Pinchot, Nov. 27, 1912, Pinchot Papers. Pocatello, Idaho, *Tribune*, Feb. 1, 1913. Boise, Idaho, *Capital News*, Feb. 28 and March 2, 1913. J. S. Bartlett to W. Wilson, Dec. 16, 1912, Pres. Appt. file, Interior Records, N.A.

Although divided on possible candidates, westerners were almost unanimously against the retention of Secretary Fisher. Borah asked the Idaho legislature to demand Fisher's recall, and Taylor, of Colorado, called for an organized protest against his continuation in office. Among those who thought that Wilson should keep him on were Ray Stannard Baker and President Taft. Fisher was personally willing to serve the new administration, if only because he feared that a crisis in conservation was inevitable when the Democratic Congress met: *Rocky Mountain News*, Jan. 13, 1913. M. D. McInery to W. L. Fisher, Jan. 3; Anon. to Fisher, Feb. 10; Fisher to M. Sullivan, Feb. 7; R. S. Baker to Fisher, Jan. 5, 1913; Fisher to Baker, Dec. 30, 1912, Walter L. Fisher Papers, Library of Congress. "Memo. found on Cabinet Table," Feb. 4, 1913, Taft Papers.

⁷ F. G. Newlands to T. J. Walsh, Nov. 14, 1912, Walsh Papers. C. Tallman folder, Pres. Appt. file, Interior Records, N.A. *Oregonian*, Nov. 27 and 29, 1912. Joseph N. Teal, "Autobiography...," typescript, copy in Pinchot Papers. San Francisco *Call*, Nov. 14–18, 1912. *Oregonian*, Nov. 29, 1912. Clippings, Franklin K. Lane Papers, Bancroft Library.

⁸ T. J. Walsh to F. G. Newlands, Nov. 8; to J. Davies, Nov. 18; to W. J. Bryan, Nov. 12 and 20, 1912, Walsh Papers.

⁹ G. Pinchot, Diary, 1912, entry for Nov. 7; Pinchot to W. Kent, Nov. 7, to L. Brandeis, Nov. 9, and J. Teal to Pinchot, Nov. 19, 1912, Pinchot Papers. Pinchot to T. Gore, and enclosure, Jan. 5, and H. L. Myers to W. Wilson, Jan. 7, 1913, Woodrow Wilson Papers, Library of Congress. F. H. Ray to T. J. Walsh, March 1; E. L. Norris to Walsh, Jan. 23 and Feb. 1, and to Wilson, Feb. 12, 1913, copy, Walsh Papers. Norris to M. E. Hay, Nov. 19, and Hay to Wilson, Nov. 22, 1912, Marion E. Hay Papers, Eastern Washington State Historical Society. Pinchot to W. Pach, Jan. 20, to Teal, Jan. 8, and to Brandeis, Jan. 24, 1913, Pinchot Papers.

¹⁰ W. Wilson to T. J. Walsh, Dec. 21, and H. L. Myers to Walsh, Nov. 22, 1912, Walsh Papers. G. Pinchot, Diary, 1913, entry for Jan. 24; Pinchot to L. Brandeis, Jan. 24, 1913, Pinchot Papers. W. J. Bryan to Wilson, Dec. 13, 1912, Wilson Papers.

R. S. Baker to W. L. Fisher, Jan. 5, 1913, Fisher Papers. Arthur S. Link, *Wilson: The New Freedom* (Princeton, 1956), p. 18.

¹¹ E. M. House to W. Wilson, Jan. 9, 1913, Wilson Papers. F. K. Lane to W. L. Fisher, Nov. 22, 1912, Fisher Papers. Lane to H. K. Asher, Oct. 22; to C. K. McClatchy, Nov. 25; to A. C. Miller, Dec. 4, 1912, and to E. M. House, Jan. 22, 1913, in Anne W. Lane and Louise H. Wall (eds.), *The Letters of Franklin K. Lane . . .* (New York, 1922), pp. 107–109, 112–113, 117–118, 124–126, and statement of Mrs. Lane, pp. 129–130.

¹² J. N. Teal to W. Wilson, March 4, 1913, Wilson Papers. T. Roosevelt to F. K. Lane, March 11, 1913, Theodore Roosevelt Papers, Library of Congress. San Francisco *Call*, March 4, 1913. *Oregonian*, March 3 and 4, 1913. Seattle *Post-Intelligencer*, March 2 and 4, 1913. G. Pinchot, Diary, 1913, entry for March 8, 1913, Pinchot Papers. E. L. Norris to T. J. Walsh, March 7; Walsh to Norris, March 18; B. E. Marden to Walsh, March 7, 1913, Walsh Papers. Helena *Independent*, March 6, 1913. Butte, Mont., *Miner*, March 17, 1913.

¹³ J. N. Teal to G. Pinchot, March 14, and Pinchot to Teal, March 21, 1913, Pinchot Papers. F. K. Lane to W. Wilson, May 22, 1913, and A. Andrews folder, Pres. Appt. file, Interior Records, N.A. Lane to A. Shaw, April 8, and to C. K. Field, April 18, 1914, in Lane and Wall (eds.), *op. cit.*, pp. 148–151. Lane later praised Ballinger because of the loyalty and affection which his staff had had for him, and because of the efficient organization he had built up in the Department. These sentiments caused Pinchot to describe Lane as an adherent of Ballinger: Pinchot's comments attached to copy of Ickes' article containing Lane's statement, Pinchot Papers.

¹⁴ Lane and Wall (eds.), *op. cit.*, pp. 139–140. E. M. Ammons to F. K. Lane, April 14; Lane to Ammons, May 19; Lane to W. Wilson, Aug. 11; Wilson to Lane, Aug. 11, 1913, G.L.O., Interior Records, N.A. Santa Fe *New Mexican*, April 8, 1914.

¹⁵ Elmo R. Richardson, "The Struggle for the Valley . . . ," *California Historical Society Quarterly*, Vol. 38, No. 3 (Sept., 1959), pp. 254–256. F. K. Lane to "My Dear Billy" (perhaps William Kent), June 10, 1914, in Lane and Wall (eds.), *op. cit.*, pp. 154–155.

¹⁶ Reno, Nev., *Gazette*, March 10, 1913. F. K. Lane to W. M. Bole, May 26, 1913; to E. F. Adams, Jan. 10, 1914; to L. F. Abbott, Jan. 12, 1915, in Lane and Wall (eds.), *op. cit.*, pp. 136–137, 144–145, 161–162. [F. K. Lane], *Report of the Secretary of the Interior* (Washington, 1913), pp. 1, 21–23. Samuel P. Hays, *Conservation and the Gospel of Efficiency* (Cambridge, Mass., 1959), p. 248.

¹⁷ *Rocky Mountain News*, March 22, 1913. C. S. Thomas to E. M. Ammons, March 20, 1913, Elias M. Ammons Papers, Colorado State Archives. F. K. Lane to W. E. Borah, *c.* Dec., 1913, William Borah Papers, Library of Congress.

Lane thought that Harding would do well to select Governor Lowden of Illinois as his Secretary of the Interior in 1921, an opinion that perhaps indicates Lane did not think the West's claim to the post a primary consideration. He praised the ultimate selection of Fall, of New Mexico, however, and thought that the senator would make "a good western Secretary," but one "quite likely to get into a row with our eastern conservation friends": Lane to G. W. Wickersham, Nov. 18, 1920, and to H. McAllister, April 22, 1921, in Lane and Wall (eds.), *op. cit.*, pp. 367 and 439. W. L. Jones to E. J. Hawkins, Aug. 29, 1913, Wesley L. Jones Papers, University of Washington Library. A. N. Brown to E. Brainerd, March 31 and Sept. 16, 1914, Erastus Brainerd Papers, University of Washington Library.

¹⁸ Los Angeles *Times*, April 5 and July 18, 1913. *Oregonian*, Feb. 3, 1913. *Capital News*, Feb. 6 and 24, 1913. *Idaho Statesman*, Feb. 13, 1913. Edward H. Thomas, "Conservation As Practiced," and Gifford Pinchot, "Conservation As Practiced . . . ," reprints from *Pearson's Magazine*, Jan. and May, 1913, in the John Crerar Library, Chicago.

¹⁹ *Inaugural Address of Elias M. Ammons, Governor of Colorado . . .* (Denver,

1913), pp. 5, 13. *Rocky Mountain News*, Jan. 15 and June 1, 1913. "Conservation from a Colorado Viewpoint—By A Critic of the Government," *Collier's Weekly*, March 15, 1913, p. 24. Ammons, article, *Farmer's Life* (Denver), Sept., 1913, copy in Conference of Western Governors file, G.L.O., Interior Records, N.A. Ammons to E. T. Taylor, Feb. 10 and May 20; to C. S. Thomas, April 4; and to W. G. M. Stone, April 4, 1913, Ammons Papers. C. P. Dodge to E. P. Costigan, Dec. 31, 1912; B. Griffith to Costigan, Feb. 26 and March 21; Costigan to editor of Grand Junction, Colo., *News*, April 7; Stone to Costigan, April 9, 1913, Edward P. Costigan Papers, University of Colorado Library. Dodge to G. Pinchot, Nov. 27, 1912, Pinchot Papers, and broadsides, "National Forests" and "Ammons, the Tool of Big Business," in folder 1853, *ibid.*

[20] G. Pinchot to W. Kent, Nov. 7; to C. R. Crane, Nov. 9; J. N. Teal to Pinchot, Nov. 19; Pinchot to S. E. White, Dec. 5, 1912; to B. A. Fowler, Jan. 2, 1913, Pinchot Papers.

[21] A. N. Brown to E. Brainerd, *c.* March, and March 31, 1913, Brainerd Papers. J. W. Bryan, *Proposed Investigation of the Forest Service . . .*, speech, copy in University of Washington Library. H. A. Slattery to G. Pinchot, July 23, 1912; Pinchot to C. L. Pack, July 9, 1913; Slattery to O. Price, May 27, 1913; and Pinchot, Diary, 1913, entries for Jan. 5, 10, and 29, Feb. 25 and 26, Pinchot Papers. W. A. Clark to W. E. Borah, Dec. 2, 1913, Borah Papers.

[22] *State versus National Control of the Public Forests From the Viewpoint of a Western State* (Portland, 1913), pp. 2–8.

[23] R. L. Wilbur to H. Hoover, Aug. 2, 1929, copy; A. B. Cammerer to H. L. Ickes, memorandum, March 19, 1934, Administrative file, State Control, Interior Records, N.A.

BIBLIOGRAPHY

BIBLIOGRAPHY

MANUSCRIPT COLLECTIONS

Library of Congress
  William E. Borah Papers
  Thomas H. Carter Papers
  Walter L. Fisher Papers
  James R. Garfield Papers
  Gifford Pinchot Papers
  Theodore Roosevelt Papers
  William H. Taft Papers
  Thomas J. Walsh Papers
  Woodrow Wilson Papers
Arizona
  Will C. Barnes Papers. Arizona Pioneers Historical Society, Tucson, and Arizona
    State University, Tempe
  E. S. Gosney Papers, Arizona Pioneers Historical Society, Tucson
  Frederic Winn Papers, Arizona Pioneers Historical Society, Tucson
California
  Edward A. Dickson Papers, University of California at Los Angeles, Library
  John P. Irish Papers, Stanford University Library, Stanford
  T. Perceval Gerson Papers, University of California at Los Angeles, Library.
  Franklin Hichborn Papers, University of California at Los Angeles, Library
  Robert U. Johnson Papers, University of California, Bancroft Library, Berkeley
  Abbot Kinney Papers, University of California at Los Angeles, Library
  Franklin K. Lane Papers, University of California, Bancroft Library, Berkeley
  Meyer Lissner Papers, Stanford University Library, Stanford
  Theodore P. Lukens Papers, Henry E. Huntington Library, San Marino
  Marsden Manson Papers, University of California, Bancroft Library, Berkeley
  James C. Needham Papers, Stanford University Library, Stanford
  George C. Pardee Papers, University of California, Bancroft Library, Berkeley
  Alice M. Rose Collection, Stanford University Library, Stanford
  Chester H. Rowell Papers, University of California, Bancroft Library, Berkeley
  John D. Works Papers, University of California, Bancroft Library, Berkeley
Colorado
  Edward P. Costigan Papers, University of Colorado Library, Boulder
Idaho
  Weldon B. Heyburn Papers, University of Idaho Library, Moscow
  C. J. Munson Scrapbooks, Idaho Historical Society
Nevada
  William S. Stewart Papers, Nevada State Historical Society, Reno
New Mexico
  Thomas B. Catron Papers, University of New Mexico Library, Albuquerque
Oregon
  Jonathan Bourne, Jr., Papers, University of Oregon Library, Eugene
  John Minto Papers, Oregon Historical Society, Portland, and Oregon State
    Library, Salem

Washington
  Richard A. Ballinger Papers, University of Washington Library, Seattle
  Erastus Brainerd Papers, University of Washington Library, Seattle
  Thomas E. Burke Papers, University of Washington Library, Seattle
  Marion E. Hay Papers, Eastern Washington State Historical Society, Spokane
  Wesley L. Jones Papers, University of Washington Library, Seattle
  Miles C. Poindexter Papers (film copies), University of Washington Library, Seattle
Wyoming
  C. Watt Brandon Papers, University of Wyoming Library, Laramie
  Bryant B. Brooks Papers, University of Wyoming Library, Laramie
  Alice Richards McCreery Collection, Wyoming Historical Society, Cheyenne
  Francis E. Warren Papers, University of Wyoming Library, Laramie

ARCHIVES

National Archives, Washington, D.C.
  Department of the Interior Records, Natural Resources Division
Colorado State Archives, Denver
  Elias M. Ammons Papers
  Henry A. Buchtel Papers
  John A. Shafroth Papers
Idaho Historical Society, Boise
  James H. Brady Papers
  Frank R. Gooding Papers
  James H. Hawley Papers
  Frank W. Hunt Papers
New Mexico Historical Society, Santa Fe
  George Curry Papers
  Herbert J. Hagerman Papers
  Miguel A. Otero Papers
Oregon State Library, Salem
  William P. Lord Papers
Utah State Archives, Salt Lake City
  John C. Cutler Papers
  William Spry Papers
  Heber M. Wells Papers
Washington State Archives, Olympia
  Marion E. Hay Papers
  Albert E. Mead Papers

PRINTED SOURCES

Baker, Ray Stannard, and Dodd, William E. (eds.). *The Public Papers of Woodrow Wilson.* 6 vols. New York: Harper and Bros., 1925–1927.
Lane, Anne Wintermute, Wall, Louise Herrick (eds.). *The Letters of Franklin K. Lane: Personal and Political.* Boston and New York: Houghton Mifflin Co., 1922.
Porter, Kirk H., and Bruce, Donald (comps.). *National Party Platforms, 1840–1956.* Urbana: University of Illinois Press, 1956.
The Works of Theodore Roosevelt. 20 vols. (National Edition). New York: C. Scribner's Sons, 1926.

FEDERAL DOCUMENTS

United States Congress. *Congressional Record.* 1893–1913. 53rd Congress through 63rd Congress. Washington, D.C.

——, *Report of the Secretary of the Interior.* 59th Cong. through 63rd Cong., 1906–1913. Exec. Doc. 1. Washington, D.C., 1906–1913.

——, House of Representatives. *Hearing Before the Secretary of the Interior on the Enlargement and Consolidation of San Francisco Mountain Forest Reserve, February 6, 1901.* 59th Cong., 1st sess., H. Doc. 613. Washington, D.C., 1906.

——, Senate. *Investigation of the Department of the Interior and of the Bureau of Forestry.* 61st Cong., 2nd sess., S. Doc. 719. Washington, D.C., 1911.

——, ——. *Preliminary Report of the Public Lands Commission, March 7, 1904.* 58th Cong., 2nd sess., S. Doc. 188. Washington, D.C., 1904.

United States Department of Agriculture, Forest Service. *Forest Reserves in Idaho.* Bulletin 67. Washington, D.C., 1905.

STATE DOCUMENTS

Arizona
Session Laws of the Eleventh Legislative Assembly of the Territory of Arizona. Phoenix, 1899.

California
First Biennial Message of Governor George C. Pardee to the Legislature of the State of California, Thirty-Sixth Session, 1905. Sacramento, 1905.

First Biennial Message of Hiram W. Johnson Before the Senate and Assembly of the State of California, Fortieth Session, January 6, 1913. Sacramento, 1913.

Inaugural Address of Governor Hiram W. Johnson Before the Senate and Assembly of the State of California in Joint Assembly at Sacramento, Tuesday, January 3, 1911. Sacramento, 1911.

Second Biennial Message of Governor George C. Pardee to the Legislature of the State of California, Thirty-Seventh Session, 1907. Sacramento, 1907.

Second Biennial Message of Governor Henry T. Gage to the Legislature of the State of California, Thirty-Fifth Session, 1903. Sacramento, 1903.

Colorado
Biennial Report of the Forest Commission of the State of Colorado for the Years 1889 and 1890. Denver, 1891.

Inaugural Address of Elias M. Ammons, Governor of Colorado, Before the Nineteenth General Assembly. Denver, 1913.

Journal of the General Assembly of the Legislature of Colorado, Seventeenth Session. Denver, 1909.

Journal of the Senate of the Legislature of the State of Colorado, Eighteenth Session. Denver, 1911.

Official Proceedings of the Colorado Conservation Commission from March, 1909 to April, 1910. Denver, 1910.

Idaho
Fifth Biennial Report of the Commission of Immigration, Labor, and Statistics, 1907–1908. Boise, 1909.

Inaugural Message of Frank R. Gooding, Governor of Idaho, to the Eighth Session of the Legislature. Boise, 1905.

Message of Frank Steunenberg, Governor of the State of Idaho, to the Fourth State Legislature. Boise, 1899.

Montana

Governor's Message Relating to Conservation, January 17, 1911. Helena, 1911.

Message of Governor Edwin L. Norris to the Eleventh Legislature Assembly of the State of Montana. Helena, 1909.

Message of Governor Joseph K. Toole to the Tenth Legislative Assembly of the State of Montana, 1907. Helena, 1907.

Message of Governor Robert B. Smith to the Fifth Legislative Assembly of the State of Montana, January 4, 1897. Helena, 1897.

Tenth Report of the Board of Agriculture, Labor, and Industry of the State of Montana for the Year Ending November 28, 1906. Helena, 1906.

Twelfth Report of the Department of Agriculture, Commerce, and Immigration of the State of Montana for the Years 1909–1910. Helena, 1910.

Nevada

Inaugural Message of Governor Tasker L. Oddie to the Legislature of 1911, Twenty-fifth Session. Carson City, 1911.

Journal of the Assembly of the Legislature of the State of Nevada, Twenty-Fourth Session, 1909. Carson City, 1909.

Message of Lieutenant and Acting Governor Denver S. Dickerson to the Legislature of 1909, Twenty-Fourth Session. Carson City, 1909.

New Mexico

Proceedings of the Legislative Council of the Territory of New Mexico, Santa Fe, January 18, 1909. Santa Fe, 1909.

Oregon

Fourth Annual Report of the Oregon Conservation Commission to the Governor, 1912. Salem, 1912.

Journal of the Senate of the Twenty-Fifth Legislature of the State of Oregon, 1909. Salem, 1909.

Journal of the Senate of the Twenty-Sixth Legislature of the State of Oregon, 1911. Salem, 1911.

Message of George E. Chamberlain, Governor of Oregon, to the Twenty-Fifth Legislative Assembly, Regular Session, 1909. Salem, 1909.

Message of George E. Chamberlain, Governor of Oregon, to the Twenty-Third Legislative Assembly, Regular Session, 1905. Salem, 1905.

Message of Jay Bowerman, Acting Governor of Oregon, to the Twenty-Sixth Legislative Assembly, Regular Session, 1911. Salem, 1911.

Message of Oswald West, Governor of Oregon, to the Twenty-Sixth Legislative Assembly, Regular Session, 1911. Salem, 1911.

Second Annual Report of the Oregon Conservation Commission to the Governor, November, 1909. Salem, 1909.

State versus National Control of the Public Forests From the Viewpoint of a Western State. Portland, 1913.

Utah

First Biennial Report of the Utah Conservation Commission, 1913. Salt Lake City, 1913.

Journal of the Eighth Session of the Legislature of the State of Utah, 1909. Salt Lake City, 1909.

Journal of the Ninth Session of the Legislature of the State of Utah, 1911. Salt Lake City, 1911.

Preliminary Report of the Utah Conservation Commission, 1909. Salt Lake City, 1909.

Washington

Journal of the Senate of the Eleventh Legislature of the State of Washington, January 11, 1909. Olympia, 1909.

Journal of the Senate of the Twelfth Legislature of the State of Washington, 1911. Olympia, 1911.

Message of Governor J. H. McGraw to the Legislature of 1897. Olympia, 1897.

Report of the State Fire Warden for the Year 1905 to the State Board of Forest Commissioners. Olympia, 1906.

Second Message of Governor M. E. Hay to the Legislature of 1911. Olympia, 1911.

Third Biennial Report of the Board of State Land Commissioners to the Legislature of the State of Washington, Sixth Regular Session, 1898. Olympia, 1899.

Third Message of Governor Albert E. Mead to the Legislature of 1909. Olympia, 1909.

Wyoming

Message of Bryant B. Brooks, Governor of Wyoming, to the Eighth State Legislature, 1905. Sheridan, 1905.

Message of Bryant B. Brooks, Governor of Wyoming, to the Tenth State Legislature, 1909. Cheyenne, 1909.

CONTEMPORARY IMPRINTS RELATING TO THE CONSERVATION ISSUE

American National Livestock Association, *Proceedings of the Twelfth Annual Convention of the American National Livestock Association Held in Los Angeles, California, January 26, 27, 28, 1909*. Denver: Smith Brooks Printing Company, 1909.

Ammons, Elias M. Untitled article, *Farmer's Life* (Sept., 1913). Copy in Conference of Western Governors file, General Land Office, Interior Records, National Archives.

"Ammons, the Tool of Big Business." Broadside in folder 1853, Pinchot papers.

Beaman, D. C. *The National Forests and the Forest Service; Address at the Sixteenth National Irrigation Congress, Albuquerque, New Mexico, September 29, 1908*. Albuquerque, 1908. 4 pp.

Bryan, J. W. "Proposed Investigation of the Forest Service . . . June 17 ,1913." Printed speech, copy in Northwest Collection, University of Washington Library.

"Conservation from a Colorado Viewpoint—By a Critic of the Government," *Collier's Weekly*, 50 (March 15, 1913), 24.

Edwards, G. W. *Conservation and Our Republic*. N.p., 1911. Copy in Bourne papers.

Greeley, William B. "The Administration of the National Forest," typescript of speech, Feb., 1909. In United States Forest Service Regional Office, Missoula, Montana.

Harris, Francis W., and Johnson, Andrew P. *The Neglected West*. Municipal Monograph No. 1. Seattle [1911?]. Copy in Ballinger papers.

Hay, Marion E. "The State's Interest in Conservation" (Olympia, 1910).

Knapp, George L. "The Other Side of Conservation," *North American Review*, 191 (April, 1910), 465–481.

Natason, ——, comp. "The Diary of a Land Fraud," W.P.A. project. Typescript, copy in Oregon State Library.

"National Forests." Broadside in folder 1853, Pinchot papers.

National Irrigation Congress. *Official Proceedings of the Seventeenth National Irrigation Congress Held at Spokane, Washington, August 9 to 14, 1909*. Spokane: Strew and Bordon Company, 1909.

Newlands, Francis G. "Speeches, Etc. of Mr. Newlands." Nevada State Historical Society.

Oregon Conservation Association. *Proceedings of the Quarterly Meeting of the Oregon Conservation Association.* N.p. [1910?]. Copy in John Minto papers, Oregon Historical Society.

Pinchot, Gifford, "Conservation As Practiced: A Specific Answer to a Specific Attack, With a Few Words on the Alleged Western Discontent with Conservation," *Pearson's Magazine,* May, 1913, 9 pp. Reprint in John Crerar Library, Chicago.

Progressive Republican League of Montana. *Resolutions Adopted by the Progressive Republican League of Montana at the Billings Conference, February 22, 1912.* N.p. [1912?]. Copy in William A. Clark Library, Los Angeles.

"A Protest Against Misrepresentation of the Conservation Policy." Broadside in folder 1853, Pinchot papers.

Proceedings of the Public Lands Convention Held at Denver, Colorado, June 18, 19, 20, 1907 by the States and Territories Containing Public Land of the United States and Lying West of the Missouri River. Denver, 1907.

Puter, S. A. D., and Stevens, Horace. *Looters of the Public Domain.* Portland: Portland Printing House, 1908.

Seattle Chamber of Commerce. *Attitude of the Seattle Chamber of Commerce on Conservation: Report Unanimously Adopted, March 22, 1910.* Seattle, 1910. Copy in Bourne papers.

Shafroth, John A. "Real Conservation and Federal Ownership," *Continental Magazine,* May, 1912, pp. 112–123. Reprint in Colorado State Historical Society.

Short, Frank H. *Address Delivered by Judge Frank H. Short of Fresno, California, at the National Conservation Congress, St. Paul, Minnesota, September 5–9, 1910.* N.p., n.d. Copy in Bourne papers.

———. *An Open Letter to Mr. Gifford Pinchot by Frank H. Short Relating to Rights of Way in Forest Reserves, Etc.* N.p. [1909?]. Copy in Bourne papers.

Should the Forests Be Preserved? San Francisco: California Water and Forest Association, 1903.

Thomas, Edward H. "Conservation As Practiced," *Pearson's Magazine,* January, 1913. Reprint in John Crerar Library, Chicago.

Titsworth, Frederick S. "Notes on the Legal Aspects of the Conservation Program," *Proceedings of the Colorado Scientific Society,* 9 (March, 1910), 315–334. Copy in Pinchot papers.

Trans Mississippi Commercial Congress, *Proceedings of the Twelfth Trans Mississippi Commercial Congress Held at Denver, Colorado, July 12–20, 1901.* Cripple Creek, Colo., 1901.

———. *Official Proceedings of the Twentieth Annual Session of the Trans Mississippi Commercial Congress Held at Denver, August 16–21, 1909.* Denver, 1909.

Underwood, J. J. *The Crime of Conservation: Written for the Times of Seattle and Many Other Newspapers.* [Seattle?], 1911. Copy in Pinchot papers.

———. "A Possible Peril to Our Republic: Why the West Became Estranged from the East," *Leslie's Illustrated Weekly Newspaper,* April 24, 1913, pp. 446–447.

Wooley, Legrand. "Federal Versus State Control of the National Forests of the United States." Unpublished bachelor's thesis, University of Utah, 1911.

NEWSPAPERS

Arizona
  Flagstaff, *Coconino Sun*
  Phoenix, *Arizona Democrat; Arizona Gazette; Arizona Republican*
  Tucson, *Arizona Star; Citizen*
California
  Big Pine, *Owens Valley Herald*
  Colusa, *Sun*
  Fresno, *Republican*
  Independence, *Inyo Independent*
  Los Angeles, *Express; Herald; Times*
  Sacramento, *Union*
  San Francisco, *Call; Chronicle*
Colorado
  Colorado Springs, *Gazette*
  Denver, *Democrat; Post; Record-Stockman; Republican; Rocky Mountain News*
  Grand Junction, *News*
Idaho
  Boise, *Capital News; Idaho Statesman*
  Coeur d'Alene, *Press*
  Pocatello, *Tribune*
Montana
  Butte, *Miner*
  Great Falls, *Leader*
  Helena, *Independent*
  Livingston, *Enterprise*
  Missoula, *Missoulan*
  Virginia City, *Madisonian*
Nevada
  Reno, *Gazette; Nevada State Journal*
  Winnemucca, *Humboldt Star*
New Mexico
  Albuquerque, *Citizen; Journal*
  Las Vegas, *Optic*
  Santa Fe, *New Mexican*
Oregon
  Oregon City, *Enterprise*
  Portland, *Oregon Journal; Oregonian*
Pennsylvania
  Philadelphia, *Public Ledger*
Utah
  Salt Lake City, *Deseret News; Salt Lake Tribune*
Washington
  Bellingham, *Herald*
  North Yakima, *Yakima Herald*
  Olympia, *State Capital Record*
  Seattle, *Post-Intelligencer; Times*
  Spokane, *Spokesman-Review*

Wyoming
Cheyenne, *Leader; Tribune-Leader; Wyoming Tribune*
Evanston, *Wyoming Press*
Lander, *Clipper*
Laramie, *Boomerang; Republican*
Pinedale, *Roundup*
Washington, D.C.
Herald

PERIODICALS

The Argonaut (San Francisco), 1897
California Illustrated Magazine (San Francisco), 1892, 1893
California Weekly (San Francisco), 1909
The Forester (Washington, D.C.), 1899
Mining and Scientific Press (Los Angeles), 1909

AUTOBIOGRAPHIES, MEMOIRS, AND REMINISCENCES

Anderson, A. A. *Experiences and Impressions: The Autobiography of Colonel A. A. Anderson.* New York: Macmillan Co., 1933.

Chatterton, Fenimore. "Autobiography of Fenimore Chatterton." Typescript, copy in Wyoming Historical Society.

Gosney, E. S. "The Arizona Woolgrower's Association, 1898–1909." Typescript, copy in Arizona Pioneers Historical Society, Tucson.

Hagerman, Herbert J. *Matters Relating to the Administration and Removal of Herbert J. Hagerman.* Printed for private circulation. 1908. Copy in Bronson Cutting papers, Library of Congress.

Hammond, John Hays. *Autobiography of John Hays Hammond.* 2 vols. New York: Farrar and Rinehart, 1935.

Keep, John H. "Early History of the Uncompahgre National Forest." Typescript, copy in Colorado Historical Society.

Langille, Harold D. "Mostly Division 'R' Days: Reminiscences of the Stormy, Pioneering Days of the Forest Reserves," *Oregon Historical Quarterly,* 57 (Dec., 1956), 301–313.

Mondell, Franklin W. "My Story: An Autobiography," *Tribune-Leader* (Cheyenne, Wyo.), July 31, 1935.

Pinchot, Gifford. *Breaking New Ground.* New York: Harcourt, Brace and Co., 1947.

Rist, Lewis R. "Historical Sketch of the White River National Forest." Typescript, copy in C.W.A. project file, Colorado State Historical Society.

Rodgers, R. A. "How and Why I Went into the Forest Service." Typescript, copy in Frederic Winn papers, Arizona Pioneers Historical Society.

Roosevelt, Theodore. *An Autobiography.* New York: Charles Scribner's Sons, 1921.

Shoemaker, Leonard C. "History of the Holy Cross National Forest." Typescript, copy in Colorado State Historical Society.

Shoemaker, Theodore. "Reminiscences." Typescript, copy in possession of Mr. Shoemaker.

Thompson, Jessie, ed. *Early Days in the Forest Service.* 2 vols. Washington, D.C.: U.S. Department of Agriculture, Forest Service, 1955.

West, Oswald. "Reminiscences and Anecdotes; Mostly About Politics," *Oregon Historical Quarterly,* 51 (June, 1951), 95–110.

Winn, Frederic. "History of Coronado National Forest." Typescript, copy in Winn papers, Arizona Pioneers Historical Society.

SECONDARY WORKS

Clar, C. Raymond. *California Government and Forestry from Spanish Days until the Creation of the Department of Natural Resources in 1927.* Sacramento: Division of Forestry, Department of Natural Resources, 1959.

Dunne, Finley Peter. *Mr. Dooley: In the Hearts of His Countrymen.* Boston: Small, Maynard and Co., 1899.

Haskett, Bert. "History of the Sheep Industry in Arizona," *Arizona Historical Review,* 7 (July, 1936), 3–49.

Hays, Samuel P. *Conservation and the Gospel of Efficiency: The Progressive Conservation Movement, 1890–1920.* Cambridge, Mass.: Harvard University Press, 1959.

Johnson, Claudius O. *Borah of Idaho.* New York: Farrar, Strauss, and Co., 1936.

Kent, Elizabeth. *William Kent, Independent: A Biography.* Privately printed, 1950.

Lauver, Mary E. "A History of the Use and Management of the Forested Lands of Arizona, 1862–1936." Unpublished doctoral dissertation, University of Arizona, 1938.

Link, Arthur S. *Wilson: The New Freedom.* Princeton, N.J.: Princeton University Press, 1956.

Morgan, Murray. *The Last Wilderness.* New York: Viking Press, 1955.

Morrill, W. J. "Forestry," in Baker, J. D., and Hafen, L. R. (eds.), *History of Colorado* (Denver: Lindeman and Co., 1927), II, 757–783.

Morrison, Paul W. "The Establishment of the Forest Service within the Roosevelt National Forest." Unpublished Master's thesis, University of Colorado, 1945.

Murray, Keith A. "Republican Party Politics in Washington During the Progressive Era." Unpublished doctoral dissertation, University of Washington, 1946.

Paschal, Joel Francis. *Mr. Justice Sutherland: A Man Against the State.* Princeton, N.J.: Princeton University Press, 1951.

Raines, William McLeod, and Barnes, Will C. *Cattle, Cowboys, and Rangers.* New York: Grosset and Dunlap, 1930.

Rakestraw, Lawrence. "A History of Forest Conservation in the Pacific Northwest, 1891–1913." Unpublished doctoral dissertation, University of Washington, 1955.

———. "Sheep Grazing in the Cascade Range: John Minto vs. John Muir," *Pacific Historical Review,* Vol. 27, No. 4 (Nov., 1958), pp. 371–382.

Richardson, Elmo R. "George Curry and the Politics of Forest Conservation in New Mexico," *New Mexico Historical Review,* Vol. 33, No. 4 (Oct., 1958), pp. 277–284.

———. "The Struggle for the Valley: California's Hetch Hetchy Controversy, 1905–1913," *California Historical Society Quarterly,* Vol. 38, No. 3 (Sept., 1959), pp. 249–258.

Rodgers, Andrew D. *Bernard Eduard Fernow: A Story of North American Forestry.* Princeton, N.J.: Princeton University Press, 1951.

Twitchell, Ralph E. *The Leading Facts of New Mexican History.* 2 vols. Cedar Rapids, Iowa, 1912.

Voss, Walter A. "Colorado and Forest Conservation." Unpublished Master's thesis, University of Colorado, 1931.

Wagoner, J. J. "History of the Cattle Industry in Southern Arizona, 1540–1940," *Social Science Bulletin Number 20* (University of Arizona), April, 1952.

Willson, Roscoe G. "'Teddy's Pets' Fought Hostility in Early Days of Forest Reserve," *Arizona Republican Magazine,* March 4, 1956, pp. 18–19.

INDEX

INDEX

Abbott, Lyman, 74
Adams, Alva, 147–148
Adams, Samuel, 136
Agriculture, Department of, 25, 63, 95, 140. *See also* Wilson, James
Alaska, 67; national forests in, 51–52, 111; coal lands in, 54, 59, 64, 65–66, 109, 112, 116, 137
Aldrich tariff (1909), 69
Allen, E. T., 27, 29
Almagordo Lumber Company, 42
American Forestry Association, 8, 12
American Mining Congress, 103–104, 120
American Stockgrowers Association, 34
Ammons, Elias M., 9, 34, 87–89, 101, 119, 122, 143, 146, 148, 153–156
Anaconda Copper Company, 1, 150
Anderson, A. A., 21
Arizona, 3, 40, 92, 139; grazing controversy in, 10–11
Arizona Woolgrowers Association, 10
Armstrong, L. K., 90–91, 95, 101

Baker, Newton D., 151
Baldwin, Elbert L., 60–61, 74
Ballinger, Richard A., 90, 92, 95, 96, 98, 102, 123, 149, 151–154, 174, 185; as Commissioner of Public Lands, 30, 47, 49–54, 61, 63, 66, 74, 111; as Roosevelt man, 38, 39, 47, 49–50, 54; on federal resource policies, 39, 52, 54, 60–62, 64, 67, 72–73, 78, 81, 111, 114, 115; early career of, 48–49; on honesty, 48–49, 52; on business, 49, 52, 61; on public office, 49–50; personal characteristics of, 50; resents Pinchot's influence, 51, 55, 63, 67–68; and coal-land policy, 52, 54, 111; and Cunningham claims, 54, 55, 66–67; appointed Secretary of Interior, 57–60, 67; and 1908 campaign, 58; and Garfield, 58, 74, 75; and water-power site policy, 61, 63, 68, 111; and Newell, 62–63; and Interior Department staff, 62–64, 100; and Reclamation Service, 63, 72; reliance of, upon Taft, 64, 68, 75–76; resigns as Secretary, 64, 69, 115, 129–133; Western support of, 65, 70, 73, 101, 103; and Glavis charges, 67, 69; self-defense of, in controversy with Pinchot, 70, 72–75, 81–82, 84, 112–115, 119; Western criticism of,

70–72, 110; and congressional investigation, 77, 80–84, 113; post-Cabinet activities of, 84, 115–116, 118–119, 134; postcontroversy policies of, 110–113, 132; and critics' campaign, 113–116; on state control of resources, 114–115; on public indifference, 115; on political reformers, 115, 119; and 1910 campaign, 124, 127, 129; as campaign issue in West, 125, 130; and 1912 campaign, 134, *See also* Ballinger-Pinchot controversy
Ballinger-Pinchot controversy: origins of, 51–52, 55, 59–64; Western publicity concerning, 56, 70; first stage of, 64, 67–69; congressional investigation of, 69, 77, 79–84; second stage of, 70–77; and split in Republican party, 71–72, 122–123; historiography of, 84–85n.; subsequent influence of, 86, 95, 100, 149–151, 155, 159
Bard, Thomas R., 16, 57
Barnes, Will C., 94
Beaman, D. C., 35, 86–87, 89, 101, 113, 156
Bliss, Cornelius N., 1, 2, 6, 15, 16, 22
Borah, William E., 30–31, 33, 102–103, 108, 125, 130, 141, 155, 157, 184
Bourne, Jonathan, Jr., 26, 72, 141–142
Bowerman, Jay, 99–100, 107, 125
Brady, James H., 99
Brady, John S., 109
Brainerd, Erastus, 72, 79, 90, 91, 96, 120, 128
Brandeis, Louis, 81, 150
Brandon, C. Watt, 26, 140
Brooks, Bryant B., 27, 99, 101, 103
Brown, Ashmun N., 90, 96, 108, 114, 120, 138, 155, 157
Browne, J. J., 91
Bryan, J. W., 157
Bryan, William J., 86, 148, 150–151
Buchtel, Henry A., 35, 36, 38, 45
Budd, James H., 14
Burke, Thomas E., 26, 74, 97, 127, 128

Cale Bill (1908), 54, 66
California: and federal resource policies, 2, 16, 37, 40, 43, 121; economic and political conditions in, 3, 33, 71, 97, 103, 151; Yosemite Park controversies in, 12–15, 16, 18, 20, 43–44,

110; progressive reformers in, 57–58, 71, 125–126, 143; and Truckee power contract, 64, 72

California Forest and Water Association, 16

Cannon, Joseph G., 69

Carey, Robert D., 140

Carr, Donald, 129

Carter, Thomas H., 1, 6, 19, 32, 33, 35, 54, 72, 89, 91, 94, 98, 108, 111, 156

Castle, Curtis, 15

Catron, Thomas B., 9

Chamberlain, George E., 19, 29, 45, 124, 148, 156

Chatterton, Fenimore, 21–22

Clagstone, Paul, 125

Clark, Clarence D., 1, 73

Clark, William A., 146, 157

Cleveland, Grover, forest reserve proclamations of, 1, 5, 7, 8, 12, 15, 17, 18

Coal Act (1904), 54, 65, 67; (1908), 66, 67

Coal lands, 35, 52, 54, 111, 112

Cobb, Calvin, 92–93

Cody, William F., 21

Collier's Weekly, 73–74, 75, 84

Colorado, 4, 33; and federal resource policies, 9, 34, 35, 39, 73, 102, 117, 122, 124, 155, 157; resource legislation in, 12, 35, 43, 87, 88, 107; political conditions in, 34–35, 86–90, 124, 142–143, 148, 155–156, 157; public lands conventions in, 35–40, 116–118; land frauds in, 53; as center of critics' campaign, 86–90, 116, 153–156

Colorado Cattle and Horse Growers Association, 34

Colorado Forestry Association, 34, 35, 45

Colorado Fuel and Iron Company, 35

Colorado Scientific Society, 96

Congress: debates on federal resource policy in, 1–2, 31, 33, 72; Westerners in, 1, 19, 23, 108, 109, 156–157; resource legislation in, 111–112, 156

Conservation Association, National, 75, 78, 91, 99, 100, 116, 120, 137

Conservation Congress, National (Seattle, 1909), 71, 89, 90; (St. Paul, 1910), 99–103, 150

Costigan, Edward P., 142–143, 156

Cowles, Will, 90, 127

Crane, W. Murray, 127, 128, 131

Cunningham, Clarence, 54, 65, 67

Cunningham claims, 54–55, 64, 65–67, 69, 74, 75, 82–83, 112, 118, 132, 137

Curry, George, 41–43, 45, 123, 141, 153

Davis, Arthur P., 62, 63, 68, 113, 132

Delta County Livestock Association, 87

Democratic National Convention (1908), 86; (1912), 145

Democrats in the West, and federal resource policies, 1, 28, 34, 37, 70, 73, 80, 83, 86, 92, 110, 120, 124–125, 126, 138, 143, 144–157 *passim*

Dennett, Fred, 51, 55, 66, 72, 81

Denver, 3, 34–36, 38–40, 53, 86, 98, 103, 119, 156

Dickerson, Denver S., 45

Dixon, Joseph, 94

Dodge, Clarence P., 27, 39, 148, 156

Dolliver, Jonathan, 79

"Dooley, Mr.," 5

Donavan, J. J., 46, 74, 97, 102

DuBois, Fred T., 32

Eberhart, A. O., 100

Eddy, J. Arthur, 86–89, 100–101, 111, 113–114, 116–119, 156

Englebright, William, 131

Fall, Albert B., 42, 109, 141, 145, 155, 157, 158, 185

Fisher, Walter L., 117–119, 150; appointed Secretary of Interior, 135–136; and Pinchot, 135–136, 137; resource policies of, 137–138; Western criticism of, 138, 152, 155, 184

Flint, Frank, 72, 80, 131

Forest and Water Association (Los Angeles), 16

Forest reserves: creation of, 1–2; in California, 2, 14–15, 20; in Oregon, 8, 28; in Wyoming, 8, 21–22; in New Mexico, 8–9; in Colorado, 9; in Washington State, 9; in Idaho, 9, 32; in Arizona, 10–11, 28; transferred to Forest Service, 25; in Montana, 28; renamed, 25; in Utah, 40–41. *See also* National forests

Forestry, Bureau of, 21, 22, 24, 25

Forestry, Division of, 6, 7, 12, 19

Forest Service: organized, 25–26; Western criticism of, 26, 29, 31, 33, 37, 39, 40, 63, 70, 72, 75, 86–104 *passim*, 109, 118, 142, 143, 146, 155, 156; employees of, 26–27, 28, 35, 36, 38, 42, 59, 67, 78; and Interior Department, 51, 55, 63, 67–68, 137; congressional investigation of, 77, 80, 81, 157

Fred Light case, 40, 88, 116
Fulton, Charles W., 19, 32, 33, 62, 73, 114

Gage, Henry, 20
Garfield, James R., 35, 39, 40, 48, 63, 110, 124, 126, 136; appointed Secretary of Interior, 23–24; on federal resource policies, 24, 44, 54, 61, 67–68, 71, 112, 154; and Pinchot, 24–25, 77, 122; Western criticism of, 44, 59, 70; and reorganization of Interior Department, 47; at Public Lands Convention, 47, 50–54; and Taft, 56, 59–60, 134–135; and Ballinger, 57–58, 63–64, 74, 75, 118; praised by Roosevelt, 60, 123; supports Pinchot in controversy, 64, 67, 82
Geological Survey, U.S., 7, 62
Gillett, James, 20, 101, 103
Glavis, Louis: as Land Office agent, 53, 54; charges against Ballinger by, 66, 67, 69, 70, 73; and congressional investigation, 78, 81–83, 136; and California episode, 126
Gooding, Frank R., 33
Gosney, E. S., 10–11
Goudy, F. C., 35, 45, 87
Graves, Henry S., 95, 122, 137, 157
Grazing. *See* Stock-raising industry
Grazing, Division of, 94
Guggenheim, Daniel, 65, 73, 80
Guggenheim, Simon, 65, 73, 80

Hagerman, Herbert J., 41, 97, 141
Hammond, John H., 58
Hanford, Cornelius N., 48, 53, 74, 90, 91, 97
Hawley, James H., 148
Hay, Marion E., 90–91, 97, 99 ff., 105–108, 119, 120, 122, 128, 138, 150
Heard, Dwight B., 27
Heney, Francis J., 19, 57, 101, 126
Hermann, A. B., 10
Hermann, Binger, 6, 10, 15, 16, 19, 21
Hetch Hetchy controversy, 43–44, 72, 110, 123, 125, 132, 137, 154
Heyburn, Weldon B., 31–32, 33, 44, 65–66, 75, 98, 108, 125, 157
Hill, James J., 100
Hill, Louis, 100–101
Hitchcock, Ethan A., 10–11, 22–23, 41, 51, 166
Hitchcock, Frank, 54, 57, 58, 63, 67, 82, 129, 133

House, Edward M., 151
Hughes, Charles, 73
Humphrey, William E., 91, 129, 142, 157
Hunt, Frank W., 9

Ickes, Harold L., 85
Idaho, 33, 92, 99, 114, 148; economic conditions in, 9, 90; and federal resource policies, 30–31, 33, 40, 93, 122; land frauds in, 30, 53; political conditions in, 30, 125
Idaho Woolgrowers Association, 33
Insurgents in Congress, 69, 77, 83, 110, 121, 129, 141
Interior, Department of, 5, 6, 54–57, 64, 68, 76, 109, 112, 114, 134, 136–137, 140, 152–153; reorganization of, 22, 23, 25, 47; congressional investigation of, 77–84
Interior, Secretary of: Western claim to post of, 6, 47, 59; Westerner as, 31, 57, 59, 60, 130, 138, 147–152, 158, 163, 172, 185
Irish, John P., 13, 15
Irrigation. *See* Reclamation Act; Reclamation projects; Reclamation Service
Irrigation Congress, National (Albuquerque, 1895), 12; (Spokane, 1909), 71, 79

Jastro, H. A., 37, 41
Johnson, Hiram, 117, 125–126
Johnson, Robert U., 13, 15, 44
Jones, A. A., 153
Jones, Wesley L., 77, 90, 91, 108, 127, 130, 155

Kent, William, 110, 122, 125, 138, 150, 157
Kerby, Frederick, 82, 83
Kerckhoff, William, 15, 16
Killian, J. B., 27, 87, 117
Kinney, Abbot, 15, 43
Knapp, George L., 96, 109
Knight, George, 57, 58
Knight, William, 15
Knox, Philander C., 57, 133

Lafferty, Abraham W., 8, 10, 142
Land and Irrigation Congress (Chicago, 1910), 96
Land Office, U.S. Public, 6, 7, 23, 31, 47, 109, 153; reorganization of, 50–51, 55
Lane, Franklin K., 73, 148, 185; career and personality of, 151–152; resource policies of, 152–156

Lawler, Oscar, 62, 67, 68, 69, 83
Lindley, Curtis H., 97
Lindsey, Ben B., 101, 124
Lord, William P., 7
Los Angeles, 3, 14, 16, 44, 93, 96, 98, 121, 122
Lukens, Theodore P., 14, 15, 16, 44
Lumbering industry: in West, 3, 4; in Oregon, 19, 124–125; in Idaho, 33; in New Mexico, 40, 97
Lummis, Charles F., 121
Luna, Solomon, 37

McGraw, John H., 29, 54, 74, 97
McHarg, Ormsby, 80, 84
McKinley, William: and forest reserves, 1–2; appointments of secretaries of Interior by, 5, 22, 25
Madison, E. H., 83
Manson, Marsden, 123
Mantle, Lee, 94
Marshall, Thomas, 147
Maxwell, George, 16
Mead, Albert E., 30, 46, 90
Merritt, E. T., 101
Mills, William, 117
Mining industry: in West, 3, 38, 104; in Colorado, 4, 34, 35; in Arizona, 12; in Oregon, 19; in California, 103; in Nevada, 103
Minto, John, 7, 8, 29, 98
Mitchell, William, 19, 151
Mondell, Franklin, 19, 20, 26, 54, 73, 91, 98, 112, 114, 157
Montana, 3, 33, 40, 61, 96, 149, 150; resource legislation in, 12, 45–46, 107–108; and federal resource policies, 28; political conditions in, 140–141
Moody, Malcolm A., 27, 47
Moore, Miles C., 54, 65, 66, 84, 91, 93, 138
Morgan, J. P., and Company, 59, 65, 67, 83
Muir, John, 2, 6, 12–15, 16, 18, 20, 44, 72, 110
Munson, C. J., 33

National Academy of Sciences, 5, 9, 24
National forests, 25, 40, 104, 157; creation of, 34; in Colorado, 35, 38, 86, 87, 88; in New Mexico, 42–43; in Alaska, 51–52, 64, 111; administrative sites in, 56; in Indian reservations, 68, 69
National Livestock Association, 36
National Parks, Bureau of, 115, 153

National Public Domain League, 89, 90, 101, 113, 117
National Woolgrowers Association, 34, 93
Needham, James C., 20, 57, 58, 71
Nelson, Knute, 80–81, 82, 111–112
Nevada, 3, 33, 45, 103, 110, 120, 148
Newell, Frederick, 18, 23, 35, 43, 137; and Pinchot, 23, 25, 117; and Ballinger, 51, 60, 62–63, 68, 110, 113, 132; and federal reclamation policies, 61, 63; and congressional investigation, 81, 83
Newlands, Francis G., 19, 20, 110, 148–149, 150, 156
New Mexico, 3, 109, 153; and federal resource policies, 37, 41–43, 101; political conditions in, 41–43, 141; resource legislation in, 45
Newspapers, Western: on federal resource policies, 2, 4, 8–11, 13, 27, 29, 34–36, 39, 41, 43, 57, 86–87, 91–93, 97, 99, 106–107, 139–143, 146; on Ballinger-Pinchot controversy, 65, 70–71, 73, 75, 77, 79, 95; on Pinchot, 93–94, 139–143; on resignation of Ballinger, 135; on appointment of Lane, 152
Norris, Edwin L., 46, 96, 101, 103, 107–108, 149
Norton, Paul, 130–131, 136

Oddie, Tasker L., 110
Oil resources: in California, 97, 103, 112; federal policy on, 112
Olympic National Monument (Wash.), 115
Oregon, 3, 7, 8, 33, 71, 90, 108, 114, 120; land frauds in, 19, 55; and federal resource policies, 37, 73, 101, 107, 121, 158; resource legislation in, 45, 107; political conditions in, 72, 107, 124, 141–142
Oregon Forestry Association, 8, 125
Osbourne, John E., 148
Otero, Miguel A., 8, 37
Overman, Lee, 157

Page, Walter H., 150, 151
Pardee, George C., 20, 43–44, 70, 102, 116, 117, 121, 123, 125, 126, 134, 148
Patterson, Thomas, 33, 34, 36, 37, 75, 87, 89
Pepper, George W., 81
Perkins, George C., 16

Perkins, George W., 59, 67, 83
Phelan, James D., 151
Pierce, Frank, 55, 62, 66, 67, 81, 83, 137, 172, 174
Piles, Samuel H., 33, 49, 54, 127
Pinchot, Amos, 123, 137
Pinchot, Gifford: and Arizona grazing controversy, 10–11; and Yosemite Park controversies, 13, 15, 44, 110; travels of, in West, 16, 25, 35, 39, 40, 70–71, 88, 103, 124; and Roosevelt, 18, 24–25, 26, 30, 33, 56, 61, 78, 102; and Interior Department, 21, 23, 46, 47, 51, 63, 67; and Wyoming grazing controversy, 22; early career of, 24; administrative techniques of, 25, 33, 34, 38, 100–102; Western supporters of, 26–27, 37, 39, 42–43, 47, 71–72, 73, 77, 93–94, 102, 112, 116–117, 121–122, 127; Western critics of, 28, 36, 37, 65, 71, 72, 86–104 *passim*, 143; and public lands conventions, 35–40, 117; on Ballinger, 51–52, 59–60; on Taft, 55–56, 69, 76; gambit against Ballinger's administration, 63–64, 67–68, 77–79; publicizes criticisms of Ballinger, 69, 70, 72, 74, 76–79, 83; and congressional investigation, 77, 81, 83, 84; and critics' campaign, 89, 93–94, 110, 111, 121, 123, 127; and state control of resources, 109, 116–117, 156–157; and Taft's resource legislation, 110–112; conservation publicity campaign of, 121–122, 124, 139, 154; and progressives' campaign of 1910, 123–128; on resignation of Ballinger, 135; and Fisher, 135–136, 137; and progressives' campaign of 1912, 139–143; as political issue in 1912, 139–143; influence of, during Wilson's administration, 146, 149, 156–157; and Lane, 152–154, 185
Poindexter, Miles C., 114, 127–129, 155, 156
Portland, Ore., 66, 98, 114, 124
Potter, Albert F., 11, 27, 34, 40, 94–95, 111
Power development, hydroelectric, in West, 4, 16, 35, 46, 56, 61, 63, 72, 96, 110–111
Pray, Charles N., 94
Price, Overton, 78
Prince, L. Bradford, 37
Progressive movement: Westerners in, 57–58, 71, 72, 102, 107, 111, 115, 117, 120, 146; and conservation issue, 122–144 *passim*
Progressive party in West, 139–144
Public Lands Commission (1903–1904), 21–22, 153
Public Lands Committee, 119–120
Public Lands Convention: (1907), 35–40, 45, 86, 149; (1911), 116–119, 122, 130, 136; (1913), 153; (1914), 153

Railroads, Western, 4, 13, 57, 100, 112, 127
Reclamation Act (1902), 19, 63, 116
Reclamation projects, 4, 10–11, 19, 27, 35, 36, 37, 38, 53, 56, 61, 63, 70, 72, 111
Reclamation Service, 7, 21, 53, 113; Western criticism of, 63, 65, 71, 72, 78, 109, 149
Republican National Committee, 5, 54, 58
Republican National Convention (1908), 57
Republicans in West, and federal resource policies, 19, 29, 32, 35, 37, 39, 41–42, 53, 55, 58, 71, 77, 82, 87–88, 90–92, 110, 123, 126, 138–139
Richards, William A., 8, 21, 23, 47, 51
Robinson, Charles D., 13
Roosevelt, Theodore, 69, 71, 73, 74, 77, 110, 150, 152, 157–158; and resource policies, 11, 21, 22, 34, 56, 61, 68, 70, 72, 78; and resource conservation, 17–18; and Pinchot, 18, 24–25, 26, 30, 33, 56, 61, 78, 102; and Western public opinion, 19, 20, 33, 44, 46; and Republican party welfare in West, 19, 32, 33, 41–43; travels of, in West, 20, 124; relations of, with "Roosevelt men," 20–21, 23, 41–43, 47, 57, 60, 61, 82; Western criticism of, 28, 65, 97, 98; on Taft, 33, 55–56, 59, 60, 78, 79, 123; creation of national forests by, 33–34, 38, 81, and Public Lands Convention, 35–36; Western supporters of, 41, 94, 100; on Ballinger, 47, 49–50, 54, 60; and Western progressives, 102, 122, 126, 127, 139, 142; and Ballinger-Pinchot controversy, 123
Ross, E. W., 29, 38, 39, 46, 90, 101
Rowell, Chester H., 71, 123, 126, 131

Salt Lake City, 3, 99–100, 101
San Francisco, 3, 16, 44, 103
Scott, Harvey, 8, 19, 57
Seattle, 3, 48–50, 59, 71, 74, 97, 114

Shafroth, John A., 37, 80, 86 ff., 100, 102, 104, 107, 116, 118, 119, 120, 145, 146, 148, 155, 156
Shaw, Albert, 78
Shipp, Thomas R., 100–101
Short, Frank H., 96, 101, 122
Sierra Club, 14, 15, 44
Smith, George O., 62
Smith, Hoke, 18
Smith, Robert D., 12
Smith, Sylvester, 104
Smoot, Reed, 40, 94, 111, 157, 166
Spokane, 90, 114, 124, 127, 128
Spry, William, 45, 94, 100, 101, 117
State control of resources: demand for, in West, 14, 22, 88, 90–91, 102, 109–110, 114, 150; legislation concerning, 105–111; and second Public Lands Convention, 116–119; as issue in Western political campaigns, 128, 144, 146; as issue in Wilson administration, 145, 156–158
State-federal coöperation in resource policy administration, 40, 46, 146, 154
State legislatures, action of, on resource policy, 1, 4, 12, 33, 45–46, 105–108
Steunenberg, Frank, 9
Stewart, Philip, 47
Stewart, William S., 1
Stock-raising industry: in West, 3–4; in Oregon, 8; in Wyoming, 8, 21–22, 27–28; in Arizona, 10–11, 28, 139; in California, 15; and federal grazing-fee controversy, 27, 34, 37, 38; in Colorado, 35, 40, 86–88; in New Mexico, 37
Stone, W. G. M., 34, 45, 119, 121, 156
Sutherland, George, 80, 112

Taft, Charles, 132
Taft, Henry, 58
Taft, William H., 33, 51, 73–74, 86, 88–89, 95, 98, 101, 154, 184; federal resource policies of, 55–56, 60, 75–76, 102, 110–112, 119; alleged disloyalty of, to Roosevelt, 56, 72; appoints Secretary of Interior, 56–60; and Ballinger, 64, 68–69, 75–76, 79; and Pinchot, 68–69, 76, 78–79; Western opinion of, 71, 93, 138; dismissal of Pinchot by, 78–79; and congressional investigation, 80, 82–83; policy differences of, with Ballinger, 110–112, 118; and Fisher, 118, 135–139, 184; and progressive faction in West, 122–123, 128; and elections of 1910, 124, 127, 128, 129, 139; and Ballinger's resignation, 131–134
Tallman, Clay, 148, 153
Taylor, Edward T., 89, 157, 184
Teal, Joseph N., 27, 45, 124, 148–149, 152, 153, 156
Teller, Henry M., 6, 36, 37, 89, 118
Thomas, Charles S., 156
Thomas, Edward H., 155
Thomson, Robert, 63
Titsworth, Frederick S., 96
Toole, Joseph, 28–29
Trans Mississippi Commercial Congress, 9, 89
Truckee Power Company, 63, 72, 110–111, 125

Underwood, J. J., 96
United Verde Mining Company, 12
U'Ren, William S., 72
Utah, 3, 33, 94; resource legislation in, 12; and federal resource policies, 37, 40–41, 45, 101–102

Vertrees, J. J., 80–82, 131

Walsh, Thomas J., 145, 149, 150
Warren, Francis E., 19, 22, 23, 122
Washington Forestry Association, 91
Washington State, 3, 33, 48–49, 90; resource legislation in, 12, 29, 30, 46; and federal resource policies, 29, 30, 59, 90–91, 114, 127–129, 143, 146; and Ballinger-Pinchot controversy, 65, 70–71, 73, 74; political conditions in, 127–129, 143, 146
Water resource development and use. *See* Power development, hydroelectric, in West; Reclamation Act; Reclamation projects; Reclamation Service
Wells, Heber M., 12, 40, 41, 80
Wells, Philip P., 137
West: and federal resource policies, 2, 5, 7, 27; complexity of economic and political interests in, 3–4; antipathy of, toward East, 5, 7, 25, 99, 103, 105–106, 114, 118, 150
West, Oswald, 120, 124–125, 148
Western Conservation League, 90–91
Western Governors, Conference of: (1910), 99–101; (1912), 119–120; (1913), 153
White, Stephen M., 15
White, Stewart E., 18, 77, 156
White, William A., 129

White House Conference of Governors, 45

Wickersham, George W., 67, 69, 75, 83, 84, 112

Wilbur, Ray L., 158

Wilson, James, 25, 35, 63, 68, 78, 88, 95

Wilson, John L., 1, 5, 46, 70, 127, 128

Wilson, Woodrow, 138; federal resource views of, 146–147, 157; Western support of, 146–148; appoints Secretary of Interior, 150–154

Woodruff, George, 62, 63

Wyoming, 3, 8, 33; and federal resource policies, 21–22, 27–28, 39, 122, 140, 148; and Public Lands Conference, 36; political conditions in, 140

Yosemite Park controversy, 12–15, 16, 18, 20. *See also* Hetch Hetchy controversy

Young, George U., 92